POSTCARD HISTORY SERIES

Randolph County

On the front cover: Please see page 14. (Gregory P. Hinshaw.)
On the back cover: Please see page 82. (Jane Lyle.)

POSTCARD HISTORY SERIES

Randolph County

Gregory P. Hinshaw

with Judy Wilson Wright, Linda L. Black, and Thomas Keesling

ARCADIA
PUBLISHING

ISBN 978-0-7385-6036-6

Published by Arcadia Publishing
Charleston, South Carolina

Printed in the United States of America

Library of Congress Control Number: 2009925182

For all general information contact Arcadia Publishing at:
Telephone 843-853-2070
Fax 843-853-0044
E-mail sales@arcadiapublishing.com
For customer service and orders:
Toll-Free 1-888-313-2665

Visit us on the Internet at www.arcadiapublishing.com

To all those who call Randolph County home

Contents

Acknowledgments

The authors would like to gratefully acknowledge those who so willingly contributed postcards from their collections for inclusion in this book. In addition to the authors, these people include Janice Harvey, Tom Harshman, Max Harter, Tom McKee, Lowell and Anna Fraze, Harold Watson, Steve Longnecker, Jeffrey Koenker, Jane Lyle, Jean Keesling, Helen Maxine Wright, Betty Cox, Edna Modisett, and the late Dott Shook. In addition Monisa Wisener, curator of the Randolph County Historical Museum; Virginia Hiatt, director of the Union City Public Library; Marcella McCormick, director of the Ridgeville Public Library; Thomas D. Hamm, archivist at Earlham College; Suzanne Robinson, director of the Washington Township (Lynn) Public Library; and Susan M. Smith, archivist at Minnetrista Cultural Center, all made images available and shared other supporting material. We would also like to acknowledge Anna Wilson, our editor at Arcadia Publishing, for her direction in this project. Without the help of these individuals, this book would not have been possible.

INTRODUCTION

The picture postcard, in vogue from about 1906 until the early 1920s, tells the story of a place's history like almost no other artifact. As the craze caught on, literally every imaginable structure and place were photographed and mailed in printed form to friends and relatives around the country. Randolph County, Indiana, was not immune to the widespread love of the picture postcard. The *Winchester Herald* remarked on December 12, 1912, that the "post card craze was 'dying out.'" The newspaper's prediction of the death of the postcard was premature, for the craze raged for more than 10 additional years, slowly waning, but never completely passing out of style. The authors have carefully assembled a wide selection of Randolph County postcards of the early 20th century (1906–1925), reflecting life in every township and nearly every place, large or small, in the county. As readers turn through the pages that follow, they will, in a sense, be carried back in time to the Randolph County of a century ago, seeing the sights seen by their great-grandparents.

Randolph County is, in many ways, like many other midwestern counties. It was originally settled, starting in 1814, largely by pioneers from the South: North Carolina, Tennessee, and Virginia. A vast majority of the earliest settlers were members of the Religious Society of Friends (Quakers). The county was organized in 1818 and was named for Randolph County, North Carolina, a heavily Quaker county from which many of the earliest settlers had emigrated. Winchester, platted in 1818, was almost certainly named for Winchester, Virginia, and has always been the county seat. Winchester was not incorporated as a town until 1838. It was incorporated as a city in 1893. The county's other incorporated towns all owe their original or continued existence to the coming of the railroads between 1852 and 1883. Ridgeville is the oldest of the other incorporated places. Platted in 1837, it did not become a place of importance until the planning of the Logansport and Union (Panhandle) Railroad in 1853, which led to the replatting of the town. The Panhandle Railroad did not arrive until 1867, and the town was incorporated in 1868. The completion of the Panhandle also created the town of Saratoga, granted a post office in 1867, platted in 1875, and incorporated in 1907. Lynn, platted in 1847, sprang to new life with the arrival of the Cincinnati and Fort Wayne (Shoo-Fly) Railroad in 1870. Even more activity came with the Indiana, Bloomington, and Western Railroad in 1882. The town was incorporated in 1883.

Union City, platted in 1849, did not take on real life until the arrival of the Dayton and Union Railroad in 1852 and the Indianapolis and Bellefontaine (Bee Line) Railroad in 1853. Union City was replatted in 1854 and incorporated as a town sometime before 1855. It was incorporated as a city in 1875. The Bee Line also gave life to Morristown (1851), now known as Parker City, and

Farmland (1852). Morristown was granted a post office, called Parker, in 1853 and incorporated as Parker City in 1894. The town board resurrected the name Parker City in 1975, and the name of the post office was changed in 1985. Farmland's post office also opened in 1853, although the town was incorporated much earlier, in 1867. The county's other incorporated towns, Modoc, platted in 1883, and Losantville (Bronson), platted in 1886, owe their existence to the coming of the Indiana, Bloomington, and Western Railroad in 1882. The same railroad gave life to Carlos, platted in 1883 but never incorporated. Bronson was incorporated in 1890, and the name was changed to Losantville in 1960. Modoc was incorporated in 1899.

In its earliest years, Randolph County became known for its abolitionism and work for temperance, two ideas closely associated with its Quaker settlers. Union Literary Institute, which opened in 1846, was a racially integrated school governed by Quakers and freemen in Greensfork Township. It was one of the first of its kind. Many stations of the famed Underground Railroad were located in the county. In its earliest years, the county was a Whig stronghold, although the collapse of the second party system gave Democrats control for a few years in the late 1840s and early 1850s. The "anti-Nebraska" crisis that led to the formation of the Republican Party caused the organization of the new party in Randolph County at a mass convention on August 19, 1854. Randolph County has remained unswervingly Republican in the years since. Between 1854 and 1910, no Democrat was elected to county office.

In the years after the Civil War, the county was thriving economically and politically. Between 1858 and 1930, Randolph County produced one U.S. senator, James E. Watson; one U.S. congressman, Thomas M. Browne; two Indiana governors, Isaac P. Gray and James P. Goodrich; three Indiana secretaries of state, William Peele, John Neff, and Union B. Hunt; and one Indiana superintendent of public instruction, Roy P. Wisehart. The county's present courthouse was built between 1875 and 1877, and the county's famous Civil War monument, the third tallest in the state, was completed in 1892.

Like other rural counties, Randolph County's growth slowed in the earliest years of the 20th century, although the county's response to urbanization made national news. Randolph County's superintendent of schools, Lee L. Driver, became a national leader in the rural school consolidation movement. Eventually the county was home to 16 township high schools, 5 township consolidated grade schools, and 2 city school systems. Numerous articles and publications in both the academic and popular press praised the county's schools. Visitors came from as far away as Canada and China to see what one federal official referred to as "the best rural schools in the country."

One electric rail line, run longest by the Indiana Union Traction Company, served Randolph County, running east to west from Union City to Parker City and beyond between 1904 and 1930. County roads were improved for use by the increasingly popular automobile, and steam railroads continued to serve an important place in the county's economic life.

Randolph County has experienced a stable population and a declining industrial base in the latter years of the 20th century and the early years of the 21st century. Passenger service disappeared from the railroads in the 1960s, and all but one of the railroads ceased to exist by 1993. A number of the county's manufacturing operations no longer exist, while those that remain employ fewer people than they once did. Many of the dominant structures of Randolph County's towns have been lost through natural disaster or economic decline. School consolidation has dramatically reduced the number of school campuses in the county, and a number of the once-thriving churches in the small towns and open country have ceased to exist.

All is not lost in modern Randolph County, however. A number of cultural activities, including an emerging arts community in Farmland and Union City, as well as the nationally known Winchester Speedway, continue to draw many visitors to Randolph County. Major economic development is presently occurring in Winchester. The county has also become known for proactive collaboration between its five school districts. Randolph County's interesting past is a key component of its promising future.

One

Winchester and Vicinity

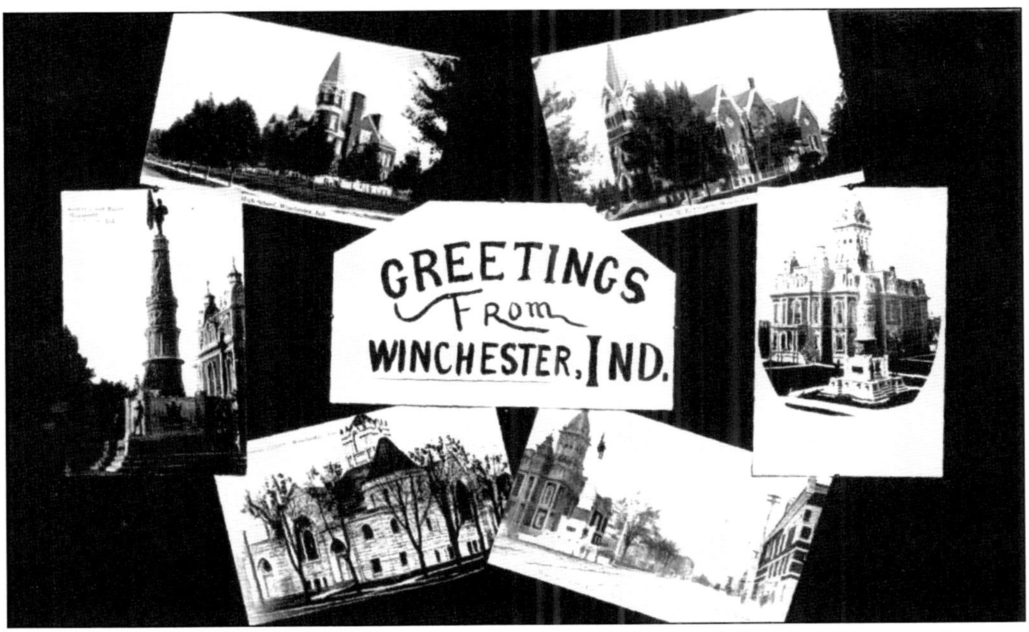

Greetings from Winchester. This composite postcard by the Shalley Art Company features, clockwise starting at the top left, Winchester High School, Winchester Methodist Episcopal Church, the Randolph County Courthouse, a view of Washington Street showing the courthouse and Civil War monument, First Presbyterian Church, and the Soldiers and Sailors Monument. (Gregory P. Hinshaw.)

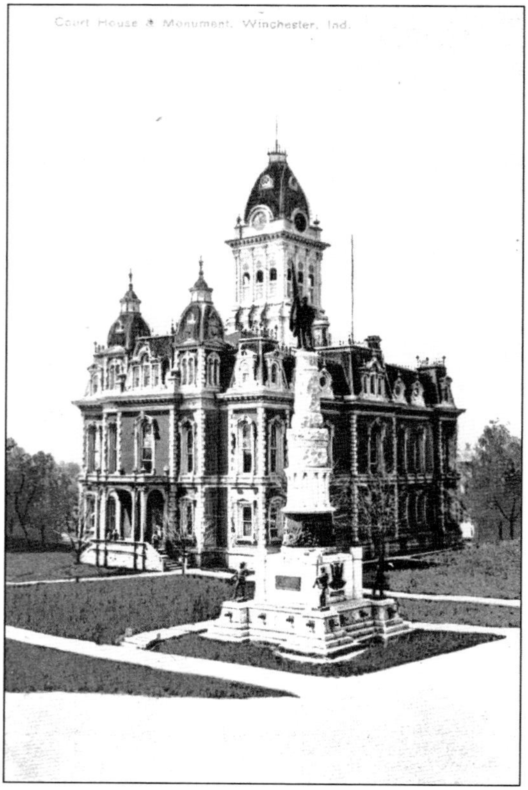

COURTHOUSE LOOKING SOUTHWEST. One of the best-known views in Randolph County is this depiction of the county's third courthouse, an Italianate structure, built between 1875 and 1877. The building was significantly altered in 1954, when after more than 50 years of debate, the central tower and mansard roof were removed. Work on the Soldiers and Sailors Monument began in 1889 and was completed in 1892. (Randolph County Historical Society.)

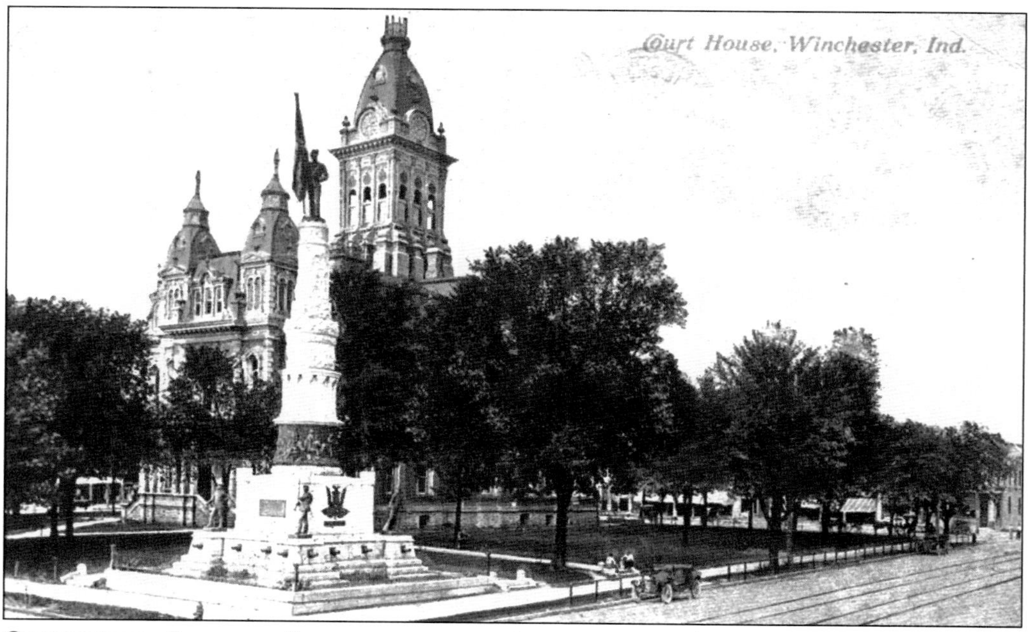

COURTHOUSE LOOKING SOUTHWEST WITH AUTOMOBILE. This view not only includes the wrought-iron fence, installed around the monument about 1907, it also shows an early automobile and hitching racks along Washington Street. (Gregory P. Hinshaw.)

COURTHOUSE LOOKING NORTH. Views of the south side of the courthouse are less common than from the north. This view shows buggies parked along Franklin Street. (Gregory P. Hinshaw.)

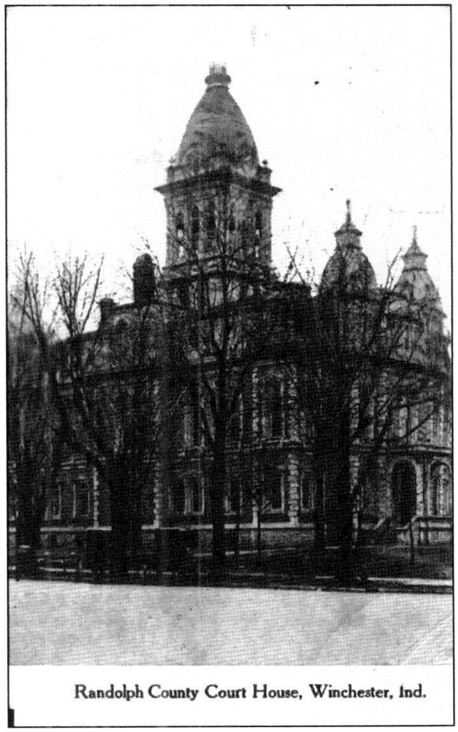

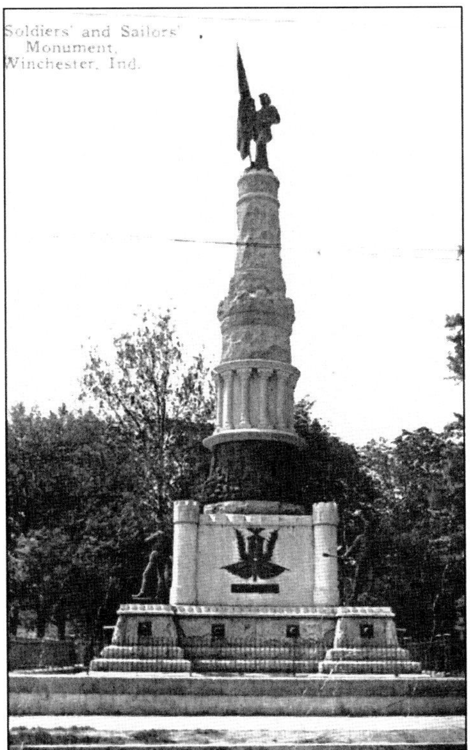

MONUMENT, NORTH SIDE. The cornerstone of the Soldiers and Sailors Monument was laid on August 15, 1889. The stonework was completed in August 1890, but it was not until July 21, 1892, that the monument was dedicated. The monument was designed by A. A. McCain, while the sculptures were done by Lorado Taft. At its completion it was the tallest monument in the state, although now it is the third tallest. (Gregory P. Hinshaw.)

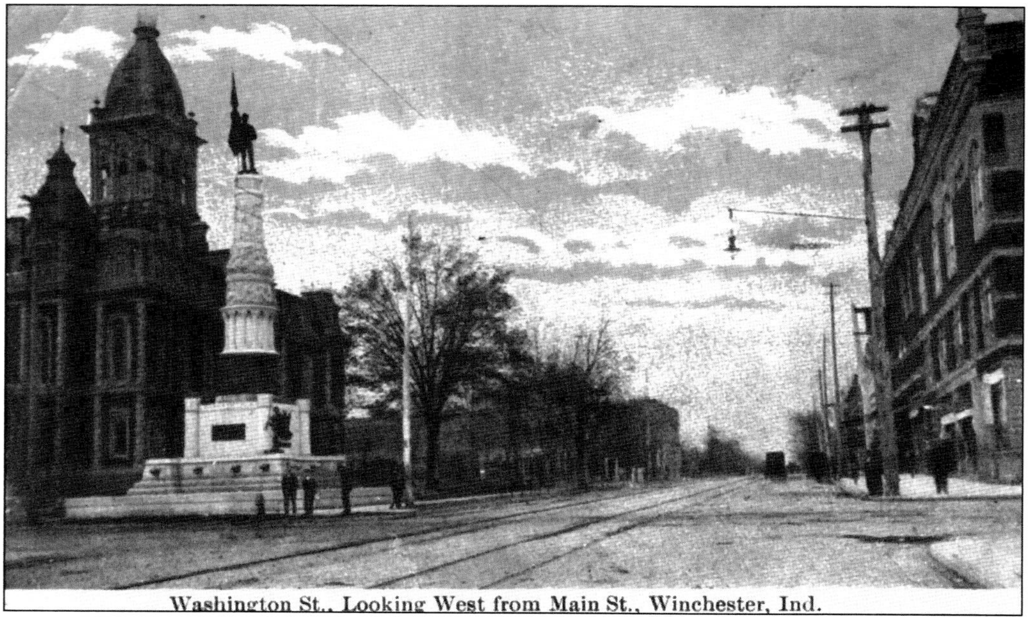

WASHINGTON STREET LOOKING WEST FROM MAIN STREET. This scene depicts a view west from Winchester's principal intersection, Washington and Main Streets. The courthouse and monument can be seen at the left, while the Knights of Pythias building is at the right. In the background is the Moorman Building, the longtime home of the People's Loan and Trust Company. In the foreground are the tracks of the Indiana Union Traction Company. (Gregory P. Hinshaw.)

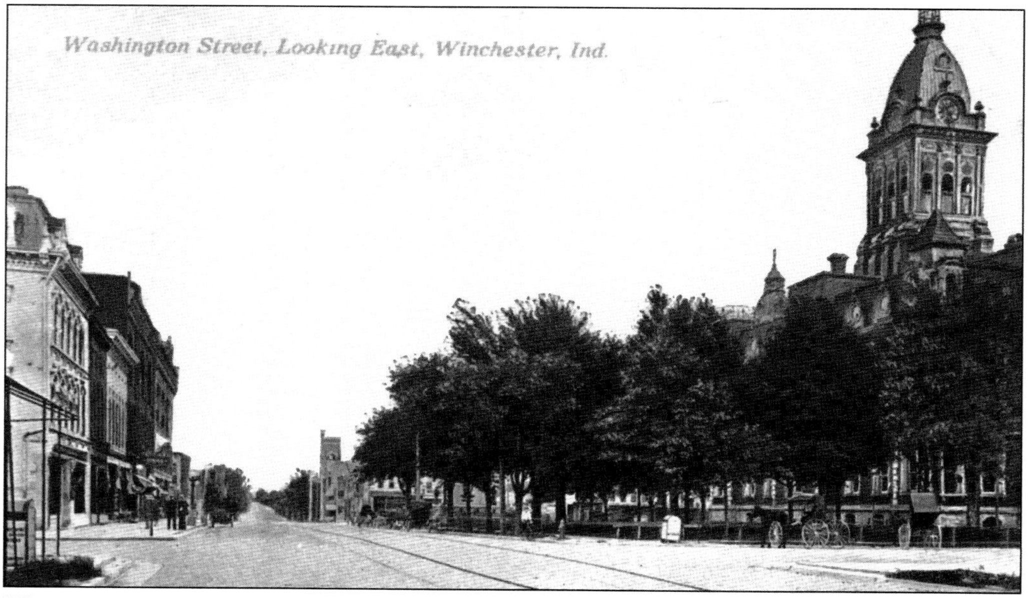

WASHINGTON STREET LOOKING EAST. This view looks east from just west of the intersection of Washington Street and Meridian Street. At the right is the courthouse, while the north side of the square is visible at the left, including the Randolph County Bank building, erected in 1860, in the foreground. In the distance is the tower of the Friends church. (Gregory P. Hinshaw.)

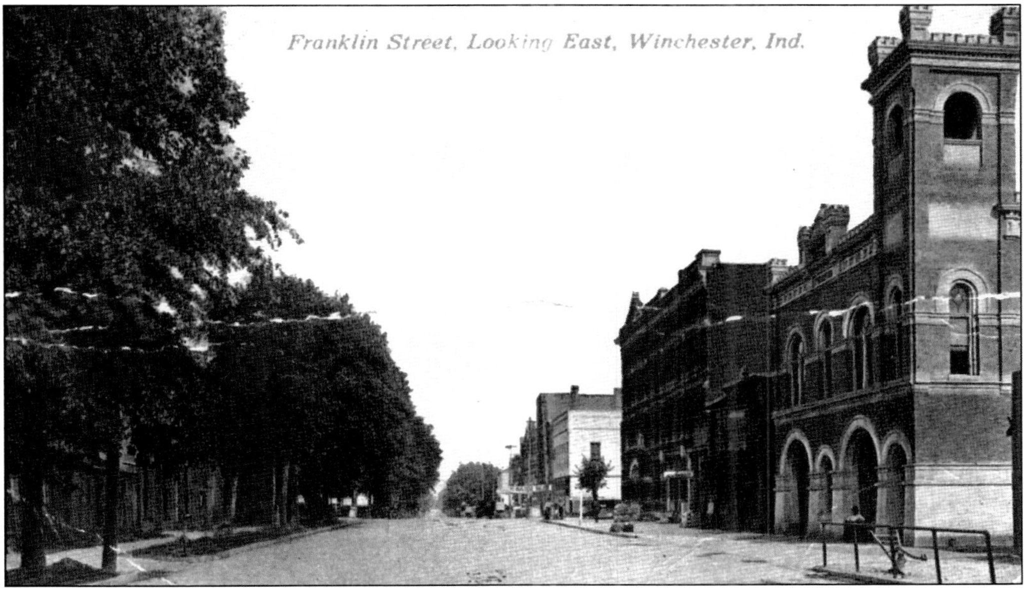

FRANKLIN STREET LOOKING EAST. This view looks east on Franklin Street from west of Meridian Street. At the right is the city hall (with tower) and the Randolph Hotel. (Gregory P. Hinshaw.)

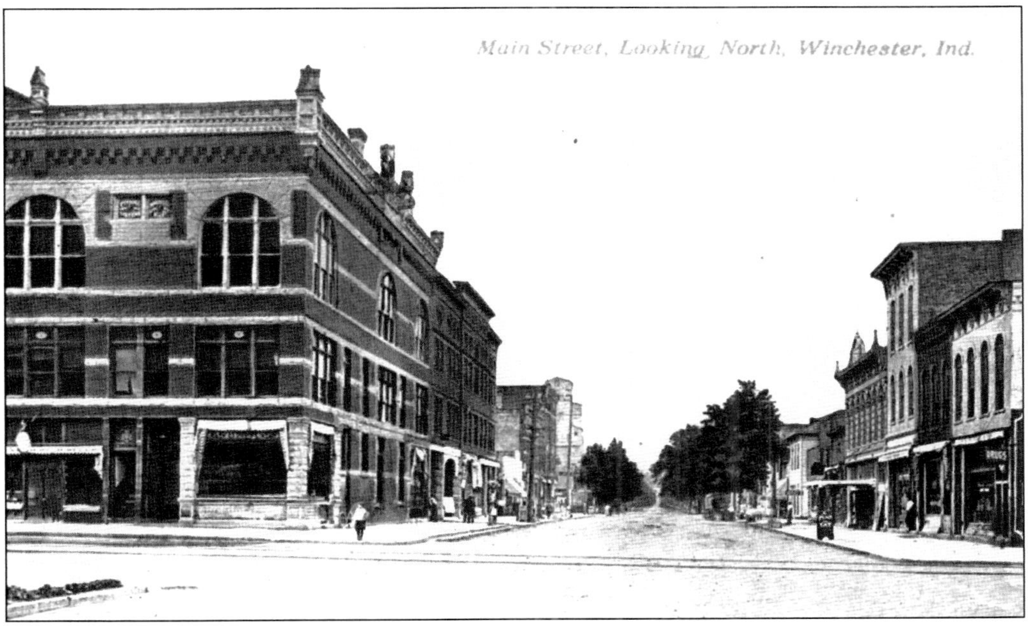

MAIN STREET LOOKING NORTH. The view looks north on Main Street from just south of the intersection with Washington Street. At the left is the Knights of Pythias building, completed in 1894. The Knights of Pythias sold their interest in the building to the Junior Order of United American Mechanics in 1951. Part of the third floor of the building was removed in 1979. (Gregory P. Hinshaw.)

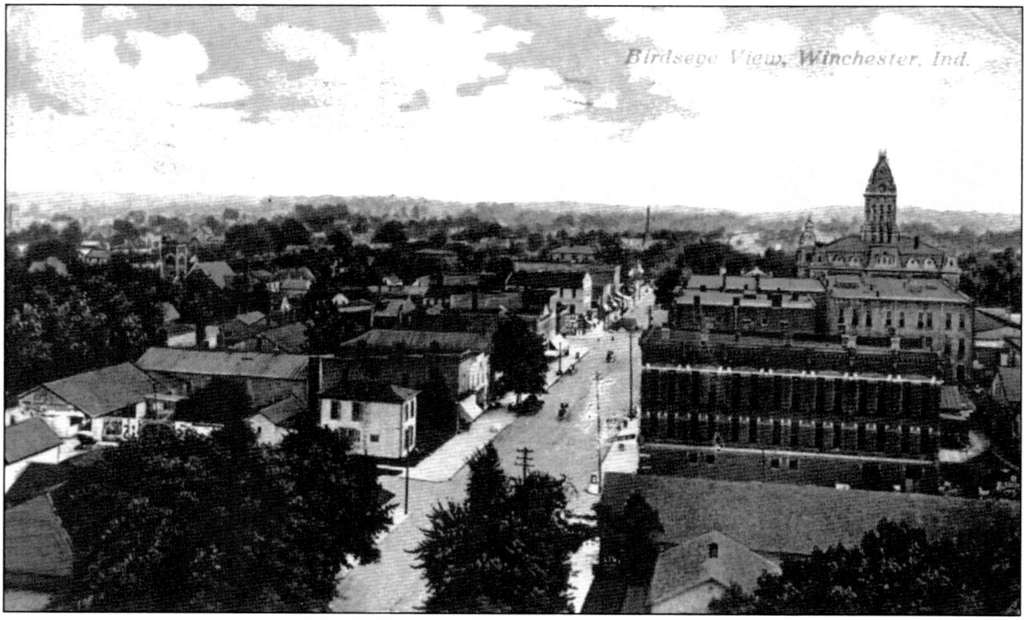

BIRD'S-EYE VIEW. This view looks south from Goodrich Brothers Hay and Grain Elevator on North Main Street. The courthouse is visible at the right, although the monument was apparently omitted by the lithographer. In the foreground at right is the hall of the Independent Order of Odd Fellows (IOOF), constructed in 1883. At center left is the tower of the Friends church. (Gregory P. Hinshaw.)

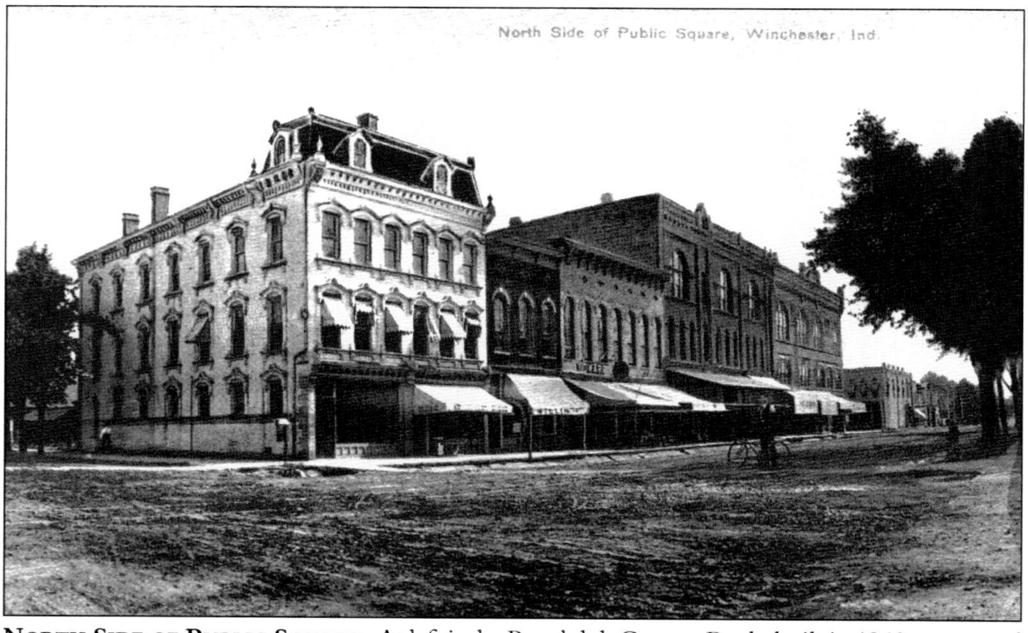

NORTH SIDE OF PUBLIC SQUARE. At left is the Randolph County Bank, built in 1860, renovated in 1877, and razed in 1957. The next two buildings were razed for expansion of the bank in 1972 and 1993. Next is the Masonic hall, constructed in 1883. It was damaged by fire in 1944, and the third floor was removed. The next building is the Pythian building. (Gregory P. Hinshaw.)

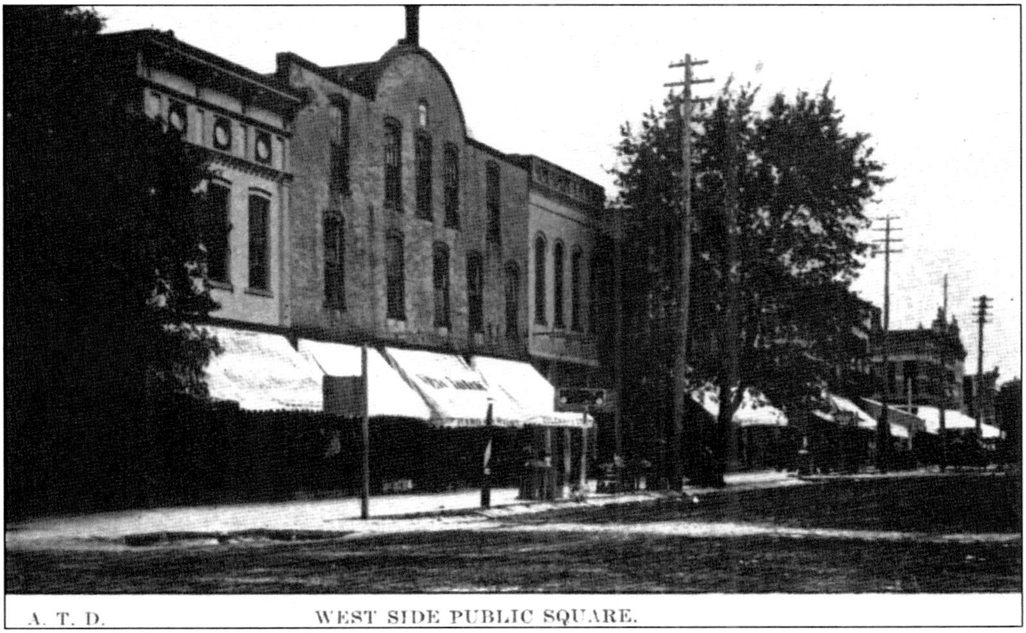

West Side of Public Square. A rare view of the west side of the public square is shown here. The building with the rounded cornice is the Canada Building. It was modernized in 1910, after this photograph. The Pretlow Block, obscured by trees, was built in 1897. The building at the far right is the Dennis Kelley Block, constructed in 1886 at the northwest corner of Meridian Street and Washington Street. It is extant, though altered. (Gregory P. Hinshaw.)

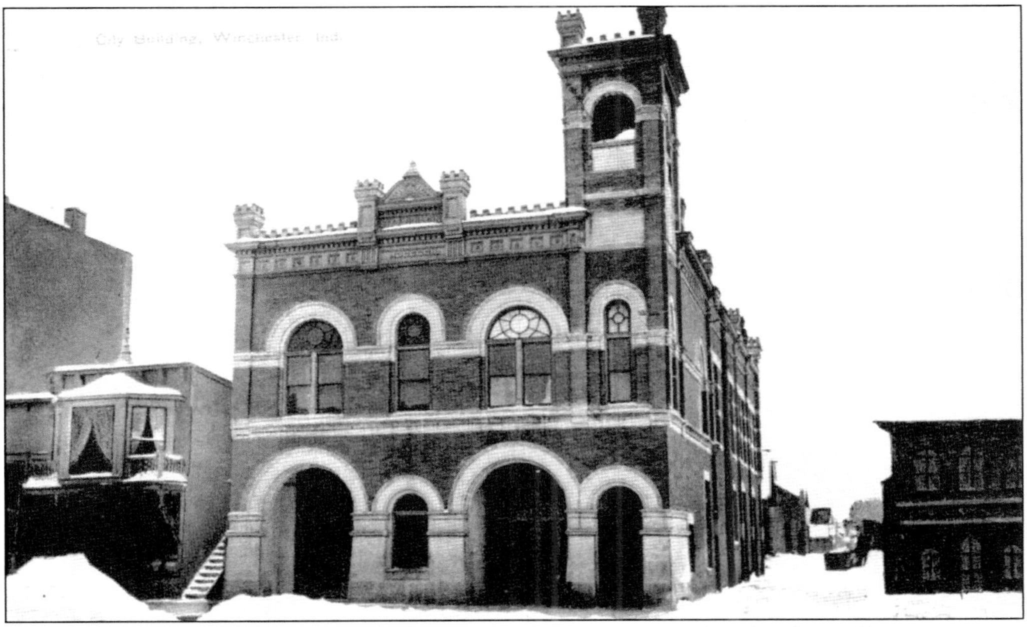

City Building. Winchester's city building, located on the south side of Franklin Street west of Meridian Street, was constructed in 1902–1903. It was used until 1984 and has since been razed. (Tom McKee.)

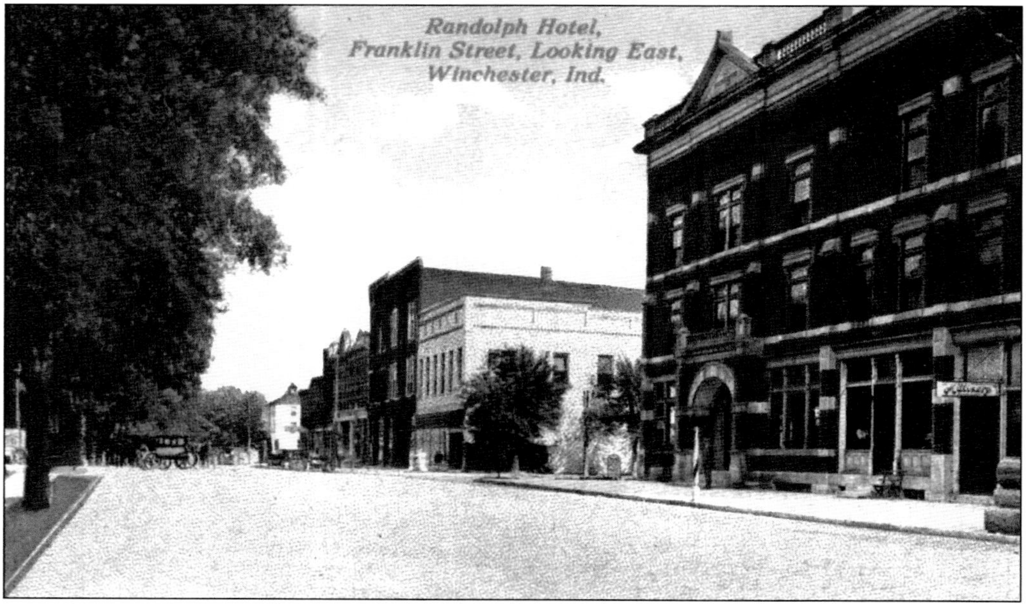

RANDOLPH HOTEL AND FRANKLIN STREET LOOKING EAST. At the right is the Randolph Hotel. Across Meridian Street are the Mills Building, erected in 1911, and the W. E. Miller Building, built in 1882 and expanded in 1889, 1902, and 1912. To the east is the Kabel Building, erected in 1902. The Franklin House, erected about 1839 by Jeremiah Smith, can be seen with a small bell tower at the far end of Franklin Street. It was razed in 1927. (Tom McKee.)

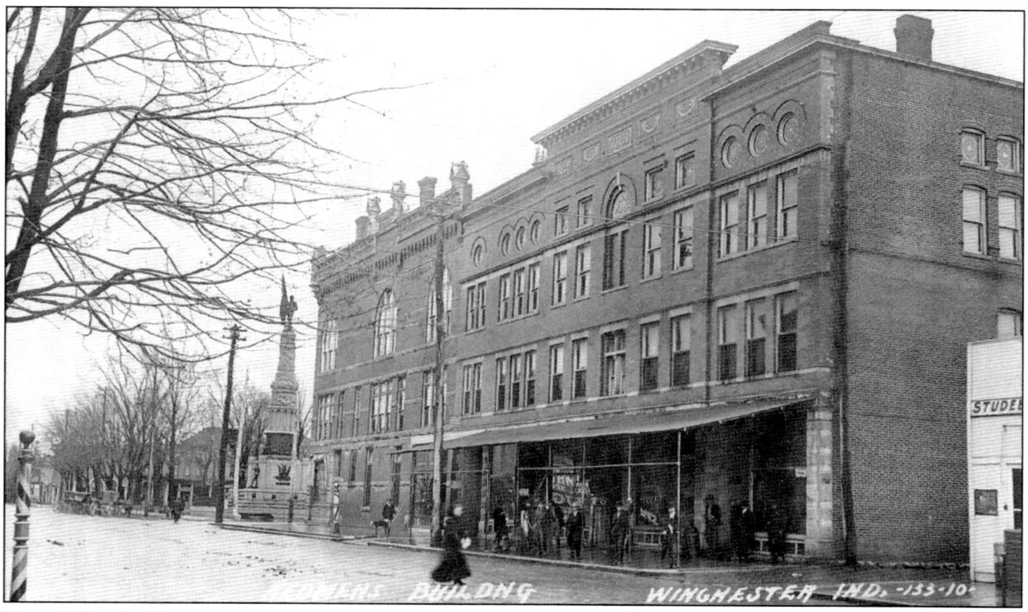

RED MEN'S BUILDING, LOOKING SOUTH ON MAIN STREET. At the right is the hall of the Improved Order of Red Men, erected in 1901–1902 and dedicated on March 2, 1902. The next building is the Knights of Pythias building, erected in 1894. The Soldiers and Sailors Monument can be seen in the background. (Jane Lyle.)

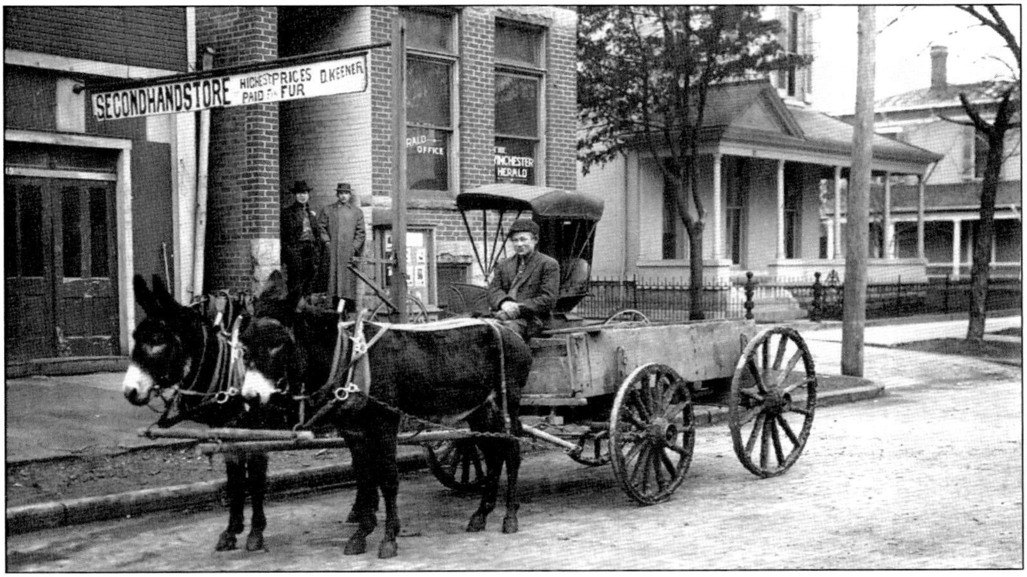

WINCHESTER HERALD OFFICE. This scene is on North Meridian Street. The office of the *Winchester Herald* can be seen. The *Herald* was established in 1875. The building depicted here was completed in 1903. The *Herald* merged with the *Winchester Journal* in 1920 to form the *Journal-Herald* and remained in the Herald Building. In 1963, the press was moved from the building, which was razed in 1966. (Jane Lyle.)

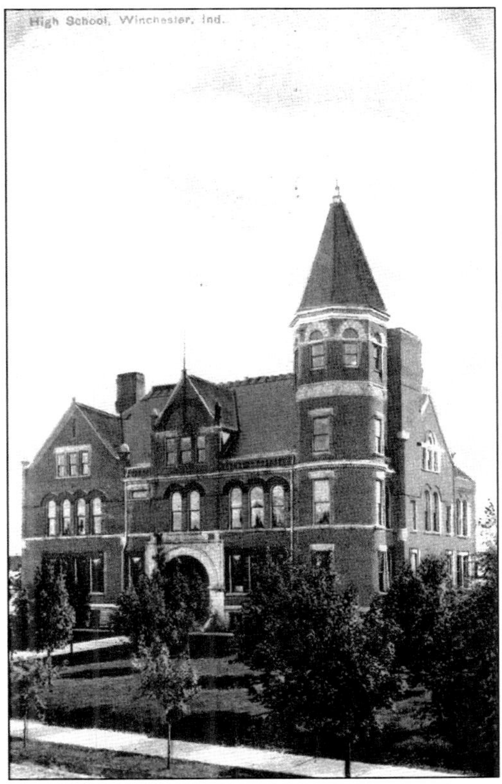

WINCHESTER HIGH SCHOOL. This building, located on the city block surrounded by South, High, Browne, and Thompson Streets, was erected in 1898–1899 by J. L. Shetterly at a cost of $15,337 to replace a building destroyed by fire on April 24, 1898. A gymnasium was added in 1923, and the field house was constructed in 1951–1952. The building was used until the spring of 1967. The school and first gymnasium were razed in 1972–1973, although the field house remains at the site. (Gregory P. Hinshaw.)

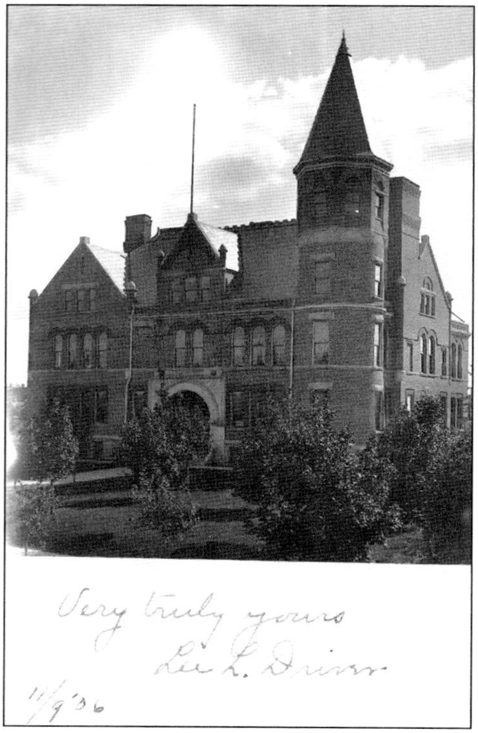

WINCHESTER HIGH SCHOOL WITH DRIVER SIGNATURE. This real-photo postcard is notable because it bears the signature of Lee L. Driver, the nationally known county superintendent of schools of Randolph County. He was the principal of this building from 1900 to 1907. (Steve Longnecker.)

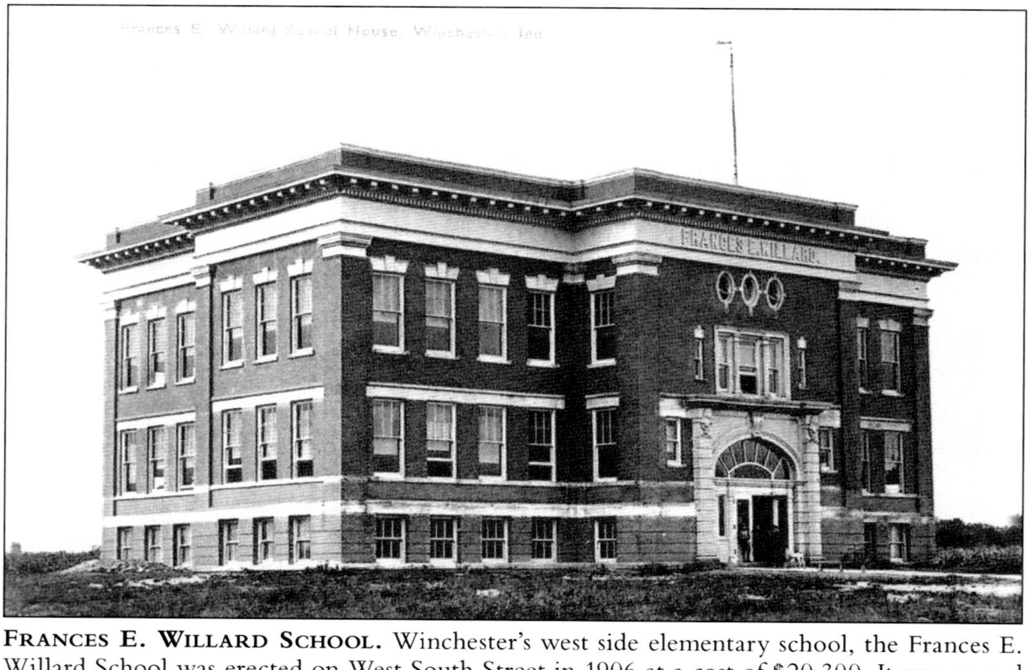

FRANCES E. WILLARD SCHOOL. Winchester's west side elementary school, the Frances E. Willard School was erected on West South Street in 1906 at a cost of $20,300. It was named for the longtime leader of the Woman's Christian Temperance Union. The building functioned until 1971, when a new building was dedicated nearby. The old building was razed soon after. (Thomas Keesling.)

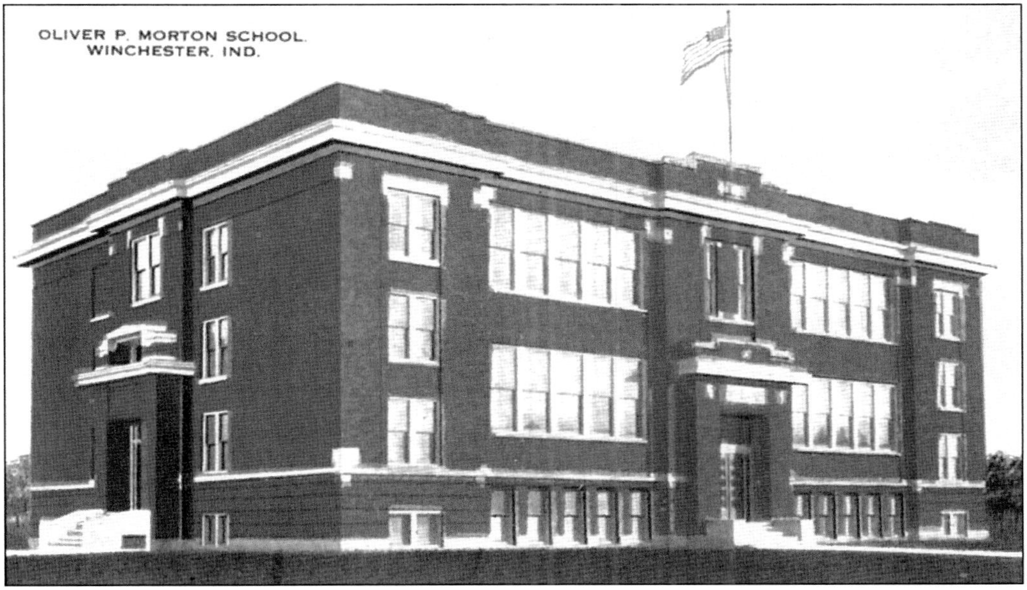

OLIVER P. MORTON SCHOOL. Winchester's north side elementary school, this building was erected in 1916 at Residence and Fourth Streets and opened in January 1917. It was named for Indiana's Civil War governor and U.S. senator. An addition was constructed in 1957. The school functioned until the spring of 1992. It was razed in the autumn. (Randolph County Historical Society.)

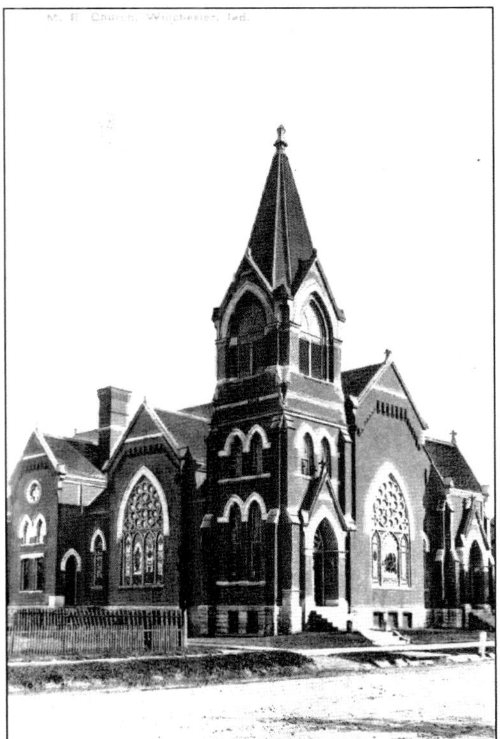

FIRST METHODIST EPISCOPAL CHURCH. This congregation is the oldest in Winchester. Methodist preaching began in the town about 1822, although no building was constructed until 1835. A brick structure was completed on the present site in 1857. A larger brick church was constructed in 1885–1886 and burned in 1899. The structure depicted here was designed by Hampton Gettinger and dedicated on December 30, 1900. An addition was made to the south side in 1962. (Gregory P. Hinshaw.)

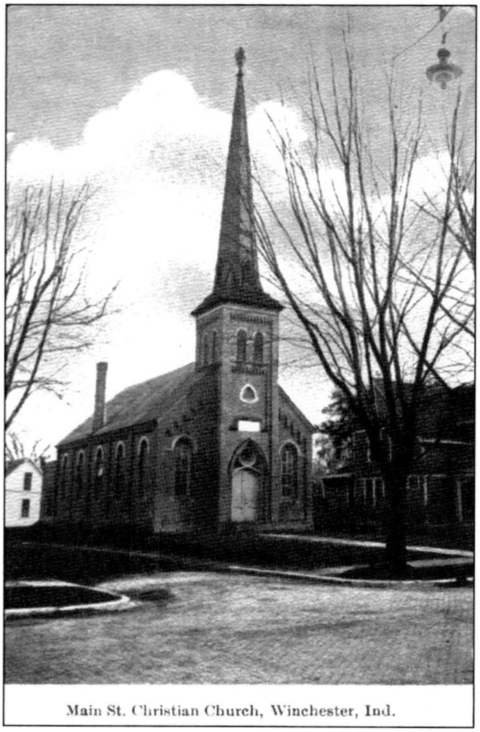

MAIN STREET CHRISTIAN CHURCH. This building stood at the southeast corner of Main and Will Streets. The congregation was organized in 1866 and originally met in the old Presbyterian church. The structure depicted here was erected in 1876 and used until 1914, when a new structure was occupied. This building was sold to the Church of the Nazarene, which used it until 1929, when a new structure was erected on the site. (Gregory P. Hinshaw.)

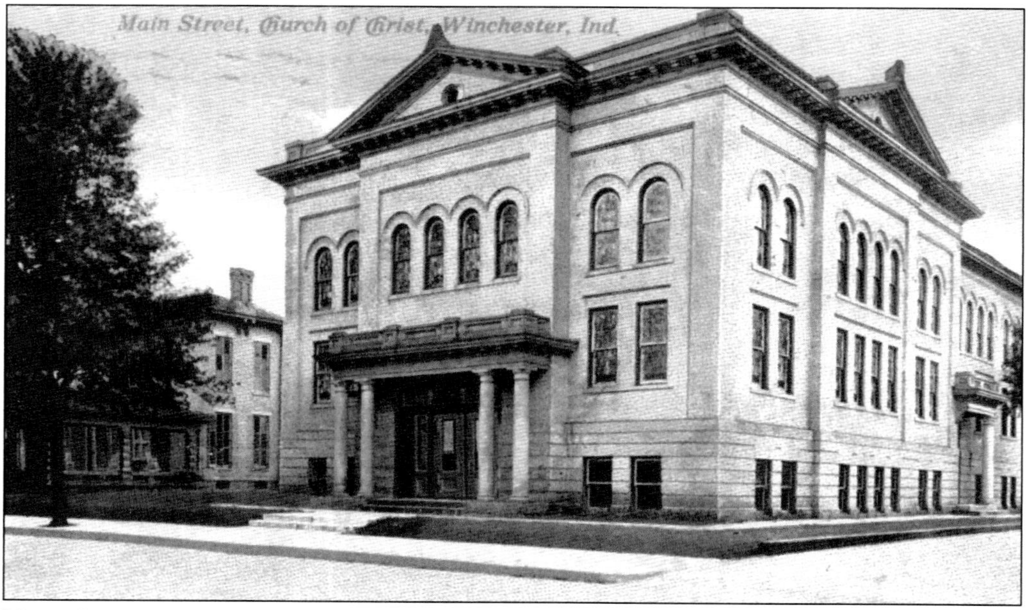

MAIN STREET CHURCH OF CHRIST. The congregation began making plans for this building, located on the west side of Main Street between Franklin and South Streets, in 1911, and the cornerstone was laid in May 1912. The building was first occupied in February 1914 and was dedicated on April 11, 1915. After denominational reorganization, the congregation became formally known as Main Street Christian Church (Disciples of Christ). (Gregory P. Hinshaw.)

FRIENDS CHURCH. Regular Friends services began in Winchester in 1873, and a Friends church was dedicated at the southwest corner of Washington and East Streets in 1874. The building was razed in 1897, and work began on the structure depicted here, which was designed by William S. Kaufman and dedicated in May 1898. This was the first Friends church to possess a pipe organ, installed in 1904. (Gregory P. Hinshaw.)

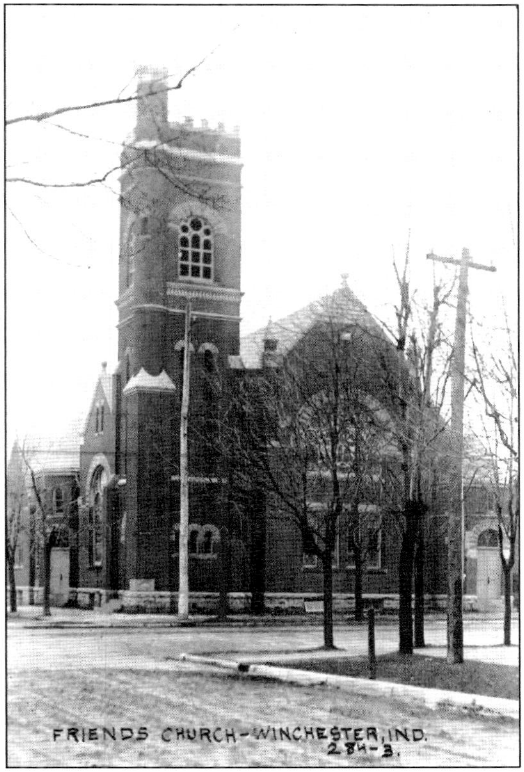

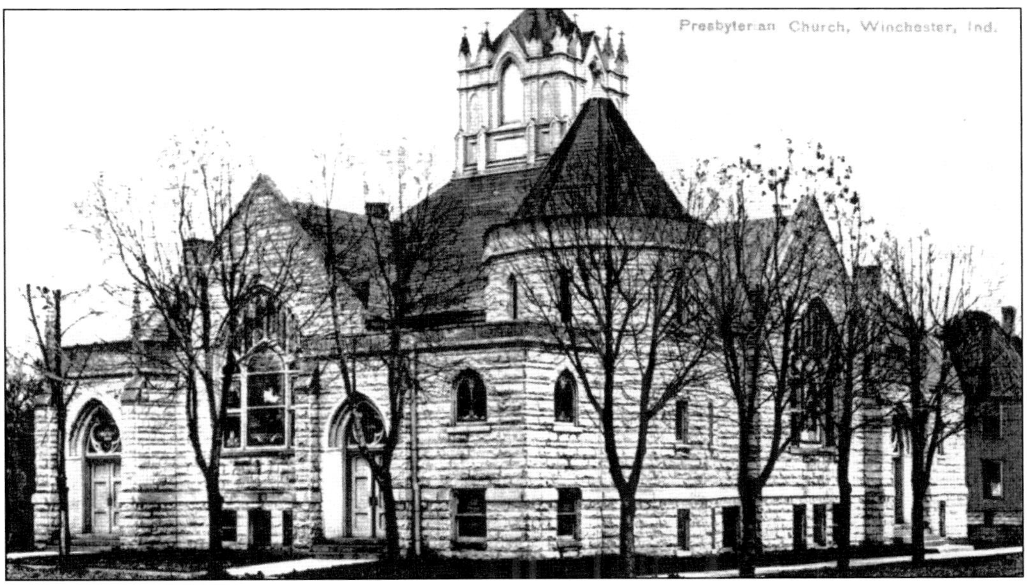

PRESBYTERIAN CHURCH. A "New School" Presbyterian Church was organized in Winchester in 1881 and met for several years in rented space. A church was completed at the northwest corner of East and Franklin Streets in 1887. The structure depicted here, designed by Hampton Gettinger, was erected east of the original building in 1903 and dedicated on May 29, 1904. An addition was completed in 1928. The central tower has since been removed. (Gregory P. Hinshaw.)

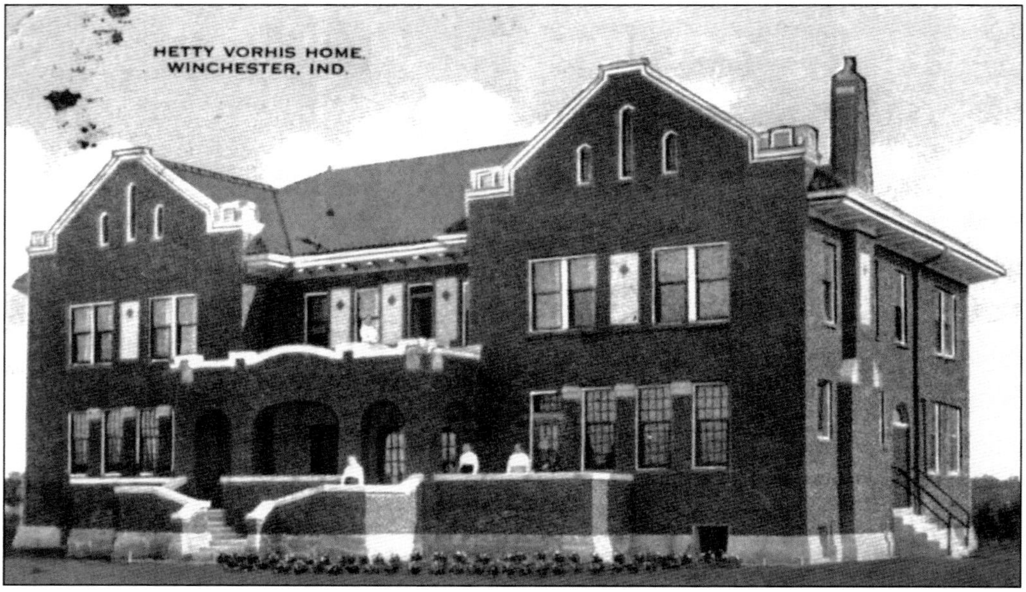

HETTY VORHIS HOME. This building was erected in 1915–1916 on Oak Street at Greenville Avenue. It was built under the direction of Hetty Vorhis as a home for "Old Women." The county acquired the structure as a hospital in 1919. The building was enlarged in 1953 and 1969–1970. A new hospital was erected nearby in 2001, and the old building became the Randolph Center for Family Opportunity, rededicated on September 20, 2003. (Gregory P. Hinshaw.)

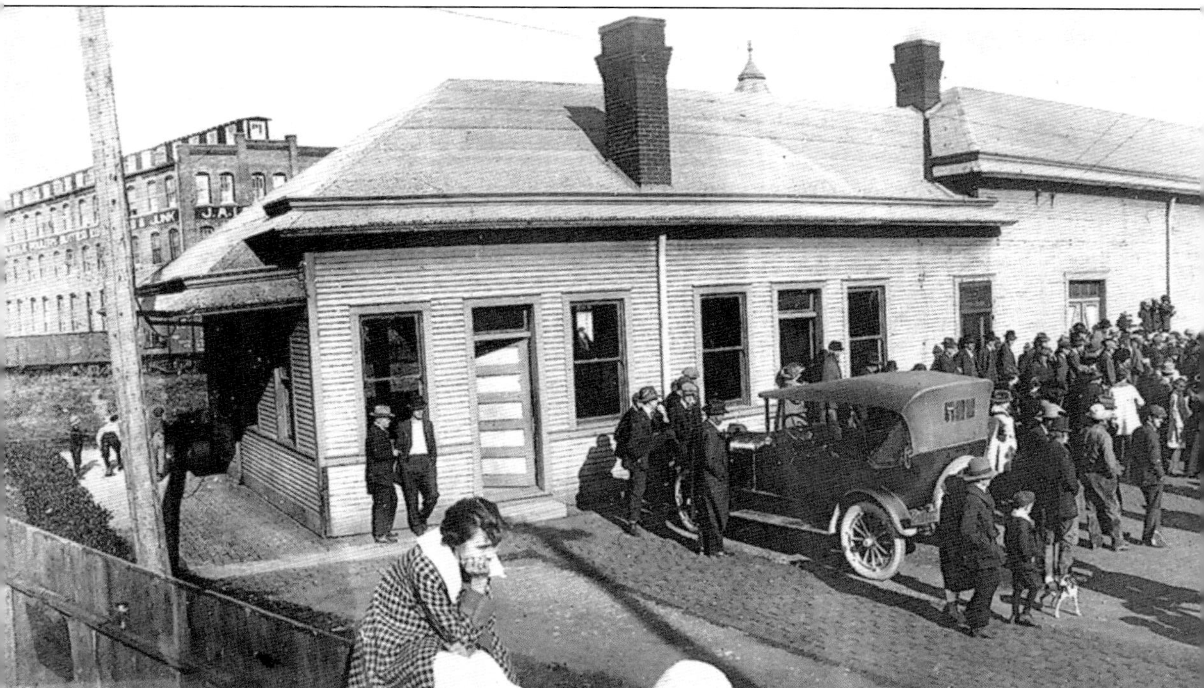

GRAND RAPIDS AND INDIANA DEPOT. This depot was constructed in 1895 on the west side of North Meridian Street. Passenger service was discontinued in 1947. The dilapidated

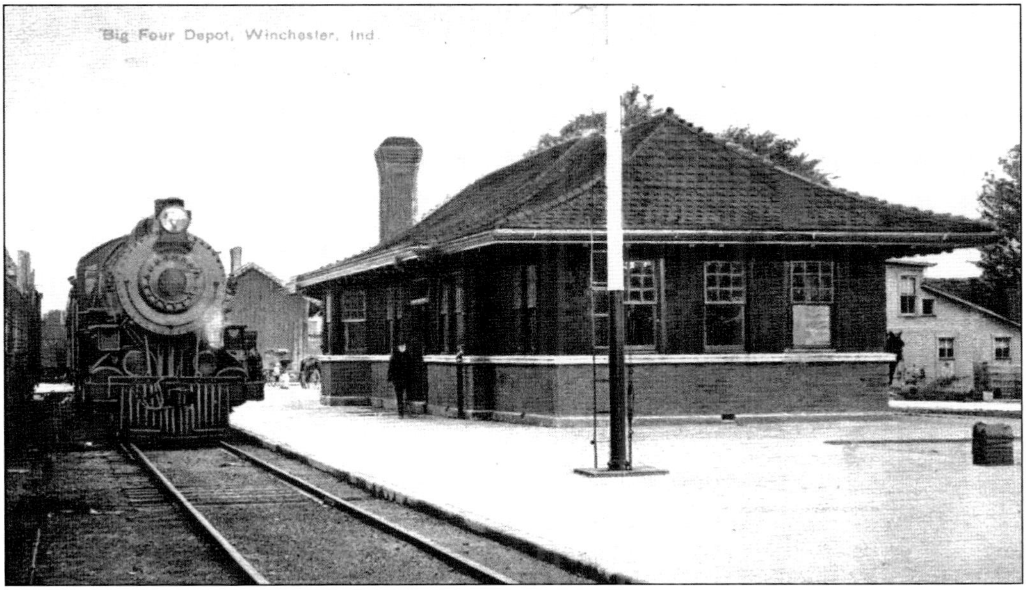

BIG FOUR DEPOT. This depot served passengers of the "Big Four," the Cleveland, Cincinnati, Chicago, and St. Louis Railroad, running east and west through Winchester. This structure, located on the east side of East Street, opened in August 1907, replacing a 50-year-old structure located farther west. This line became a part of CSX in 1999. Passenger service was discontinued in the 1960s. The building remains and is used for storage by CSX. (Harold Watson.)

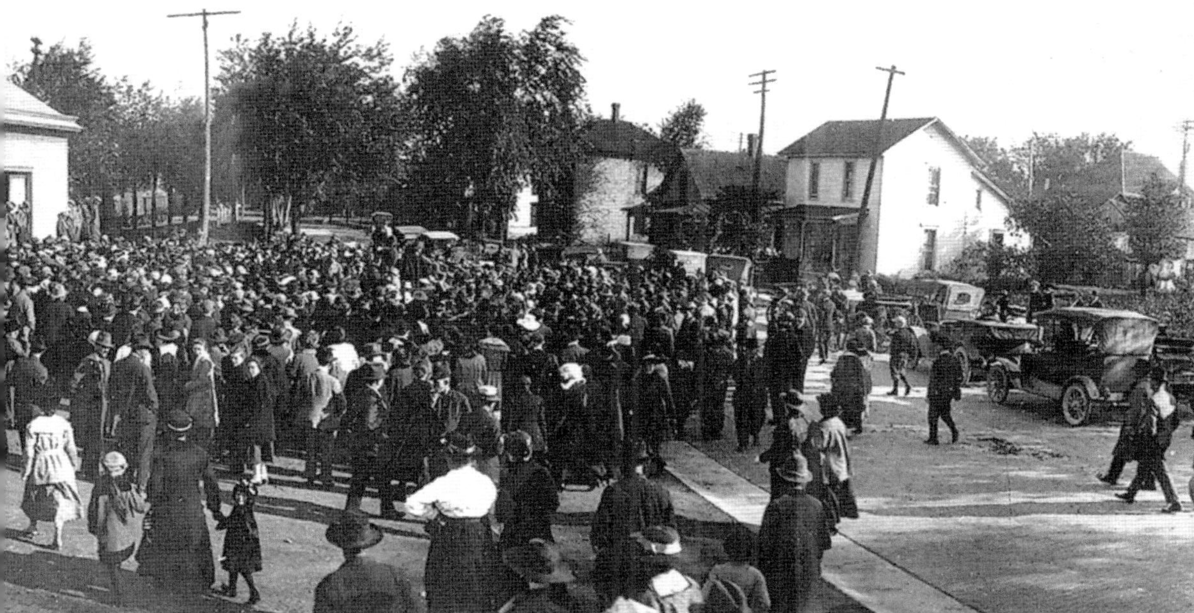

structure was razed in 1973. Freight traffic was discontinued in 1975. (Randolph County Historical Society.)

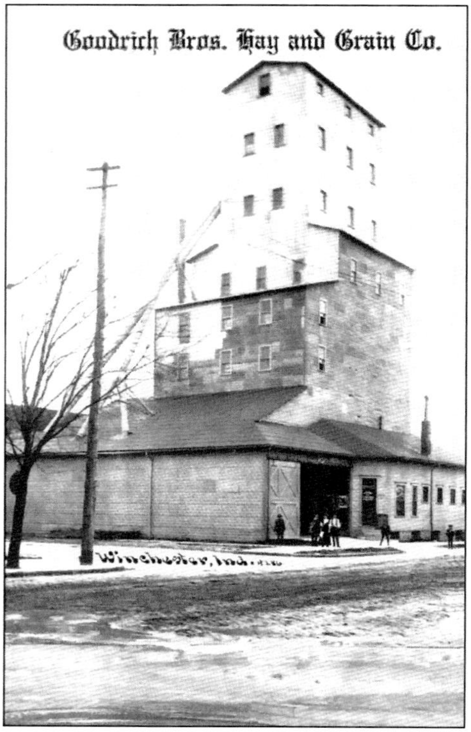

GOODRICH BROTHERS HAY AND GRAIN COMPANY. This structure was built in 1892 and was moved to the west side of North Main Street south of the railroad in 1905. It burned in May 1913. A new building was built in 1913–1914. The elevator closed in 1971 and was razed in 1973. Goodrich Brothers Hay and Grain Company was incorporated in 1898 and eventually operated approximately two dozen grain elevators in Indiana. (Thomas Keesling.)

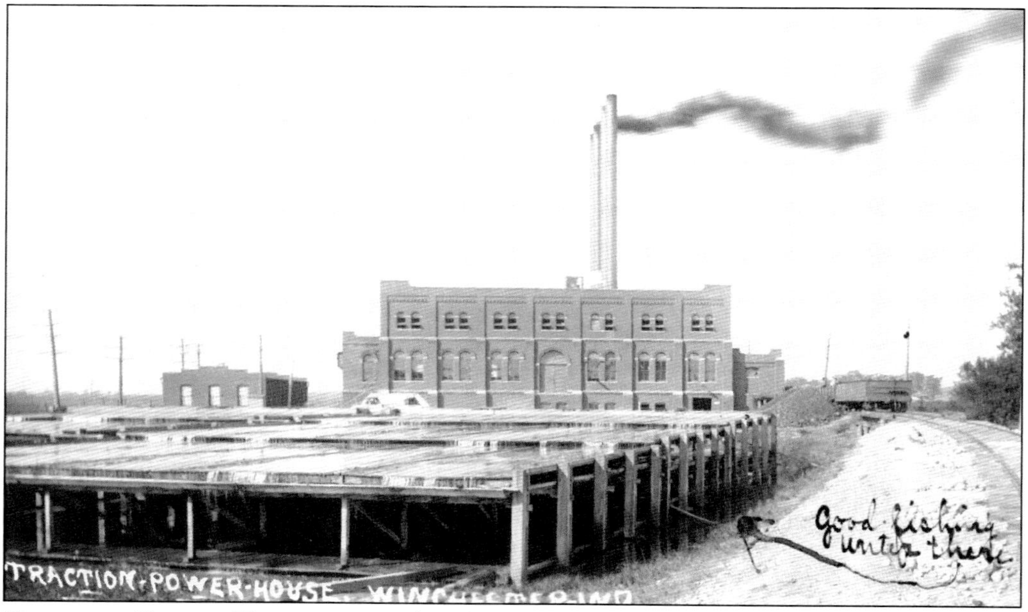

TRACTION POWER HOUSE. Located at the western edge of Winchester, this structure was built in 1903 and generated the electricity to power several miles of the Indiana Union Traction Company's line in Randolph County. In the foreground is the cooling basin. Nearby, although not pictured here, was the carbarn, used for housing traction cars. Only a portion of the structure remains today on the grounds of Omega Enterprises. (Tom McKee.)

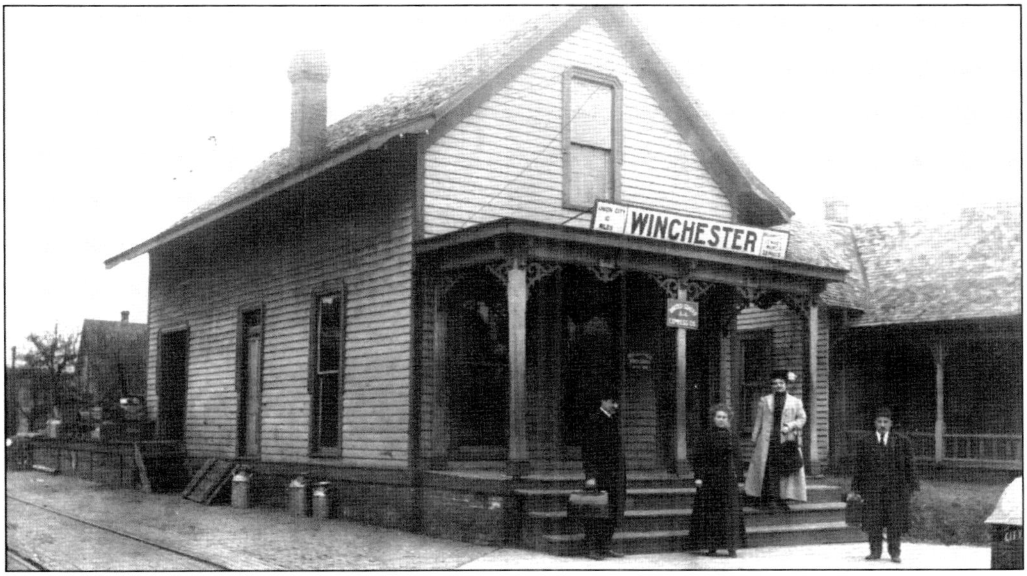

Indiana Union Traction Company Depot. Located on the south side of Washington Street west of Meridian Street, this structure was one of two depots of the Indiana Union Traction Company in Winchester. In addition to identifying the city, the sign also gives the distances to Union City, Muncie, and Indianapolis. The structure is no longer extant. The man on the right is Fernando B. Mullen. The woman at the left is Bertha Shockley, the station agent. (Randolph County Historical Society.)

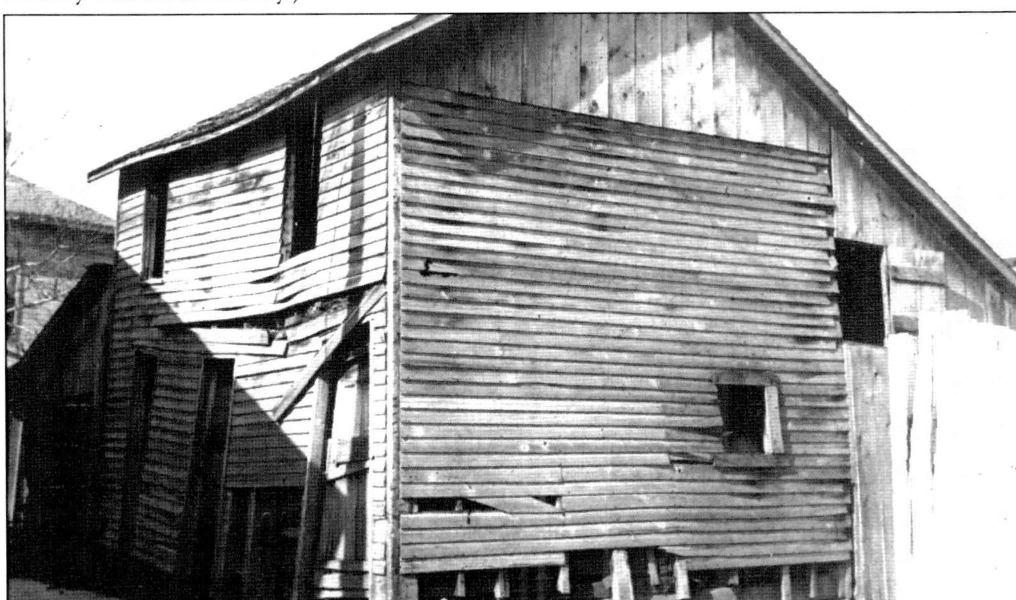

David Haworth Frame House. The structure depicted here was erected by David Haworth, a Tennessee native and Quaker, in 1824–1825 on lot No. 10, northeast square. It was the seventh house (and second frame structure) built in Winchester. It was later converted for other use and moved, but it survived until 1912, when it was razed. This photograph was taken by Newton Haworth, a grandson of David Haworth, in 1910. (Gregory P. Hinshaw.)

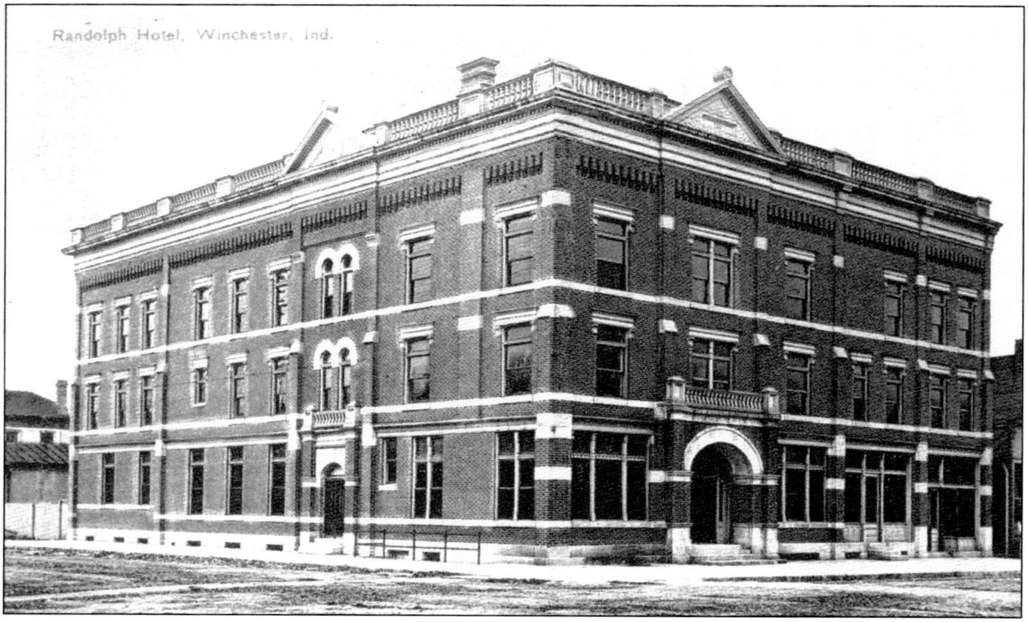

RANDOLPH HOTEL. Located at the southwest corner of Franklin and Meridian Streets, the Randolph Hotel opened in June 1904. It became the Beachler Apartments in 1971. The building's appearance remains original. (Judy Wilson Wright.)

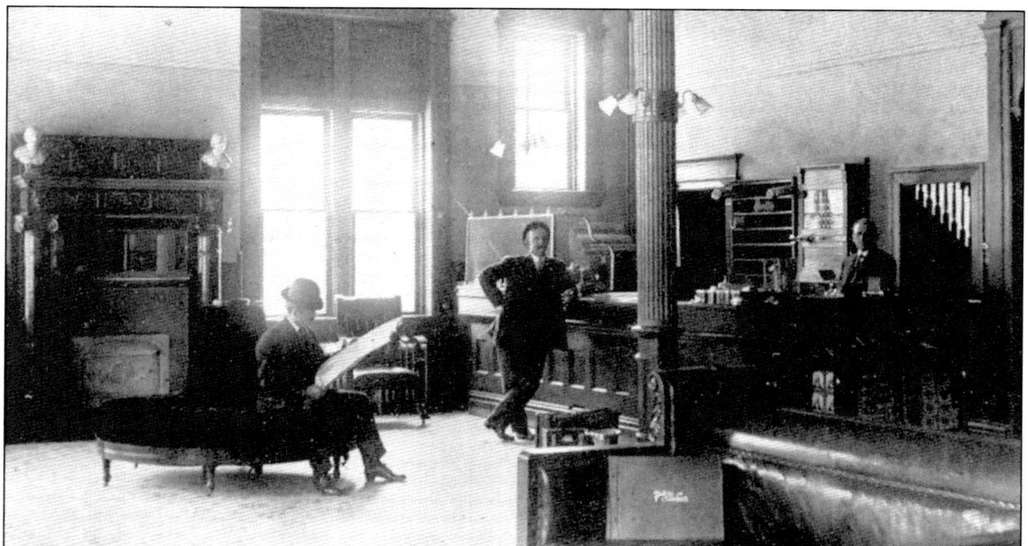

LOBBY OF RANDOLPH HOTEL. The lobby of the Randolph Hotel, opened in 1904, was located in the north room of the first floor. (Max Harter.)

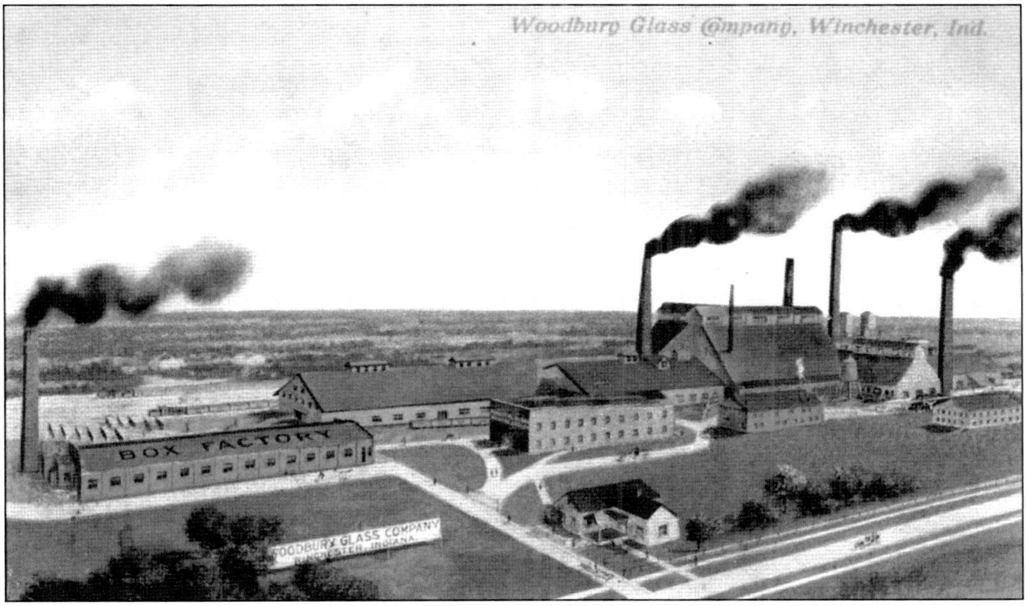

WOODBURY GLASS FACTORY. Woodbury Glass Factory was organized in July 1893 in Parker and moved to Winchester in November 1904, locating on the east side of the city. It burned in 1917 and was rebuilt the same year. The factory was purchased by Turner Glass in 1920 and became General Glass in 1930. It became Anchor-Hocking sometime between 1936 and 1939. (Gregory P. Hinshaw.)

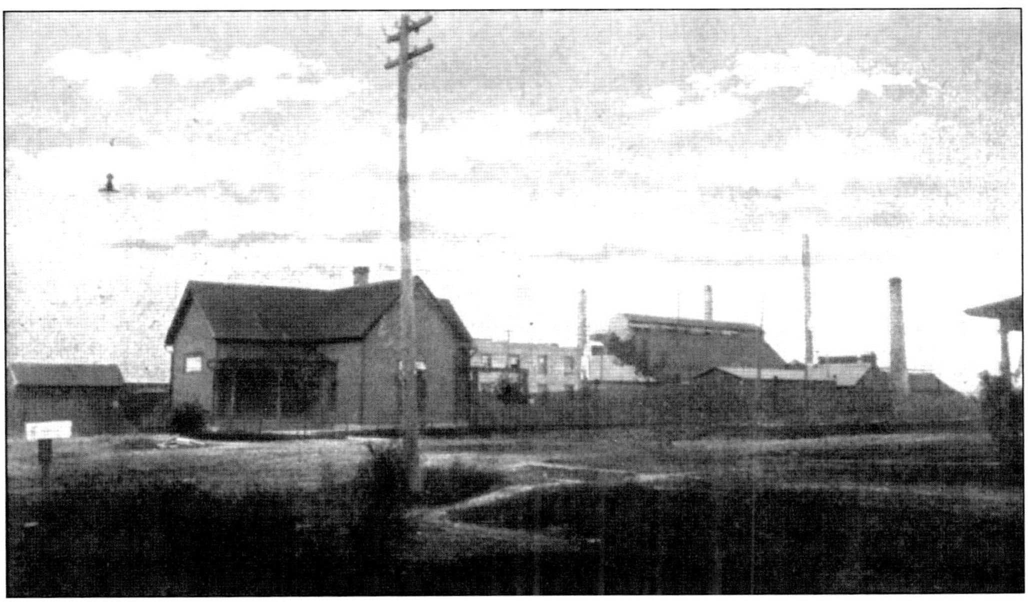

WOODBURY ENTRANCE. This view shows the office of the Woodbury Glass Company, which stands at the northeast corner of Plum and North Streets in Winchester. (Lowell and Anna Fraze.)

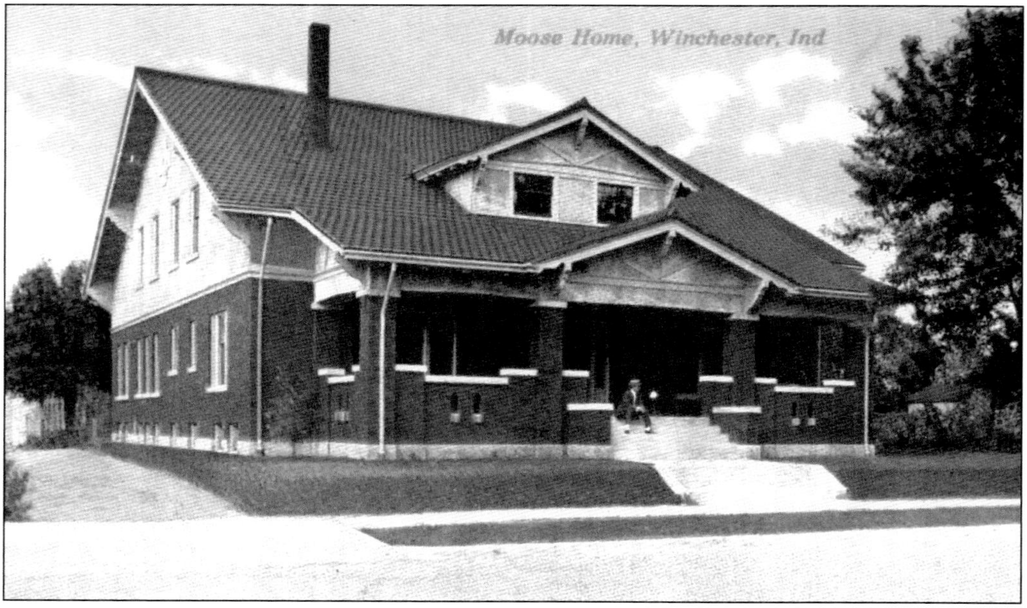

Moose Home. This structure, erected on the north side of North Street west of East Street in 1914, was the home of the Randolph Lodge No. 827, which was organized in 1913. In 1924, the lodge went into bankruptcy, and the building was abandoned. It was purchased by the Winchester Lodge No. 56, Free and Accepted Masons, in 1944. It has remained the home to Winchester's Masonic organizations in the years since. (Judy Wilson Wright.)

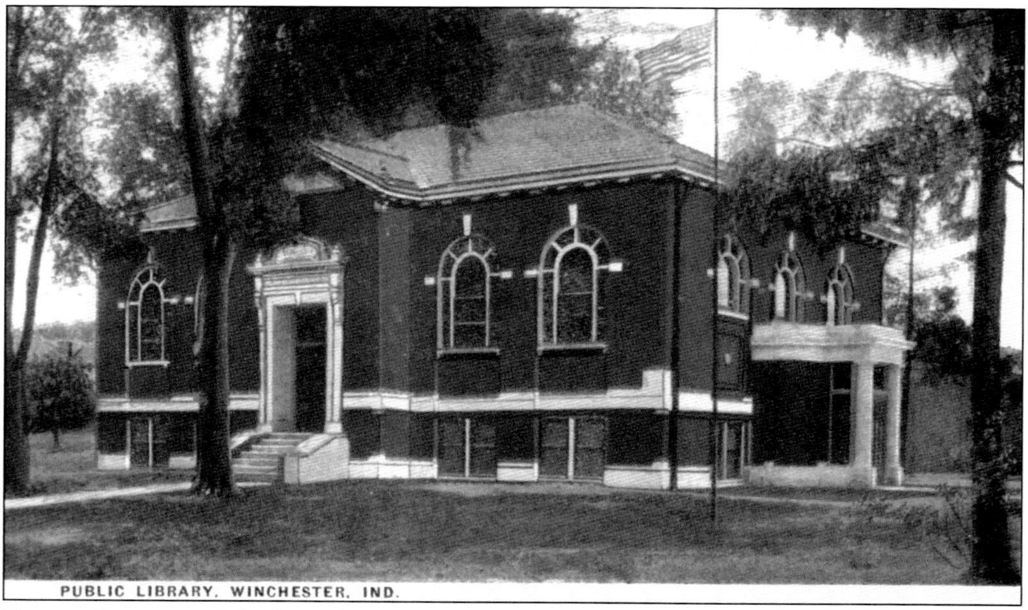

Public Library. Winchester's Carnegie Library was erected in 1915–1916 at the southwest corner of East and North Streets. Winchester did not have a public library until an association was organized in 1906. No permanent location was established until 1911. This structure was used until 1993, when a large addition was made to the west of the building. The original building is used for special purposes and storage. (Gregory P. Hinshaw.)

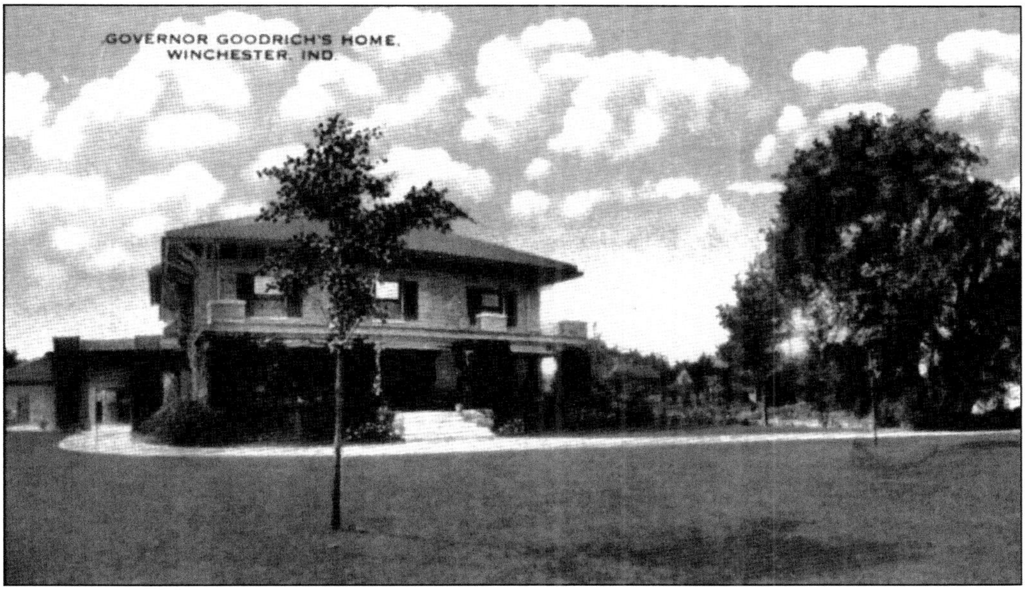

GOVERNOR GOODRICH'S HOME. James P. Goodrich, a Winchester resident, served as governor of Indiana from 1917 until 1921. He built this residence on East South Street, west of High Street, in 1912. The home remained in the possession of the Goodrich family until it was razed in 1976. (Gregory P. Hinshaw.)

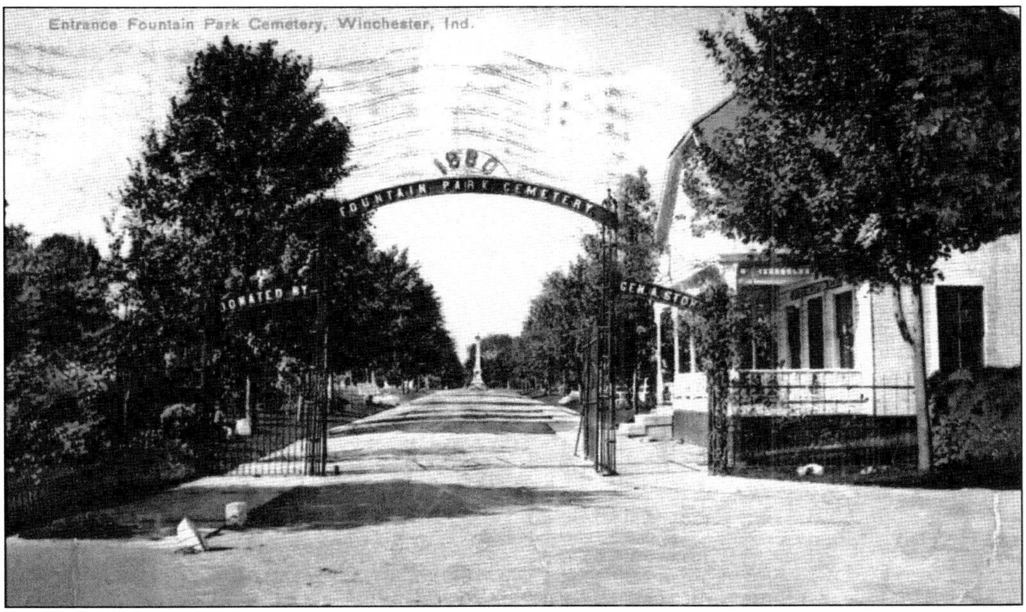

ENTRANCE TO FOUNTAIN PARK CEMETERY. Fountain Park Cemetery, located at the south edge of Winchester, was donated to the city by Gen. Asahel Stone in 1880. For many years, this iron gate marked the entrance to the cemetery. The caretaker's house, seen at right, was built in 1883 and razed in 1971. (Gregory P. Hinshaw.)

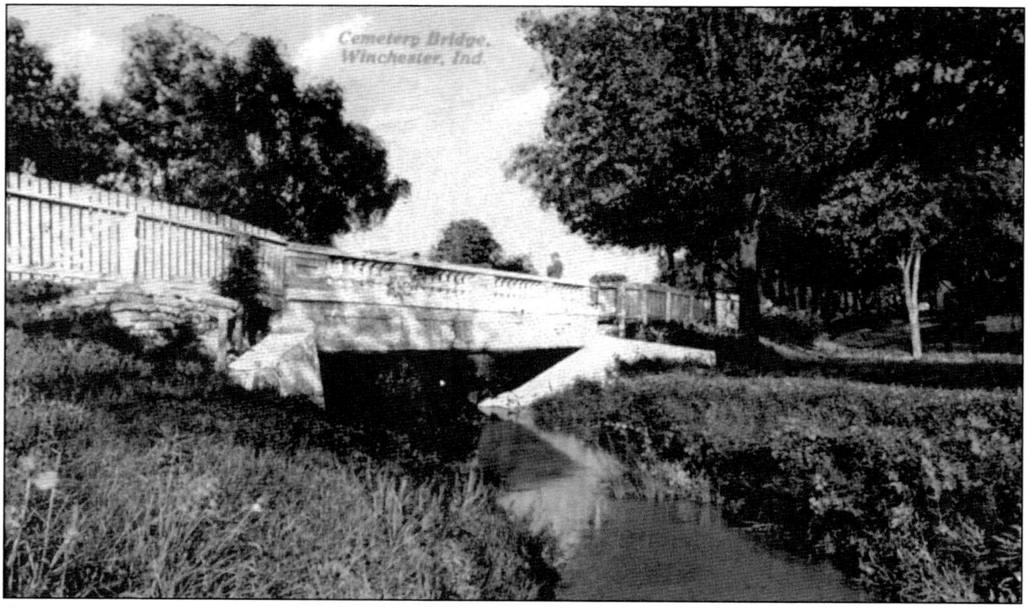

CEMETERY BRIDGE. The bridge depicted here carried South Main Street across Salt Creek at the northwestern edge of Fountain Park Cemetery. A modern bridge was built in 2001. (Gregory P. Hinshaw.)

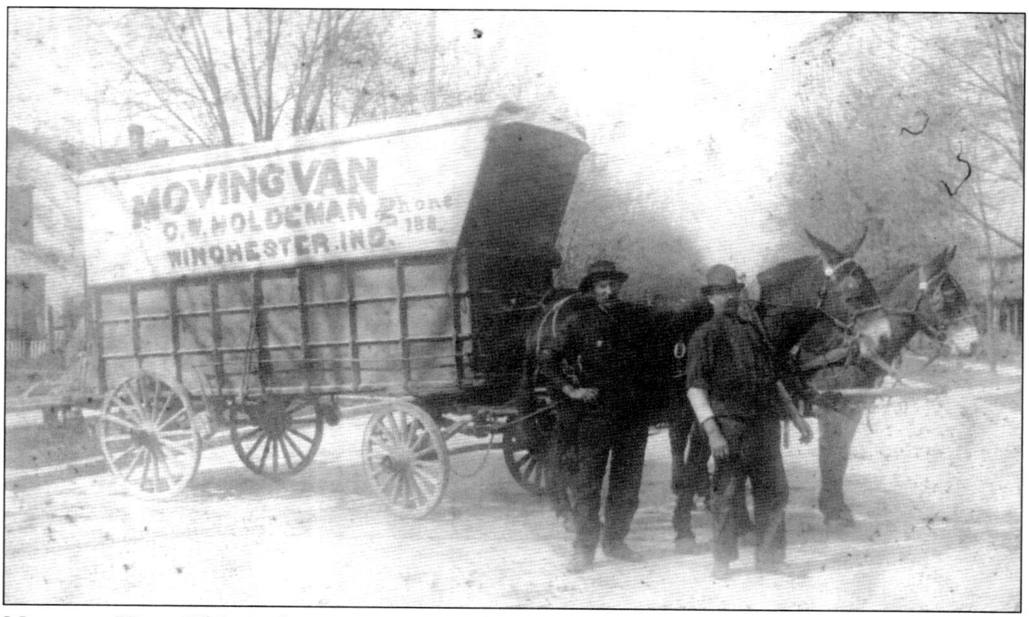

MOVING VAN. This is the moving van of C. W. Holdeman of Winchester. (Minnetrista Cultural Center.)

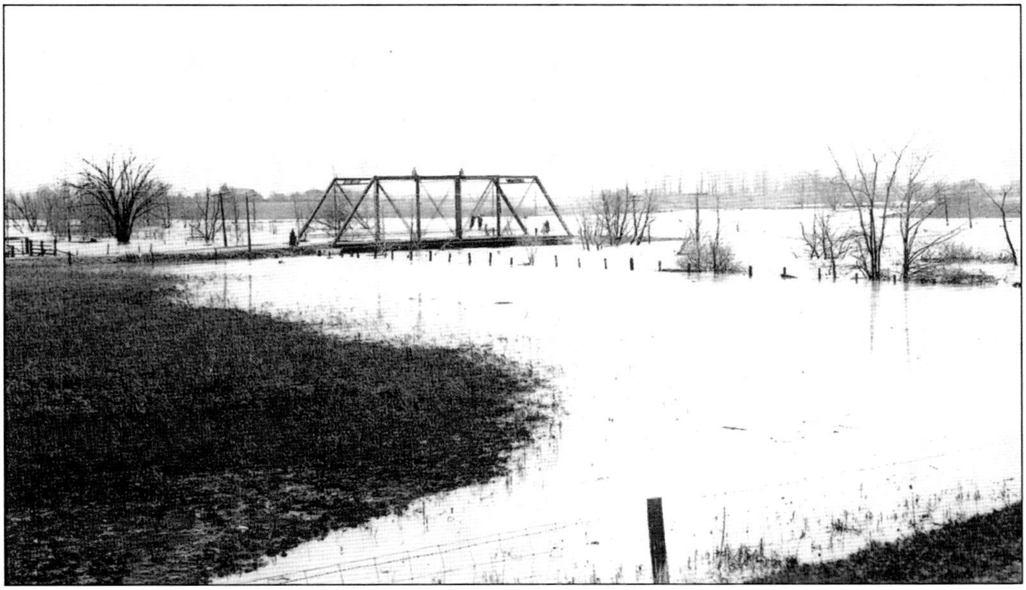

FLOOD AND BRIDGE, 1913. In 1913, a massive flood devastated the Midwest. Randolph County was not immune. This photograph shows White River flooding over the bridge on the Deerfield Pike (now old U.S. Highway 27), north of Winchester. (Randolph County Historical Society.)

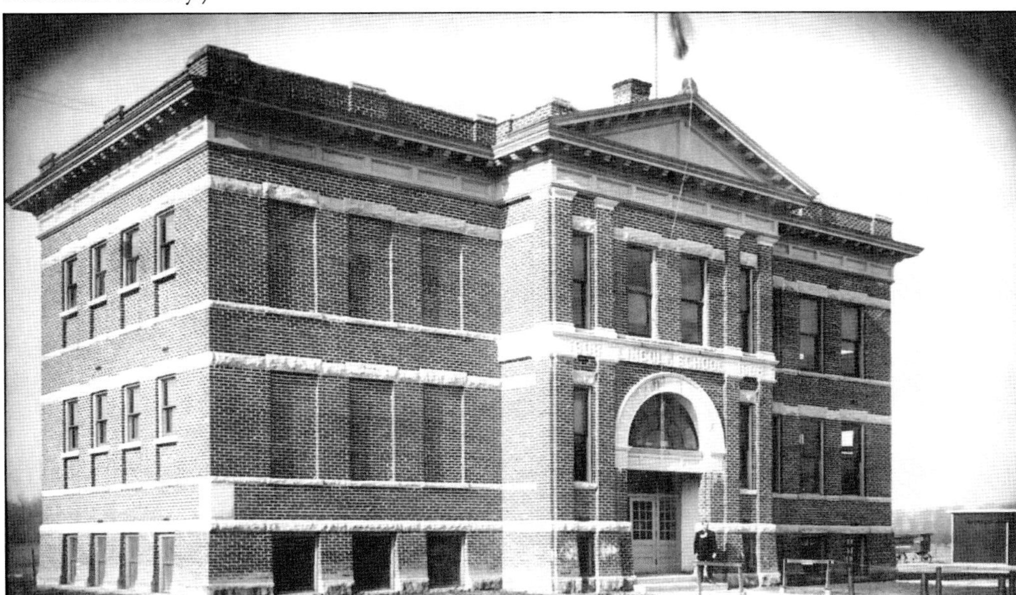

LINCOLN SCHOOL. Lincoln School, located five miles west of Winchester, was dedicated on the centennial of Abraham Lincoln's birth. Eventually all the students in western White River Township were sent to Lincoln. A high school course was added in 1910. High school students were transferred to McKinley School, east of Winchester, in 1950, and elementary grades were transferred to McKinley in January 1957. The building was razed in 1971–1972. (Randolph County Historical Society.)

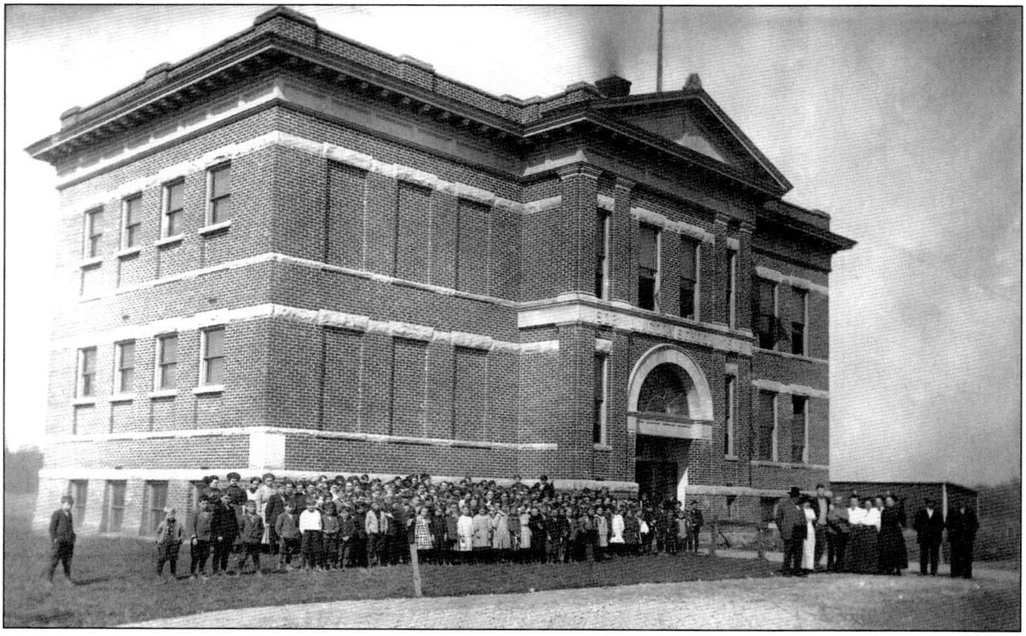

Lincoln School and Students. This postcard shows a group of students outside Lincoln School. Often erroneously credited as the first consolidated school in the nation, it was not even the first consolidated school in the county, but it was a widely known early model of rural school consolidation, constructed under the leadership of Lee L. Driver. (Steve Longnecker.)

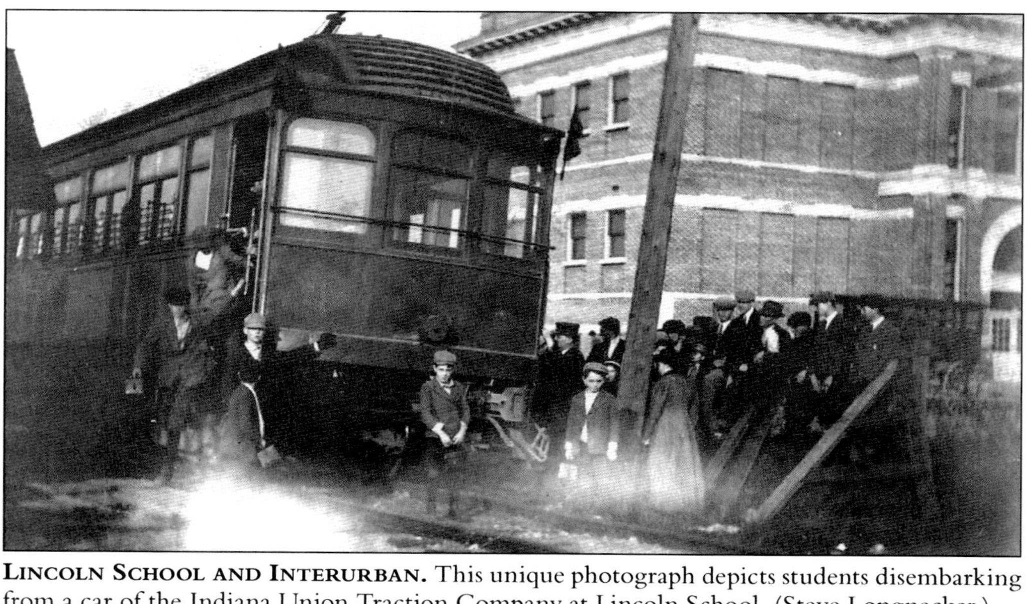

Lincoln School and Interurban. This unique photograph depicts students disembarking from a car of the Indiana Union Traction Company at Lincoln School. (Steve Longnecker.)

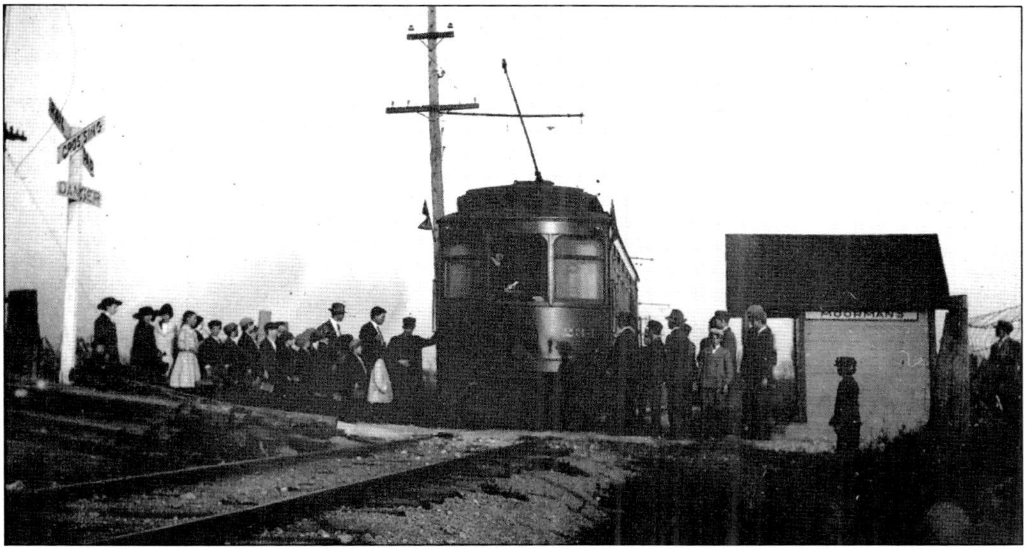

INTERURBAN AT MOORMAN'S STOP. This photograph depicts students of Lincoln School waiting to board a car of the Indiana Union Traction Company at Moorman's stop, which stood near the school. (Steve Longnecker.)

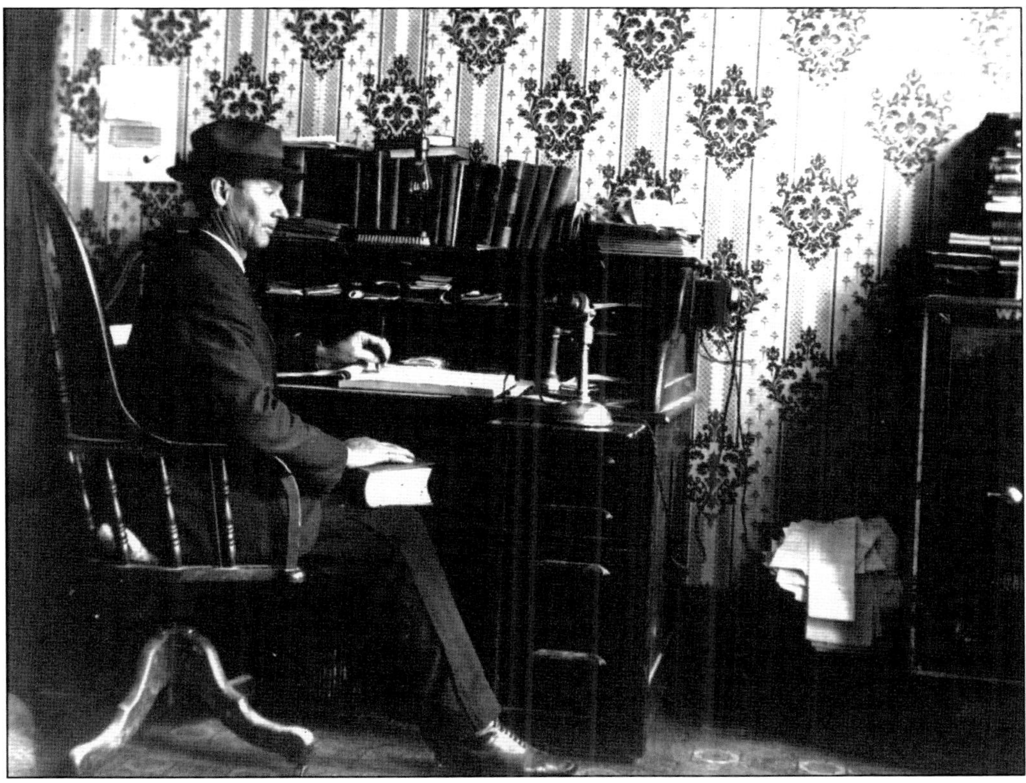

WILLIAM J. WILLIAMS. William J. (Billy) Williams served as trustee of White River Township from 1905 until 1909. It was Billy Williams who worked with Lee L. Driver to construct Lincoln School. (Judy Wilson Wright.)

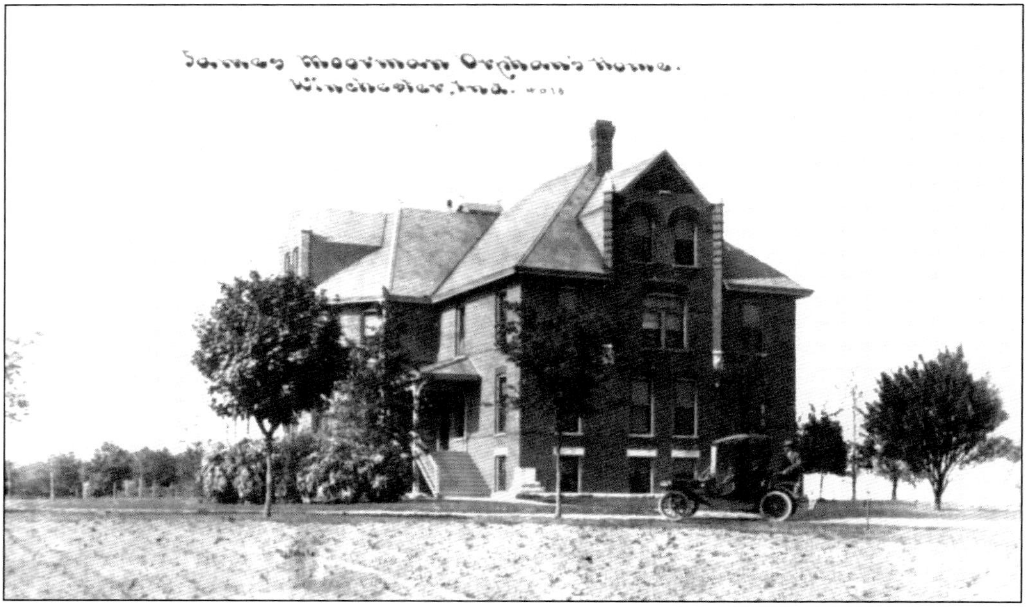

JAMES MOORMAN ORPHANS' HOME. James Moorman ordered that an orphans' home be established by the terms of his 1888 will. The home was established on a farm two miles west of Winchester the same year. The 52-room structure depicted here was erected in 1898–1899. By 1960, it was the only privately owned orphanage in the state. The home closed in 1961. In 1968, the property was sold, and the house was razed in 1973. (Gregory P. Hinshaw.)

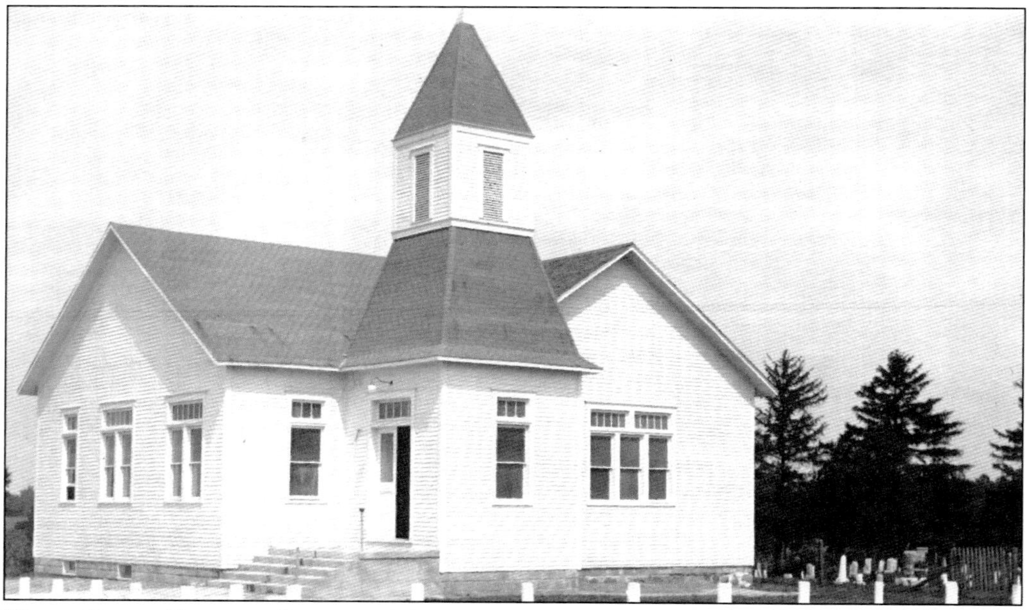

WHITE RIVER FRIENDS CHURCH. White River Friends Church was organized in 1818 and is the oldest congregation of any denomination in the Winchester community. Benjamin Cox, one of the first three county commissioners of Randolph County, was the organizer of the congregation. The building depicted here is the third, erected in 1883. The building was significantly enlarged in 1919–1920, as depicted here. It was enlarged in 1973–1974. (Gregory P. Hinshaw.)

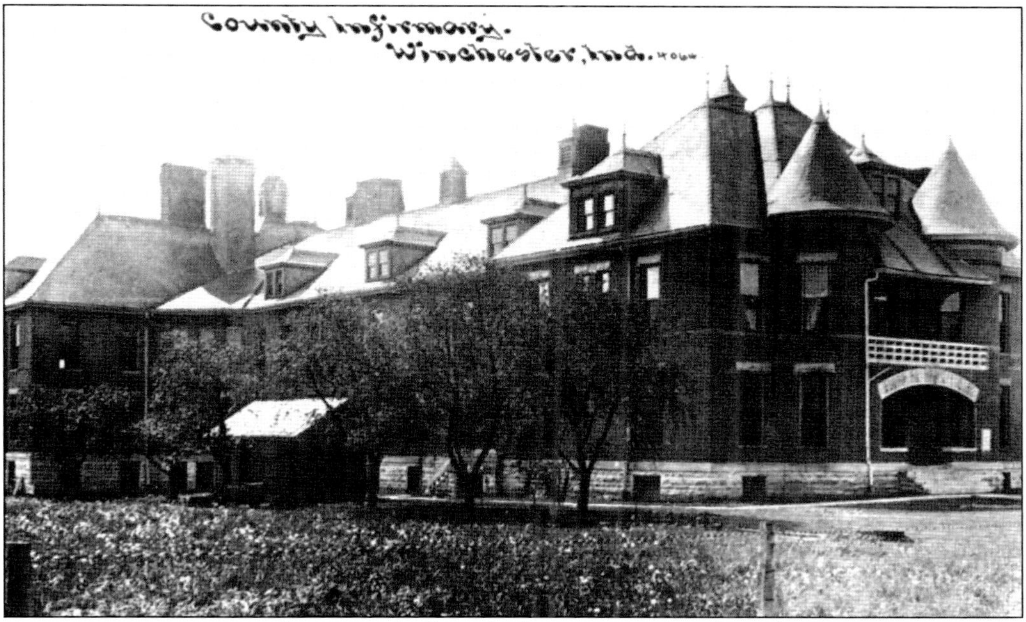

COUNTY INFIRMARY. A house was built at the "County Asylum," south of Winchester on the Lynn Pike, in 1852. The structure burned in 1854 and was replaced in 1855. In 1899, the structure depicted here was constructed at a cost of approximately $40,000. It continued to function until 2005, when the residents were moved to private facilities. The contents of the building were sold at auction in 2008. (Gregory P. Hinshaw.)

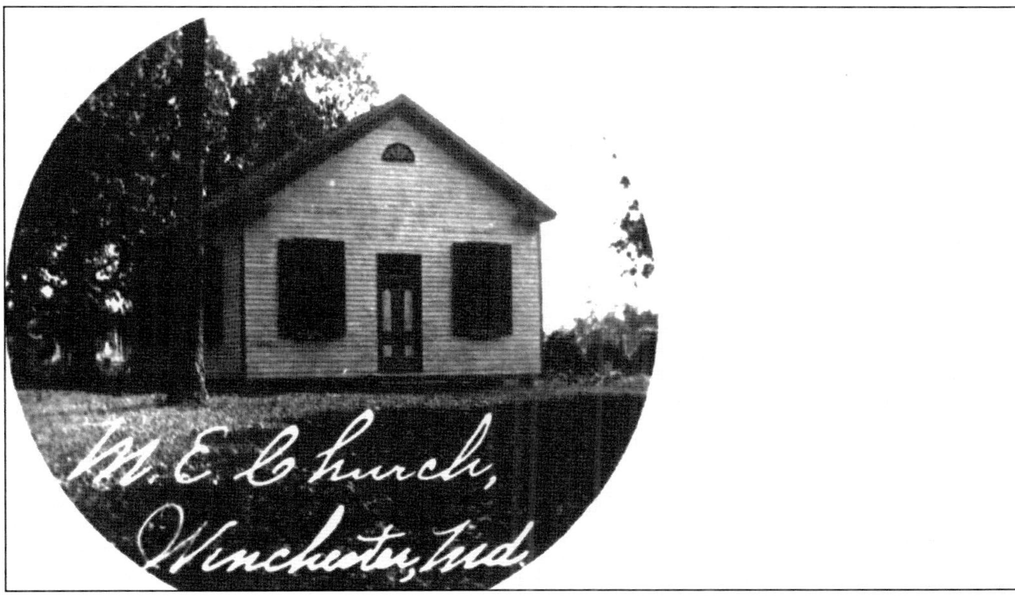

MOUNT ZION METHODIST EPISCOPAL CHURCH. This postcard depicts the Mount Zion Methodist Episcopal Church, located southeast of Winchester. The congregation, originally known as Kennedy's, was a preaching point as early as 1822. A log church was built about 1836. The present structure was erected in 1868. It was remodeled in 1892. After this photograph was taken, it was remodeled again in 1910–1911 and again in 1962. (Gregory P. Hinshaw.)

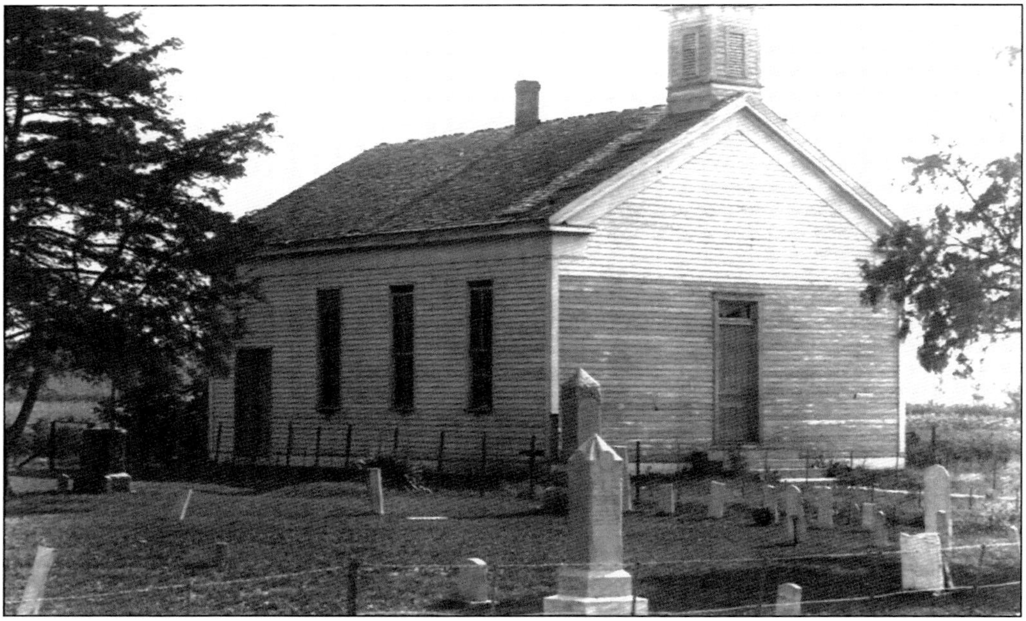

Maxville Methodist Episcopal Church. A preaching point existed at "Sumwalt's" as early as 1822. A church building was constructed about 1838. It burned in 1847. The structure depicted here was dedicated in 1858. The belfry was added in 1907. A new church was erected in 1914, and this structure was removed and made into a house in 1915. It was destroyed by fire in 1925. (Betty Cox.)

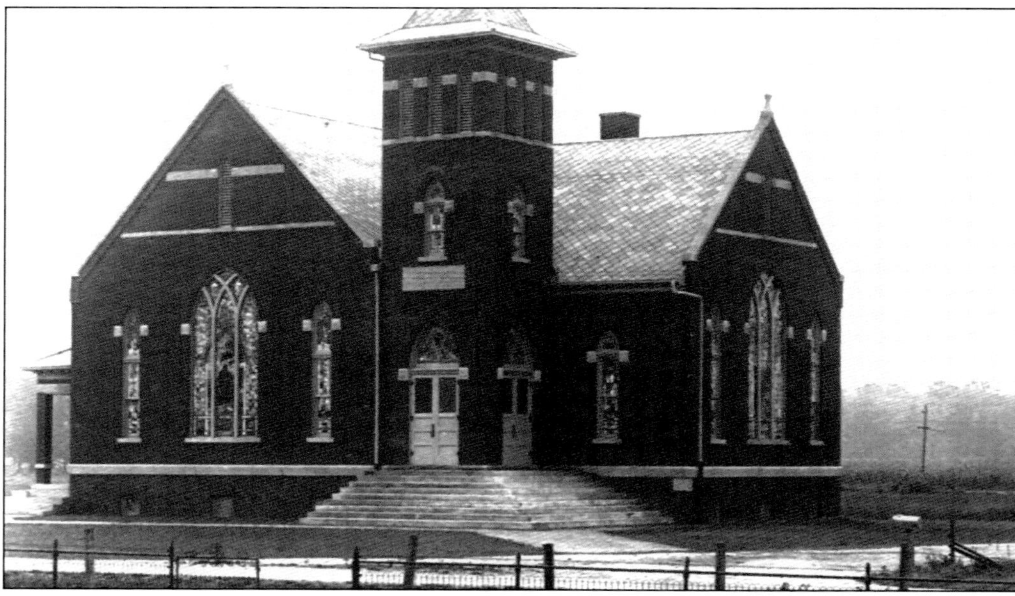

New Maxville Methodist Episcopal Church. Plans began for a new church at Maxville in 1913. This structure was dedicated on August 9, 1914. Much of the needed funding was provided by Martha F. Davis, the widow of Dr. Lewis N. Davis of Farmland, as a memorial to her husband. The congregation disbanded about 1930, and the structure was sold in 1936. Since 1968, Maxville Community (now Christian) Church has used the building. (Betty Cox.)

Two

Union City and Vicinity

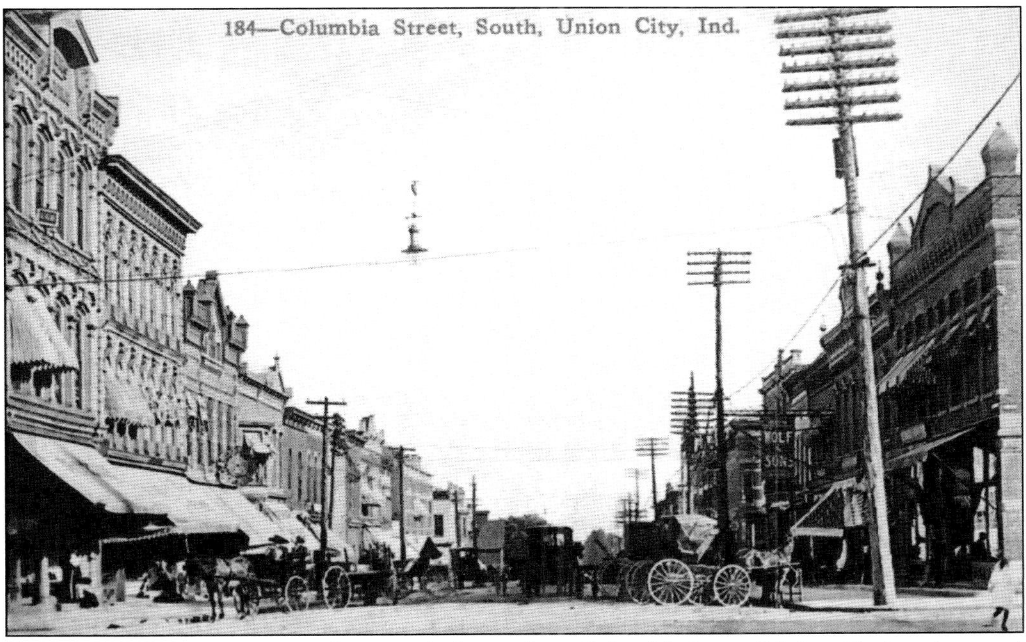

Columbia Street South. This view looks south on Columbia Street (Union City's main street) from Oak Street. At left in the foreground is the Bowers Building, erected in 1875 and destroyed by fire in 1997. Many of the buildings in this view were erected between 1883 and 1889. Two buildings on the right were destroyed by fire on April 13, 2005. (Judy Wilson Wright.)

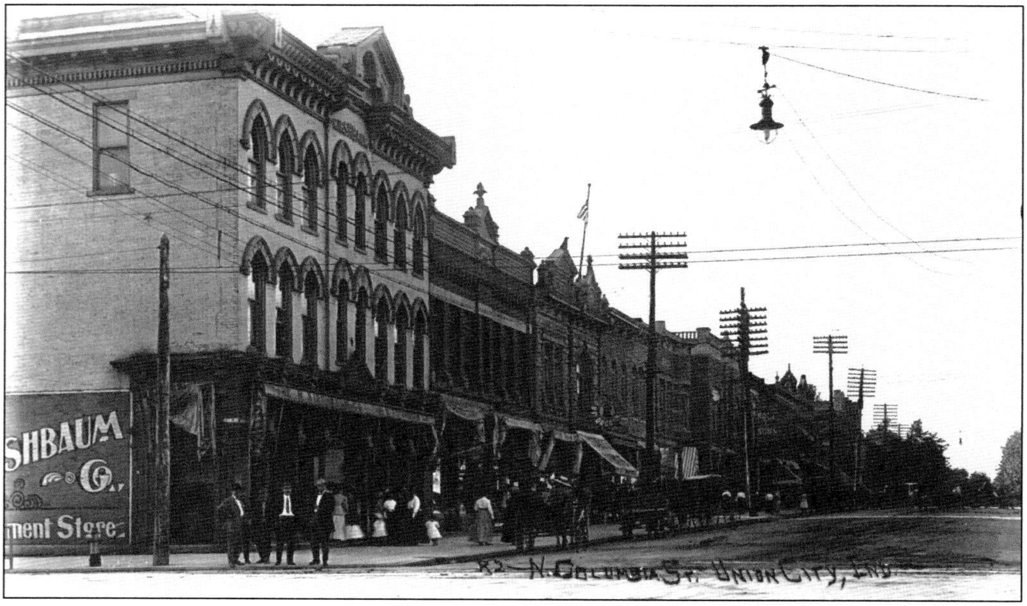

North Columbia Street. The view shows the west side of Columbia Street, north from Pearl Street. At the left is the Kirshbaum building, erected about 1870. It was occupied by Kirshbaums, a department store, which closed in 1976. The next building is the Jackson Building, erected in 1892. (Lowell and Anna Fraze.)

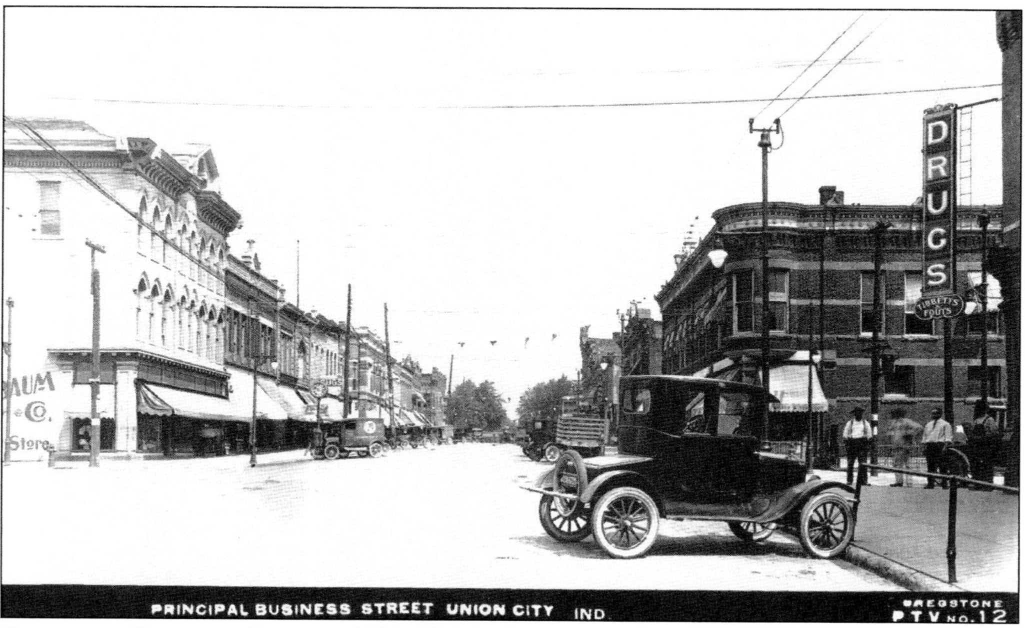

Principal Business Street, 1923. This is also a view of North Columbia Street from Pearl Street. At the left is the Kirshbaum building. At right is the Kerr Block, erected in 1898. The Kerr Block housed the Tibbetts and Fouts Drug Store. The truck on the left side belonged to the Reitenour Jewelry Company. (Jane Lyle.)

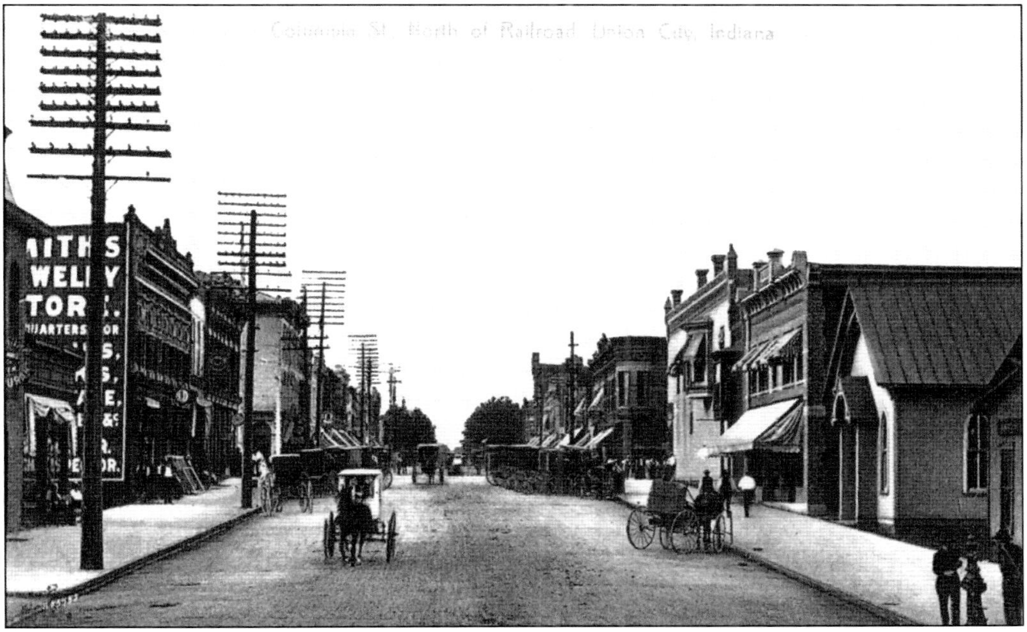

Columbia Street North of the Railroad. This view also looks north on Columbia Street from between the railroad and Pearl Street. (Jane Lyle.)

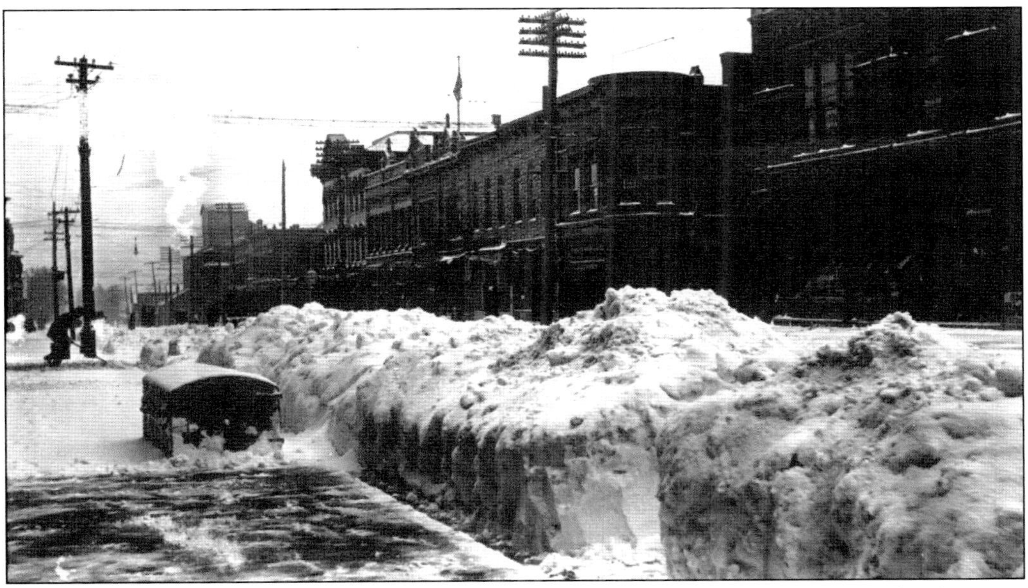

Columbia Street with Snow. Columbia Street, looking south from just south of Oak Street, is depicted here in the midst of winter in 1912. The Kirshbaum building can be seen at the far end of the street. Even farther south is the Southside Elevator, which was destroyed by fire in recent years. (Judy Wilson Wright.)

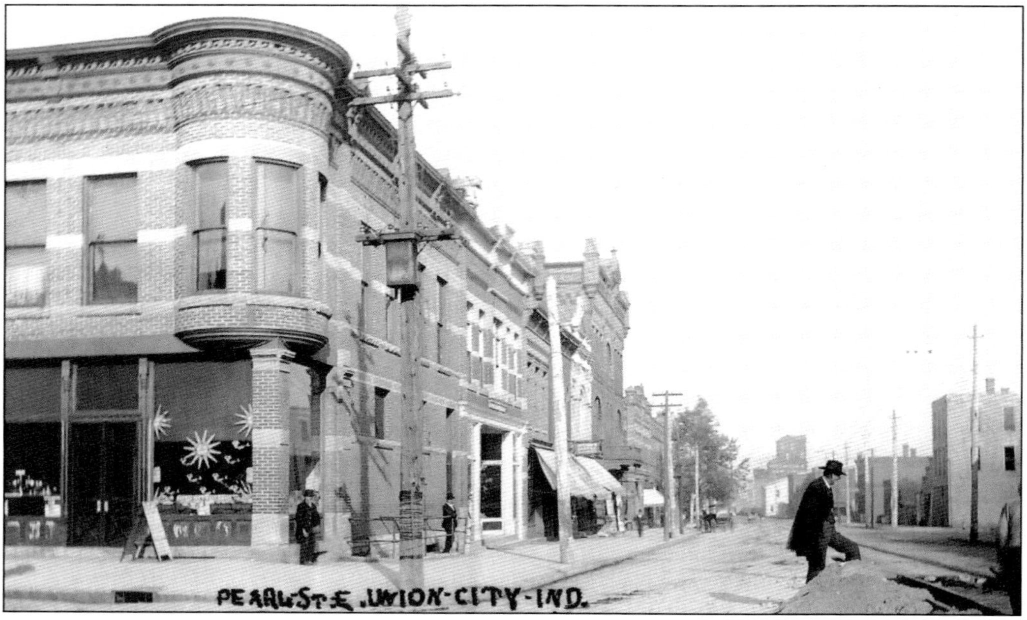

PEARL STREET LOOKING EAST. This view depicts the Kerr Block at the northeast corner of Pearl and Columbia Streets. The Rosenbush Building, built in 1904, is the next building to the east. The building with the large cornice in the background is the Union Grand Theatre. (Jane Lyle.)

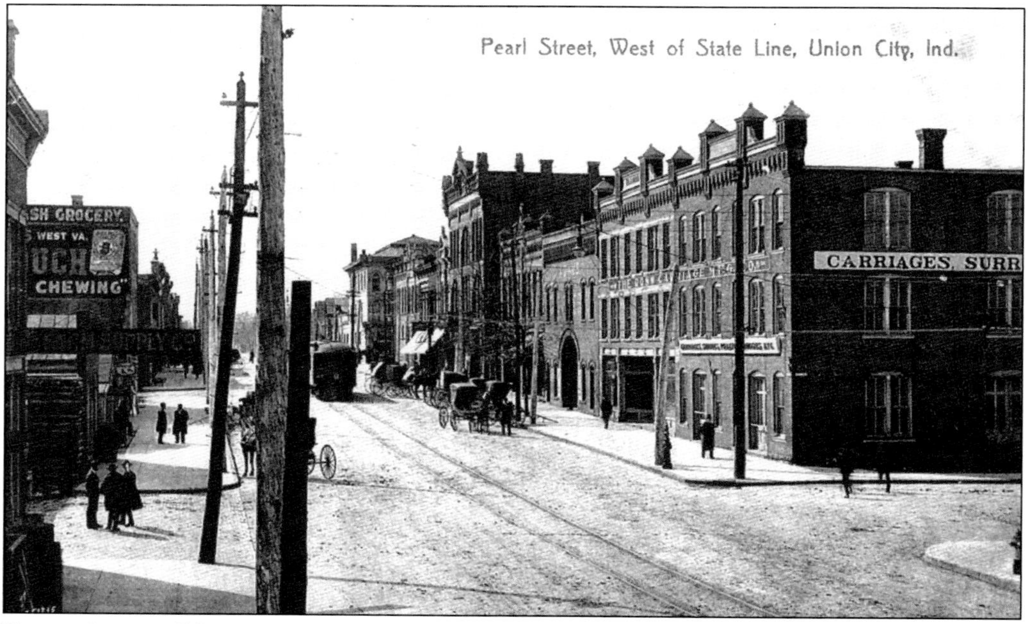

PEARL STREET WEST OF STATE LINE. Pearl Street is depicted here, looking west from the state line. The building at the right was the Ross Carriage Company. It was destroyed by fire in 1955. Next, with the rounded arch entrance, is the Adams Livery Stable. The next building, erected in 1893, is the only one in the near part of this view that remains extant. The next building is the Union Grand Theatre. (Max Harter.)

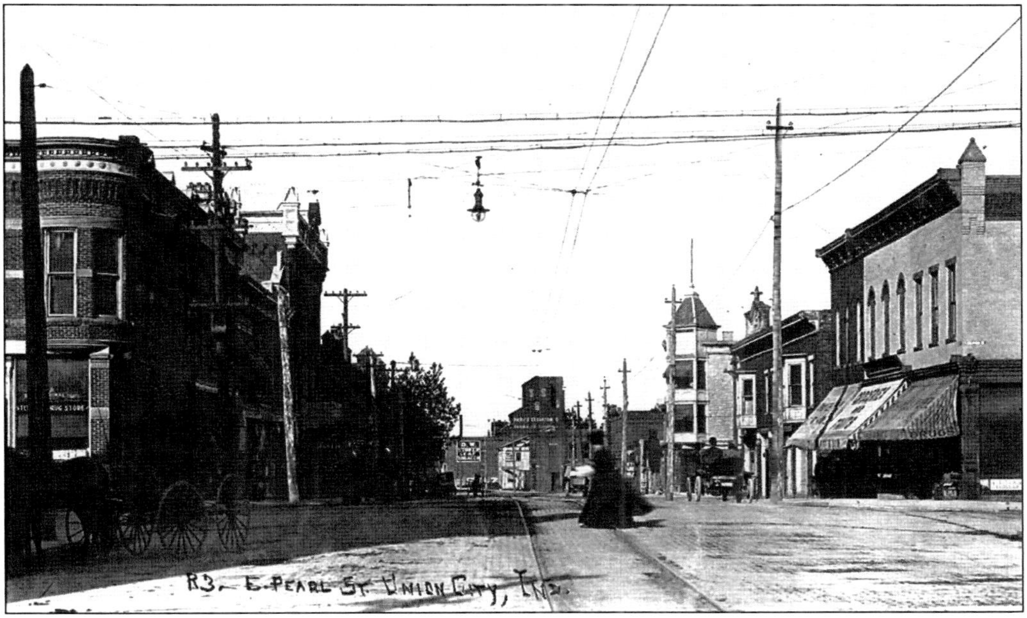

East Pearl Street. This photograph depicts Pearl Street, looking east from Columbia Street. The tracks of the Indiana Union Traction Company can be seen in the middle of the street. The building with the tower housed the Union Trust Bank until being razed in 1966. The grain elevator at the far end of the street is in Ohio. (Janice Harvey.)

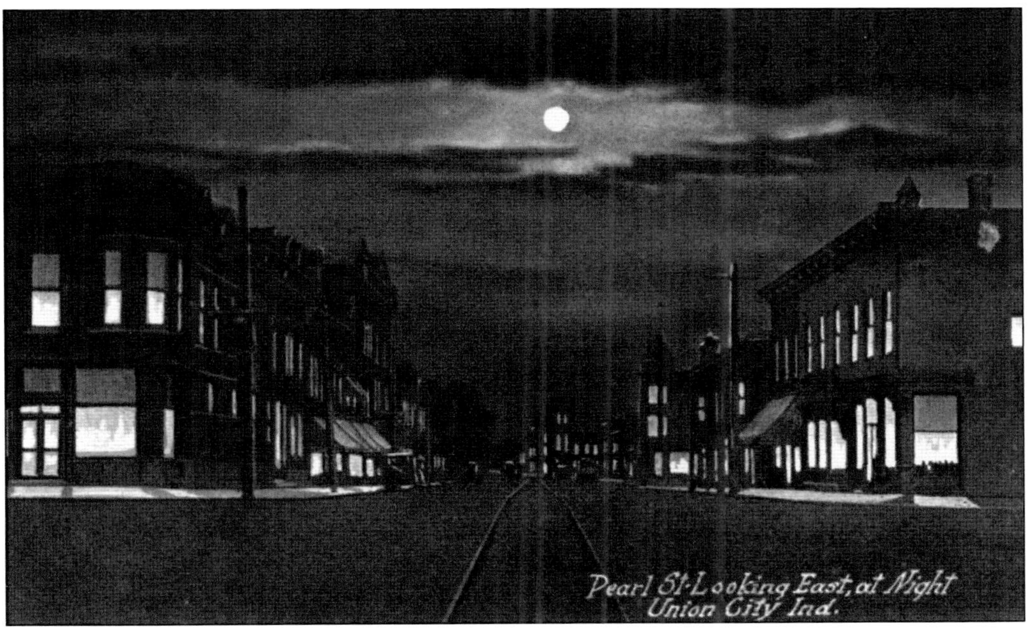

Pearl Street Looking East at Night. This unique view artistically represents the same view as the previous image; however, the view depicts a night scene, with a full moon overhead. (Judy Wilson Wright.)

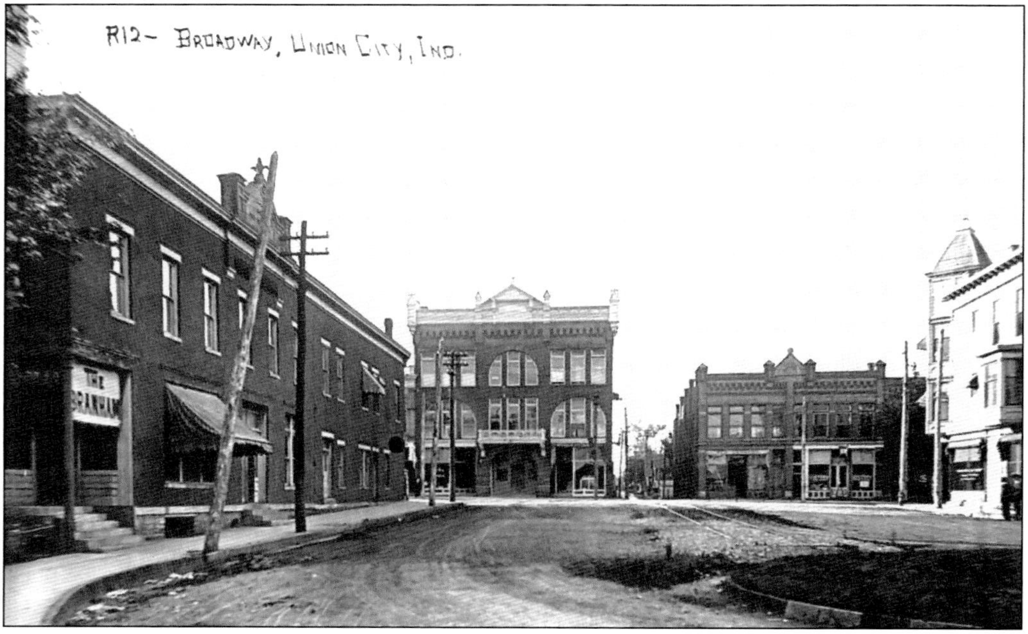

BROADWAY. This view looks north on Broadway toward Pearl Street. The traction line is at right. At the left is the Branham Hotel, erected in 1856 and razed in 1970. At the right is the Union Trust Bank, razed in 1966. In the background is the Union Grand Theatre, originally built in 1891 as the Pythian Opera House. It was destroyed by fire on June 1, 2002. (Jane Lyle.)

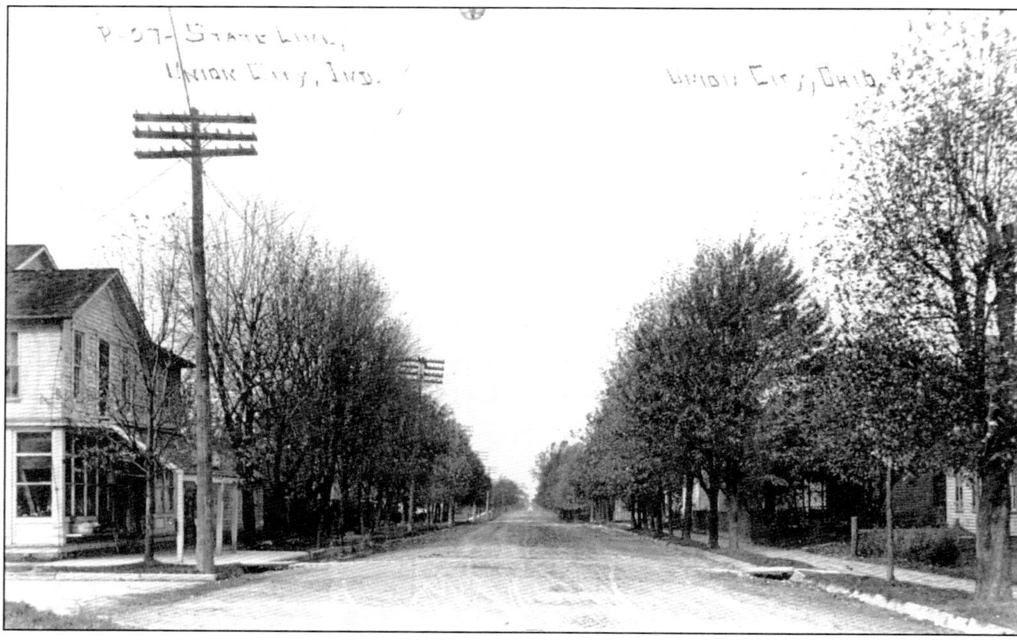

STATE LINE. If Union City is known for anything, it is that it is the "Hub of Two States." This card visually demonstrates this fact, showing Indiana on the left and Ohio on the right. (Judy Wilson Wright.)

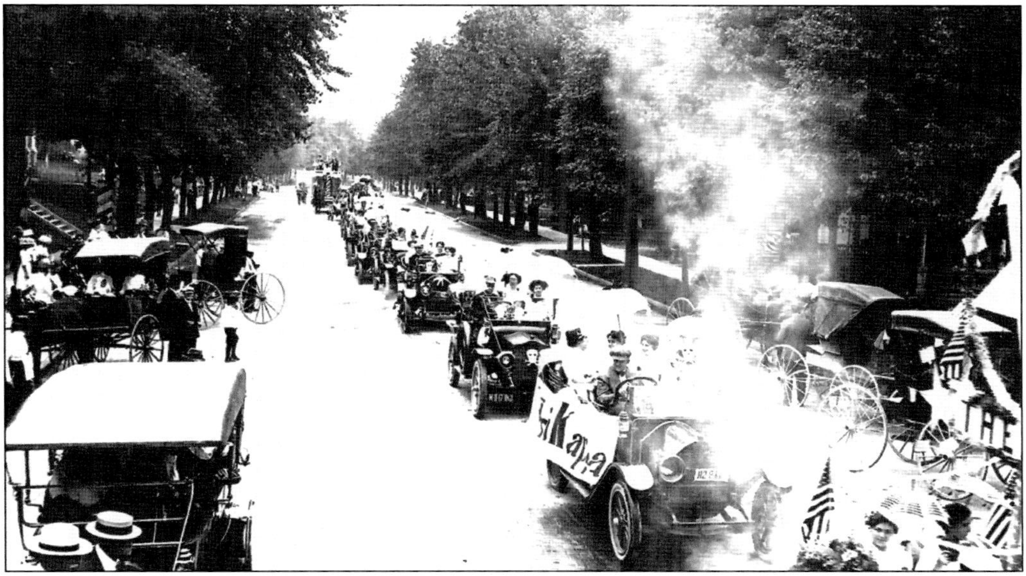

Union City Parade with Tri Kappas. This is a parade in Union City. In the first car are representatives of the Tri Kappas. Union City's Psi Chapter of the sorority was organized on January 4, 1907. (Union City Public Library.)

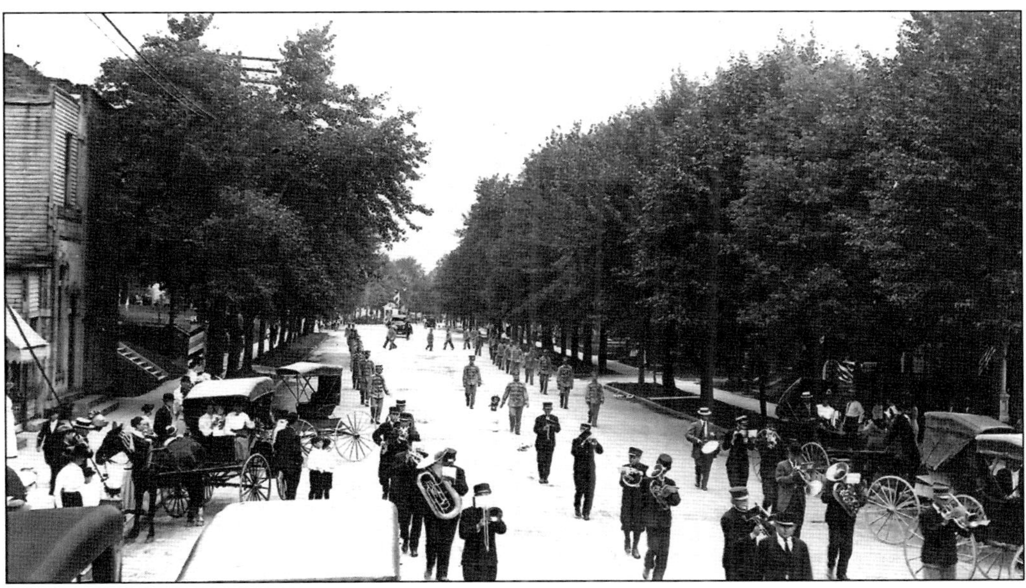

Union City Parade with Band. The parade depicted in the previous picture also included a marching band, depicted here. (Union City Public Library.)

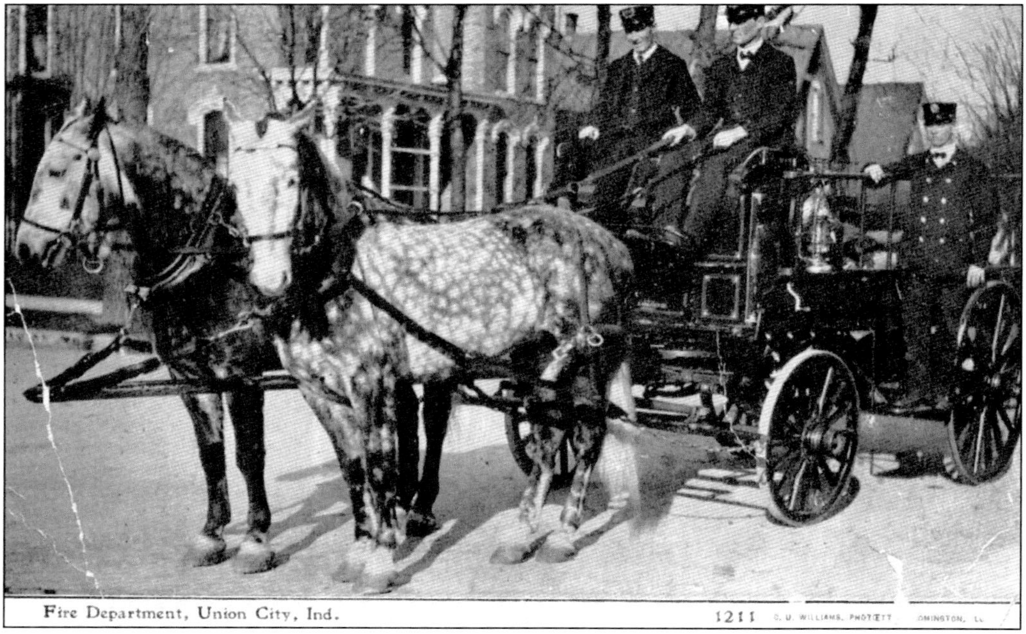

FIRE DEPARTMENT, 1916. Union City's fire department used this wagon from 1905 until 1919. The men on the wagon are, from left, Lon Harless, fire chief; Nat Coby, driver; and Thurman Constable. The horses are Prince, at left, and King, at right. (Max Harter.)

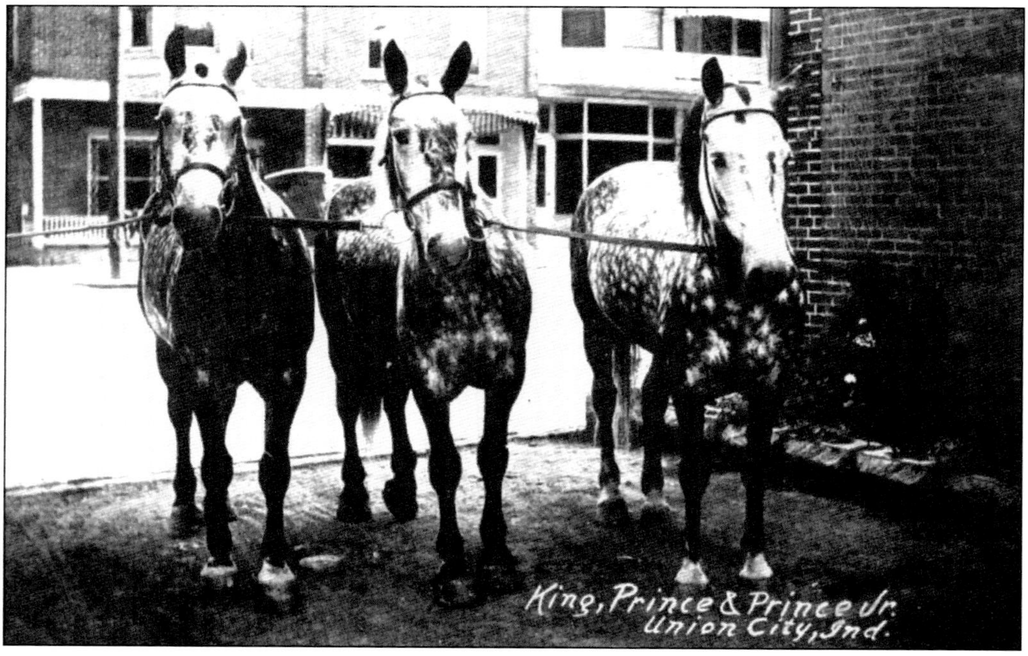

KING, PRINCE, AND PRINCE JR. These horses were owned by the Union City Fire Department. One account said, "You could set your clock at 12:00 O'clock noon by Prince. He would get nervous and put his ear to the edge of the stall so he could hear the Water Works whistle at 12:00 O'clock." (Max Harter.)

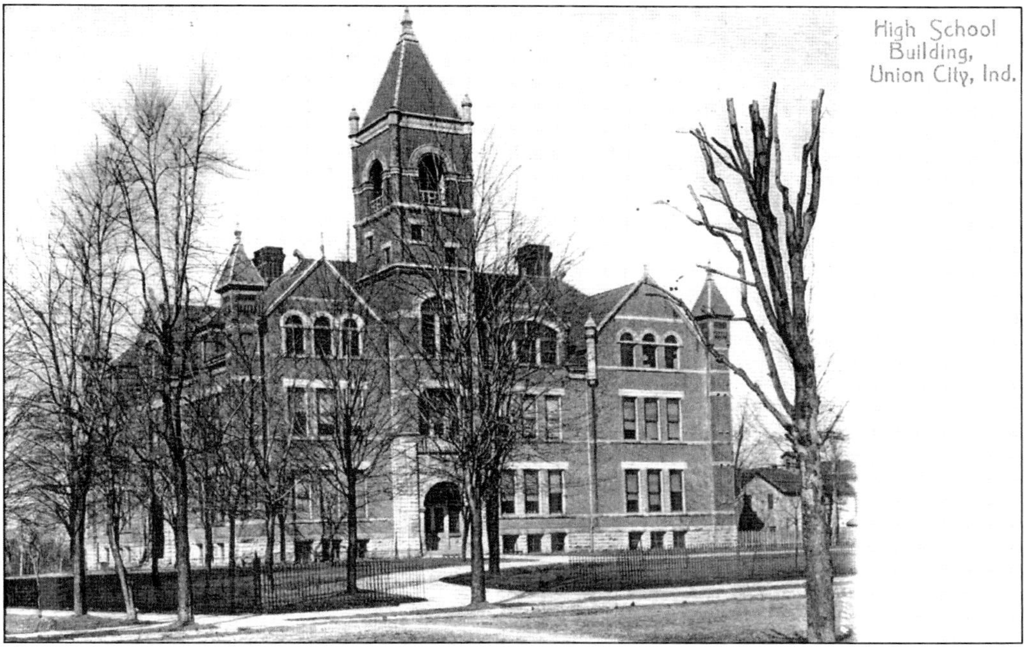

HIGH SCHOOL. This structure was erected in 1891 under the direction of Hampton Gettinger, a local architect. The building stood at the northeast corner of Oak and Walnut Streets. It was destroyed by fire on February 17, 1919. A new building was erected on the lot in 1920. The 1920 building was used as a high school until 1957 and as a middle school until 2003. (Union City Public Library.)

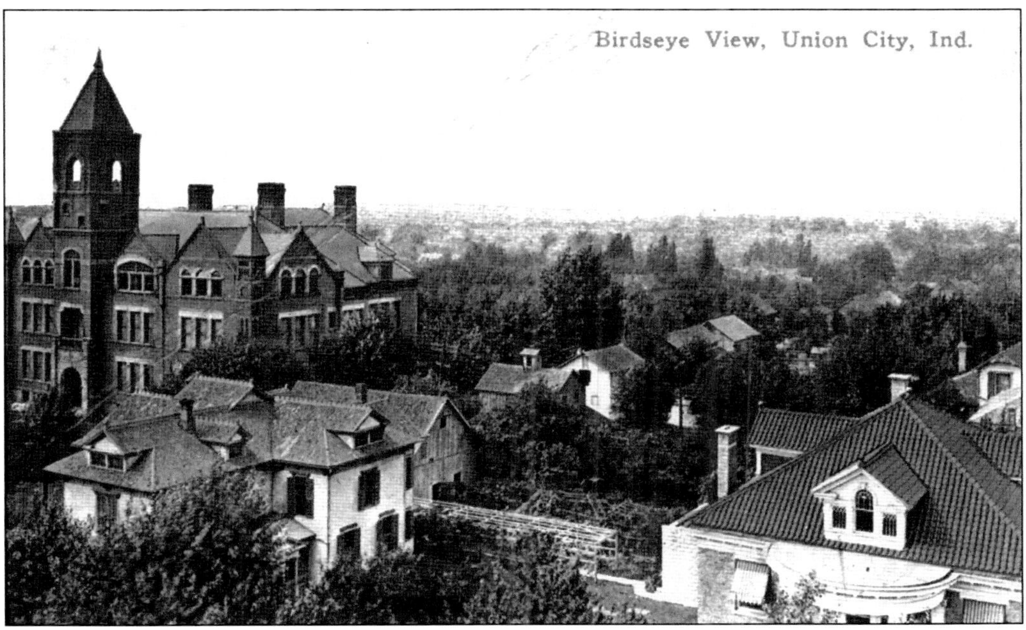

BIRD'S-EYE VIEW. The 1891 high school building is shown at the left of this picture, which was taken from the tower of the Methodist Episcopal church. (Gregory P. Hinshaw.)

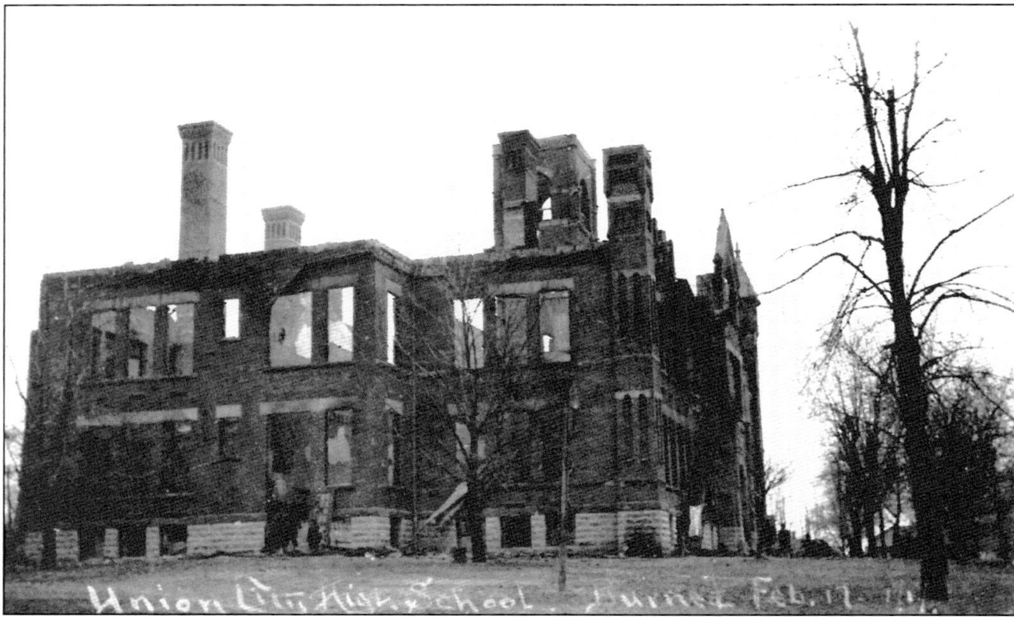

UNION CITY HIGH SCHOOL AFTER FIRE. This postcard shows the remains of the 1891 high school building after its destruction by fire on February 17, 1919. (Max Harter.)

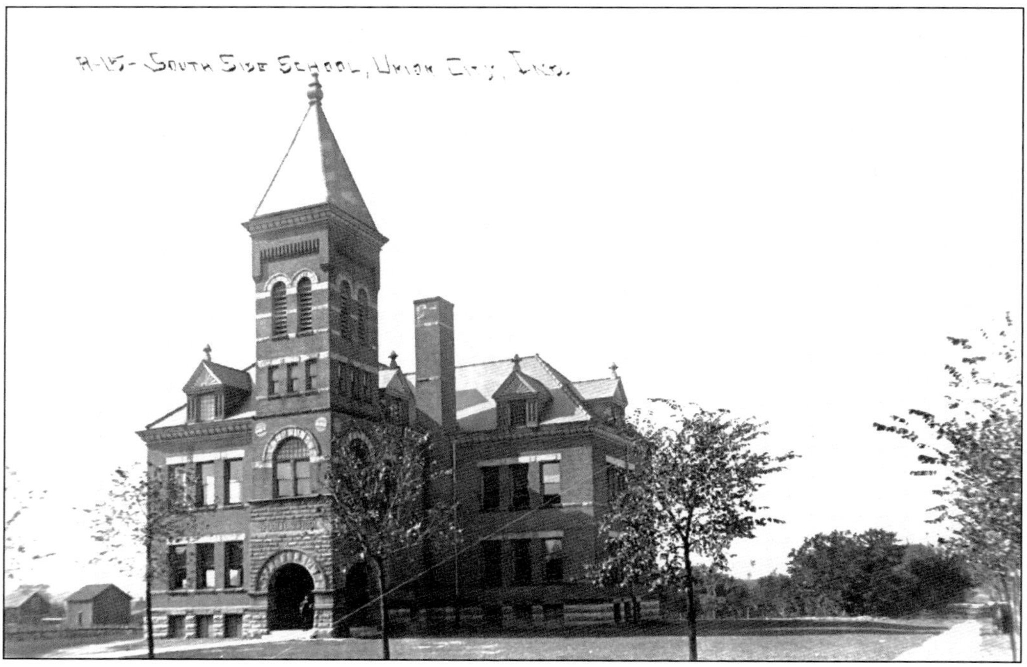

SOUTH SIDE SCHOOL. Southside School, or South Ward School, was built in 1895–1896 on the southwest corner of South Howard Street and South Street according to plans drawn by Hampton Gettinger. It closed in 1940. The contents were sold in 1944. It was later used as a youth center and was sold in September 1948. It was razed in 1979. (Gregory P. Hinshaw.)

METHODIST EPISCOPAL CHURCH, 1907. The Methodist Episcopal Church in Union City was organized in 1851. A church was built on Columbia Street in 1859. It was replaced in 1869 with a brick church at Oak and Plum Streets. The building was enlarged in 1880. A clock tower was completed in 1890. This postcard depicts the structure in 1907 just before it was razed to make room for the present building, constructed from 1907 to 1909. (Gregory P. Hinshaw.)

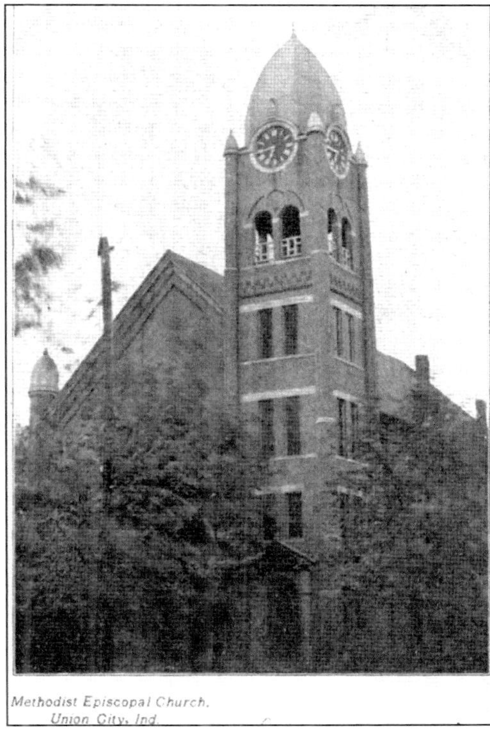

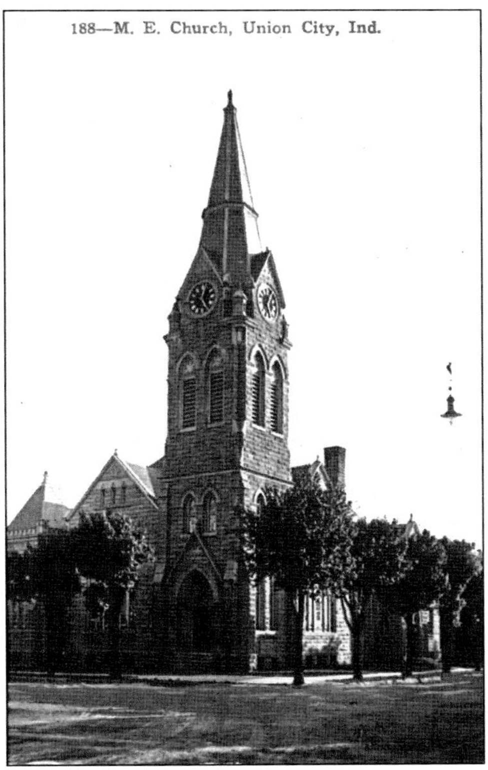

METHODIST EPISCOPAL CHURCH, C. 1909. This structure was erected between 1907 and 1909 at a cost of $30,000 on the site of the previous building. Aside from the addition of an educational unit in 1967, the building has remained virtually unchanged in the century since its erection. After the merger of the Methodist Church and the Evangelical United Brethren Church in 1968, the congregation became known as Wesley United Methodist Church. (Gregory P. Hinshaw.)

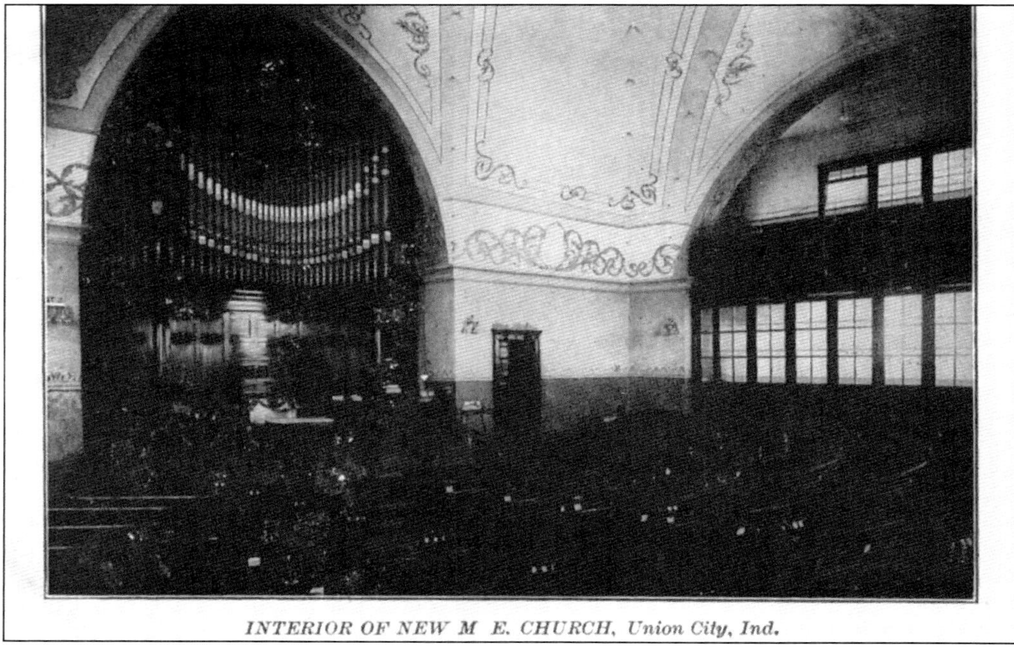

INTERIOR OF NEW METHODIST EPISCOPAL CHURCH. The "new" Methodist Episcopal church was dedicated on March 21, 1909, and included an organ, shown here, donated by Mrs. M. H. Mendenhall. The organ was replaced in 1948. (Janice Harvey.)

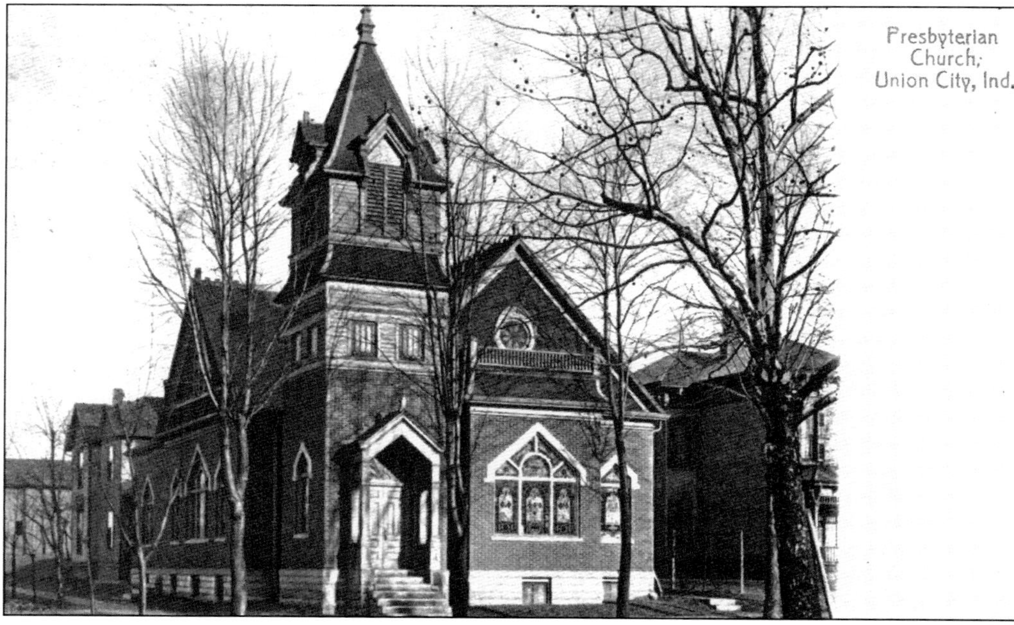

PRESBYTERIAN CHURCH. Union City's Presbyterian church was organized in 1836 in Hillgrove, Ohio. A church was constructed at the corner of Union and Oak Streets in 1862 or 1863. A new building was constructed at the southeast corner of Howard and Hickory Streets in 1879. The building depicted here was constructed in 1903–1904 and dedicated on November 20, 1904. In 1968, an addition was completed, and the church was covered with siding. (Gregory P. Hinshaw.)

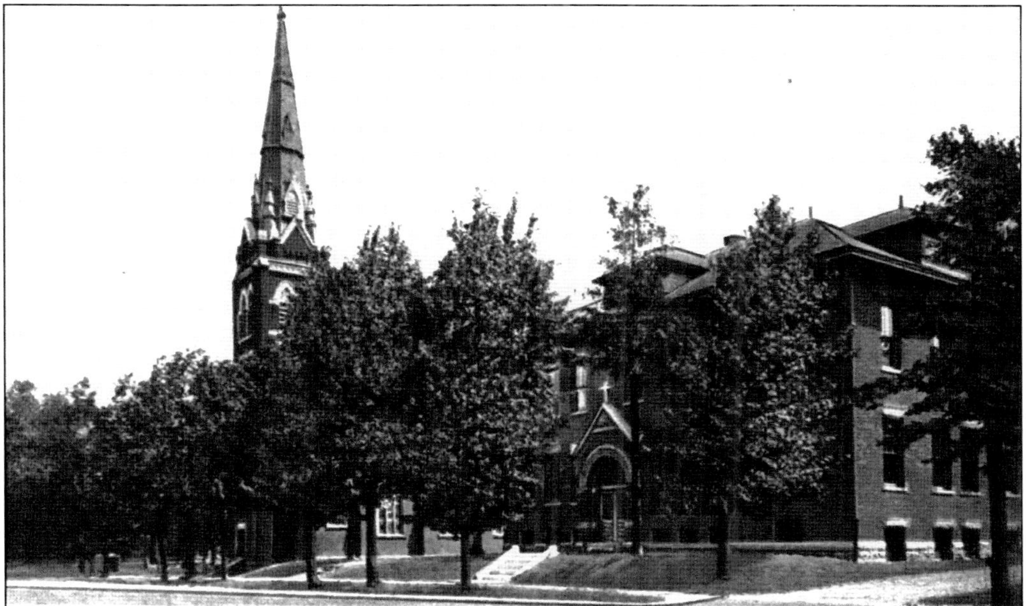

ST. MARY'S CATHOLIC CHURCH AND SCHOOL, UNION CITY, IND.

ST. MARY'S CATHOLIC CHURCH AND SCHOOL. This congregation was organized in 1854. A church was constructed on Plum Street, north of Oak Street, in 1865. The present church was designed by Hampton Gettinger and begun in 1891. A Catholic school was organized at a very early date and originally occupied a building on Hickory Street. Later a brick school was constructed on Plum Street. St. Mary's Catholic School closed in 1970 and has since been razed. (Gregory P. Hinshaw.)

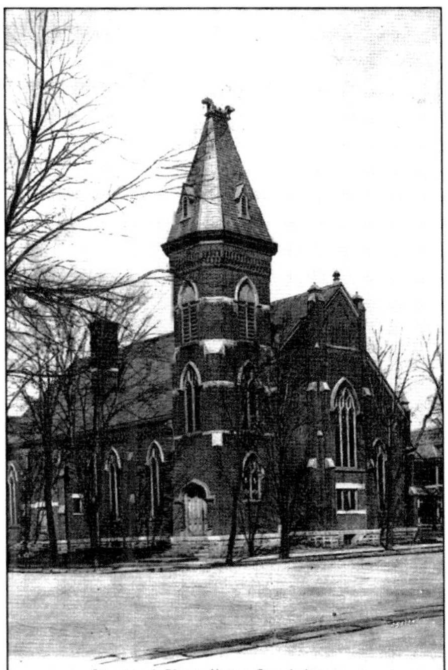

Church of Christ, Union City, Indiana

CHRISTIAN CHURCH. Jeremiah Smith, the founder of Union City, was a member of the Disciples of Christ. He gave a lot on West Oak Street to be used for a church. A frame building was constructed on the site between 1853 and 1858. A new brick church was completed on the lot to the west in 1878. It was extensively remodeled in 1901. The building was covered with stucco in the 1920s. (Gregory P. Hinshaw.)

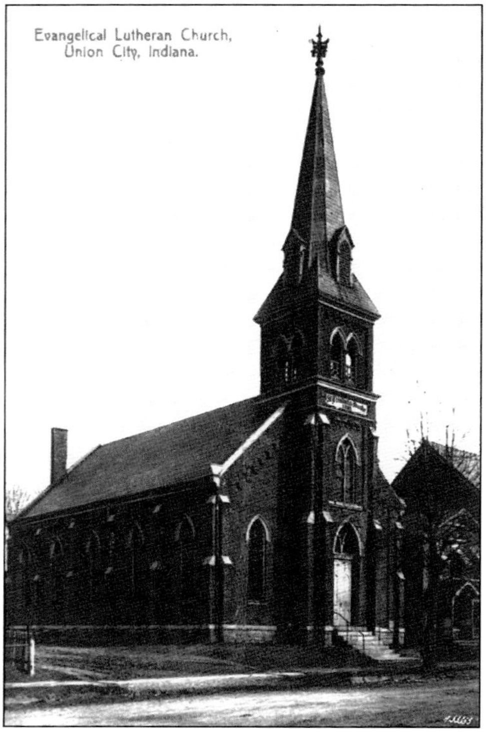

EVANGELICAL LUTHERAN CHURCH. Trinity Evangelical Lutheran Church was organized in 1857. A frame church building was erected on Plum Street in 1860–1861. The building depicted here was erected in 1885–1886. A new church was erected in 1967 on State Road 28 at Jackson Pike. The building depicted here was razed in 1970. The congregation was affiliated with American Lutheran Church, which merged into the Evangelical Lutheran Church in America in 1988. (Gregory P. Hinshaw.)

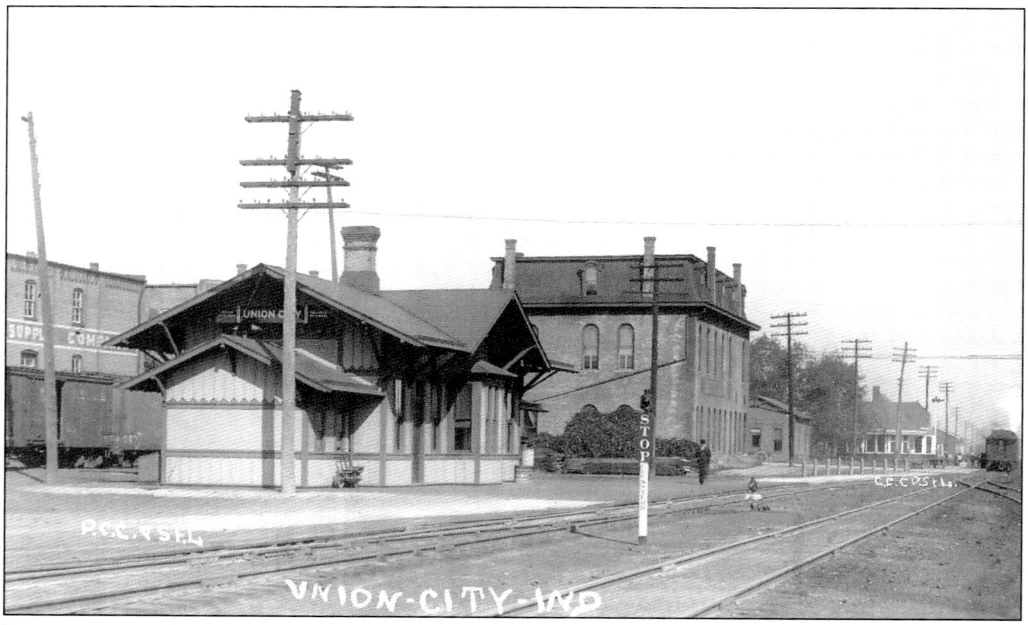

PITTSBURGH, CINCINNATI, CHICAGO, AND ST. LOUIS RAILROAD STATION. The Pittsburgh, Cincinnati, Chicago, and St. Louis Railroad depot stood on the north side of the railroad west of Columbia Street. The building was used until 1913, when a new depot opened. The Branham Restaurant can be seen in the background, while the Big Four depot can be seen even farther down the tracks. (Jane Lyle.)

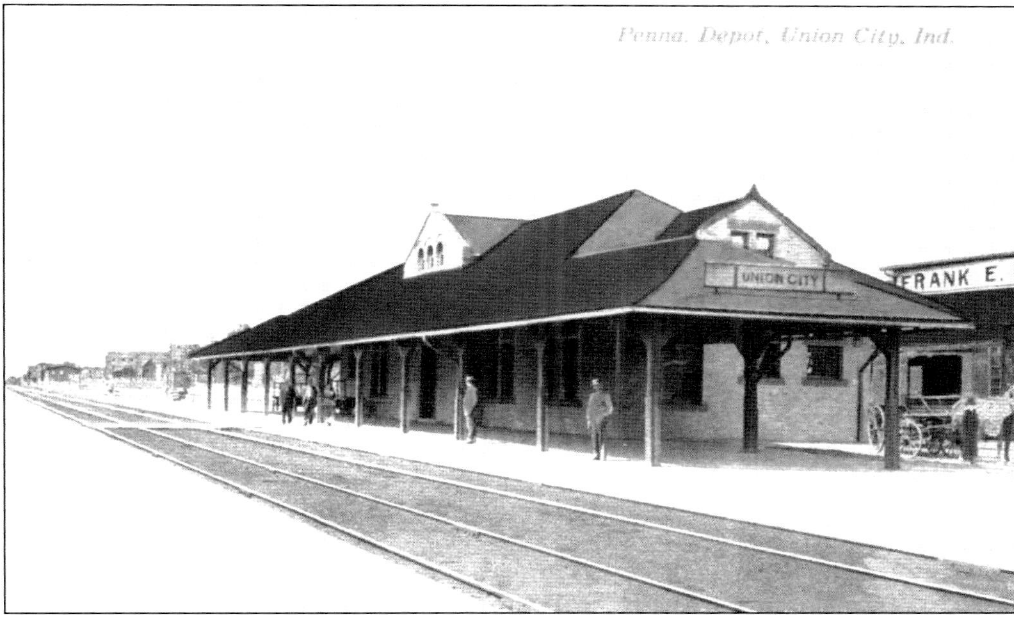

PENNSYLVANIA RAILROAD DEPOT. The Pennsylvania Railroad depot depicted here was constructed in 1912–1913 and opened in May 1913. The structure was purchased by the Art Association of Randolph County in 1980 and is now used as its headquarters. (Lowell and Anna Fraze.)

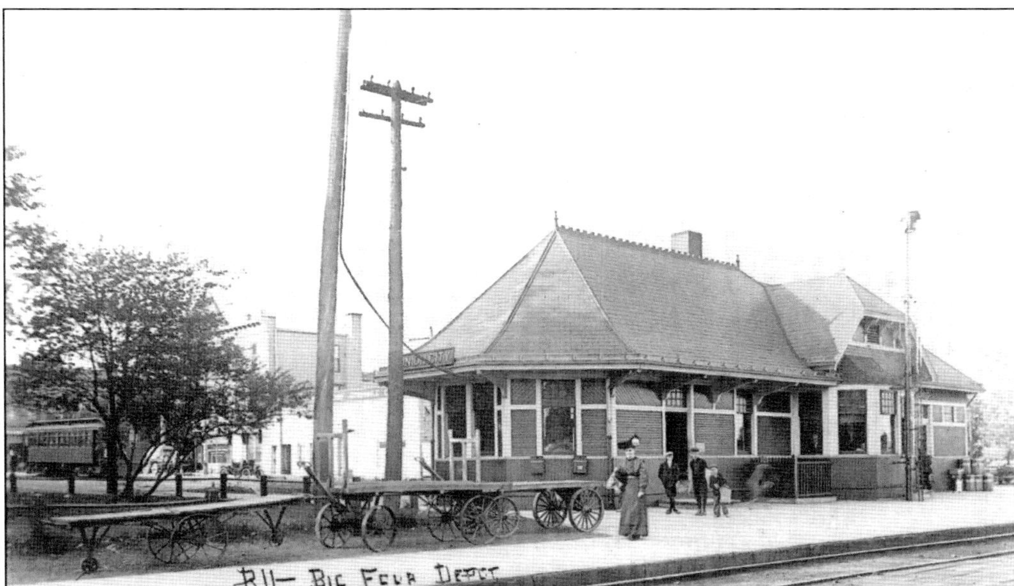

BIG FOUR DEPOT. The Big Four depot was located on the north side of the railroad, at the end of Broadway. A car of the Indiana Union Traction Company can be seen behind the building, at the left of the photograph. The Broadway Automobile Company can be seen in the background to the left of the depot. The Big Four depot was razed in 1952. (Jane Lyle.)

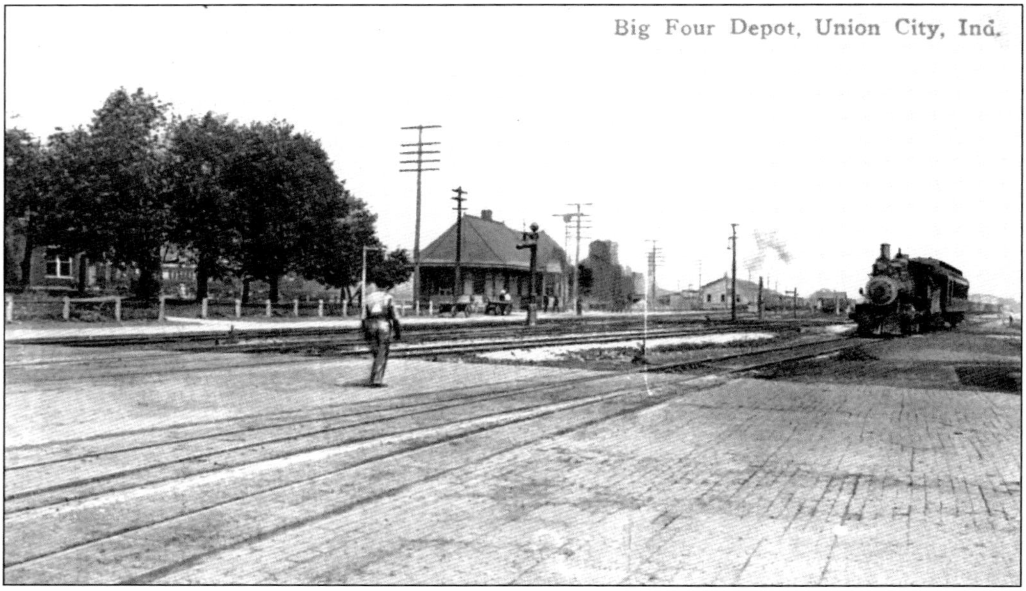

Big Four Depot and Train. The Big Four depot is shown here with the crossing watchman guarding the intersection as a small Dayton and Union passenger train approaches. This train used a turntable to turn around for the return trip to Dayton. The last of these trains ran in 1950. The Pierce Elevator, on the Ohio side, and the freight depot can be seen in the distance. (Gregory P. Hinshaw.)

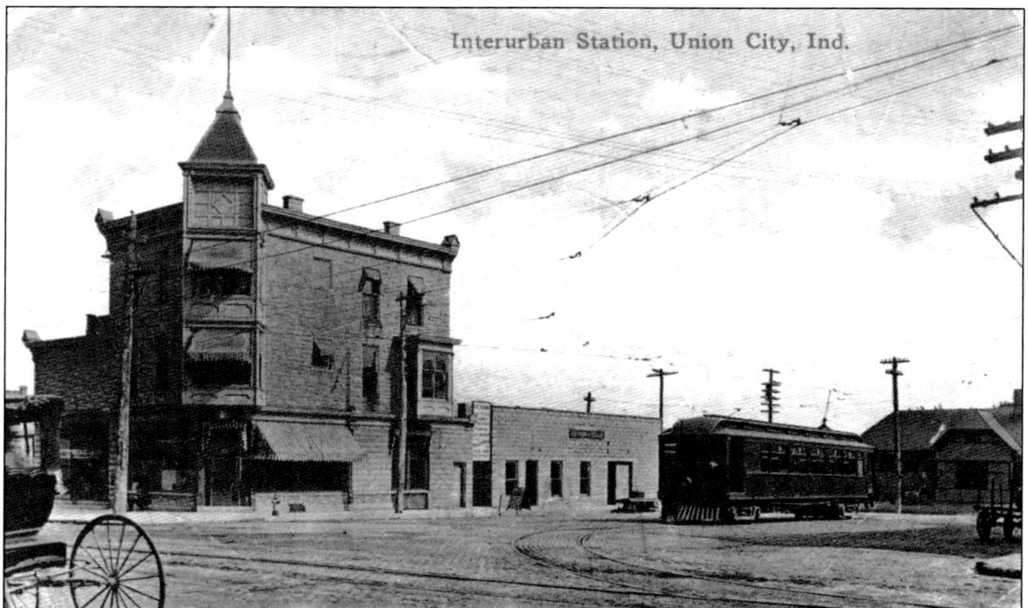

Interurban Station. This view looks to the southeast, down Broadway from Pearl Street. At the right of the photograph is the Big Four depot. The structure in the center was used for a time as the station of the Indiana Union Traction Company, whose car is shown. The bank building, at the corner of Broadway and Pearl Street, was razed in 1966 for the expansion of the Union Trust Bank. (Gregory P. Hinshaw.)

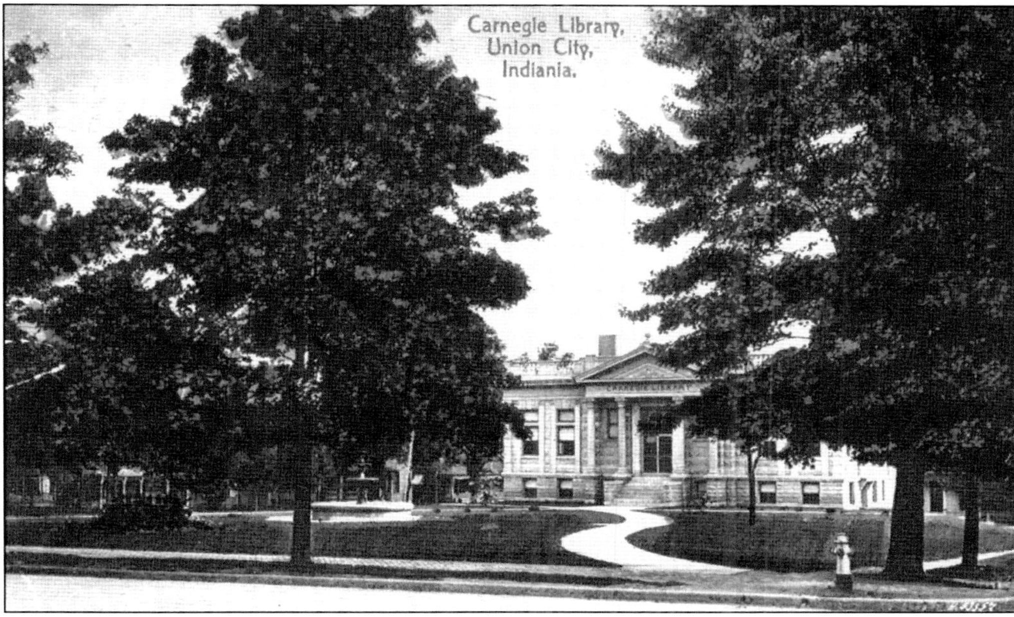

Carnegie Library. Union City's Carnegie Library is located on North Columbia Street on a lot donated to the city in 1880 by James Moorman for a park. The structure was erected in 1904 and has been in constant use with minimal alteration ever since. (Union City Public Library.)

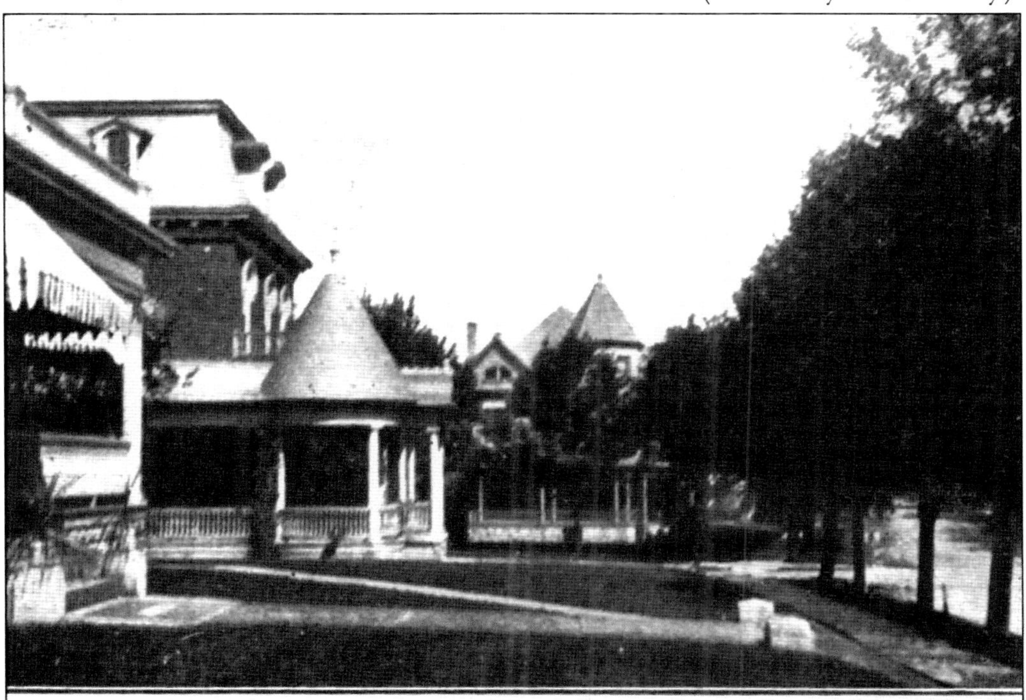

North Columbia Street. This view shows several fine residences on Columbia Street, north of downtown. (Max Harter.)

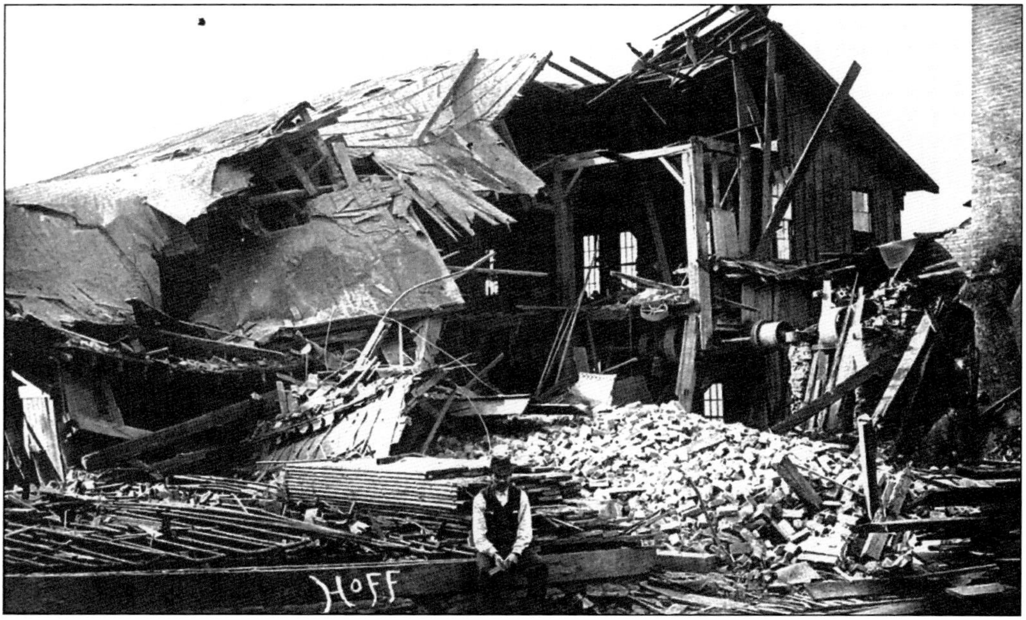

LUMBER MILL. The Witham-Bowen Lumber Company is shown here after being destroyed in 1910. A boiler explosion caused the destruction. The company was owned by Grace Witham and Reuben and Flossie Witham and was located at 201 South Columbia Street. (Max Harter.)

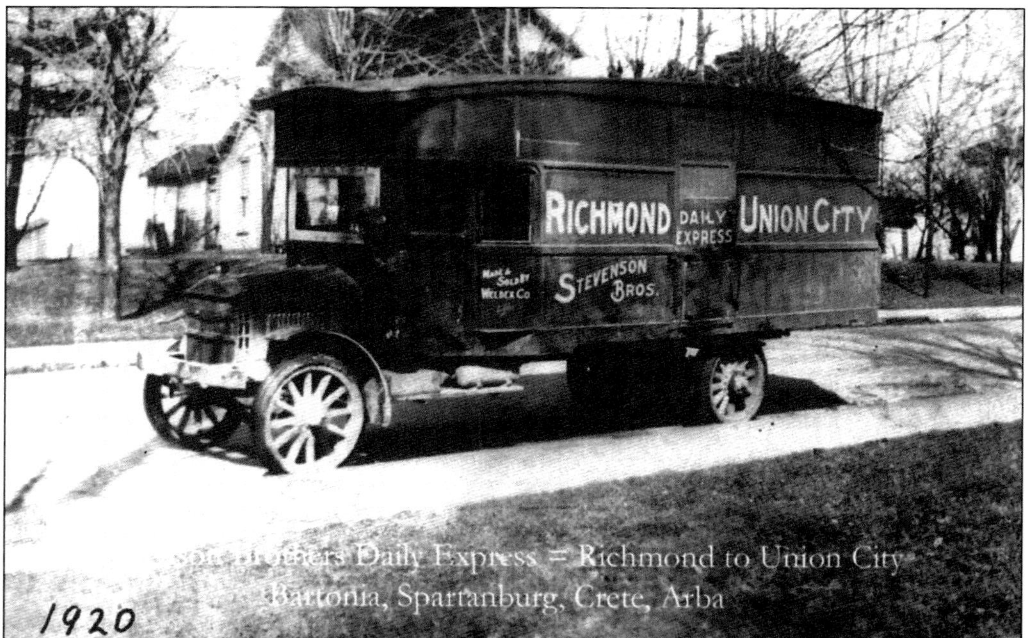

STEVENSON BROTHERS DELIVERY TRUCK. The Stevenson Brothers delivery truck made daily trips between Union City and Richmond via Bartonia, Spartanburg, Crete, and Arba. (Linda L. Black.)

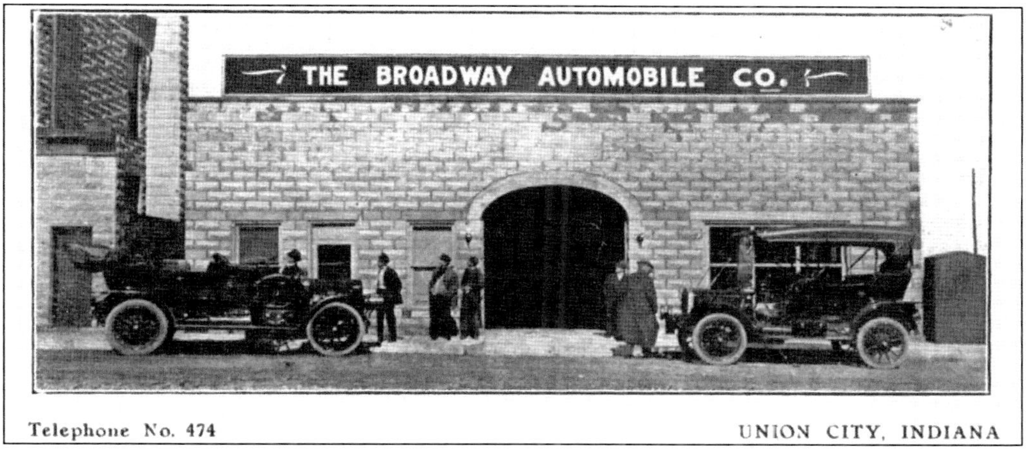

BROADWAY AUTOMOBILE COMPANY. Little is known of this company, which seems to have been housed in the former traction station on the east side of Broadway. (Max Harter.)

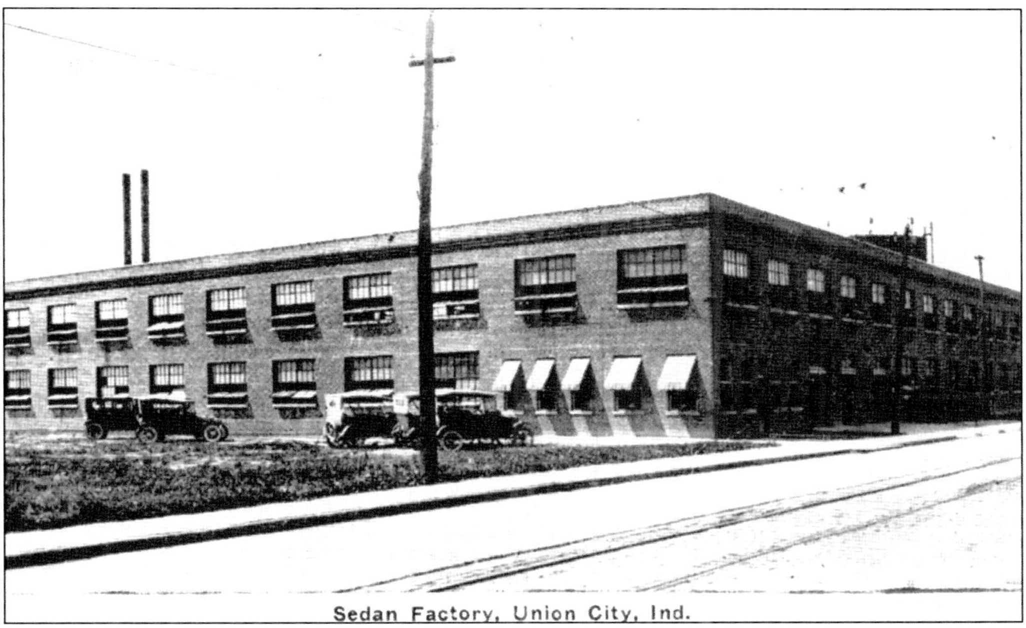

SEDAN FACTORY. The Sedan Body Company was affiliated with the Union City Body Company and was located on West Pearl Street. This building, erected in 1925, housed the offices of the International Seat Corporation and the bus company. This became the east building of the Union City Body Company. (Janice Harvey.)

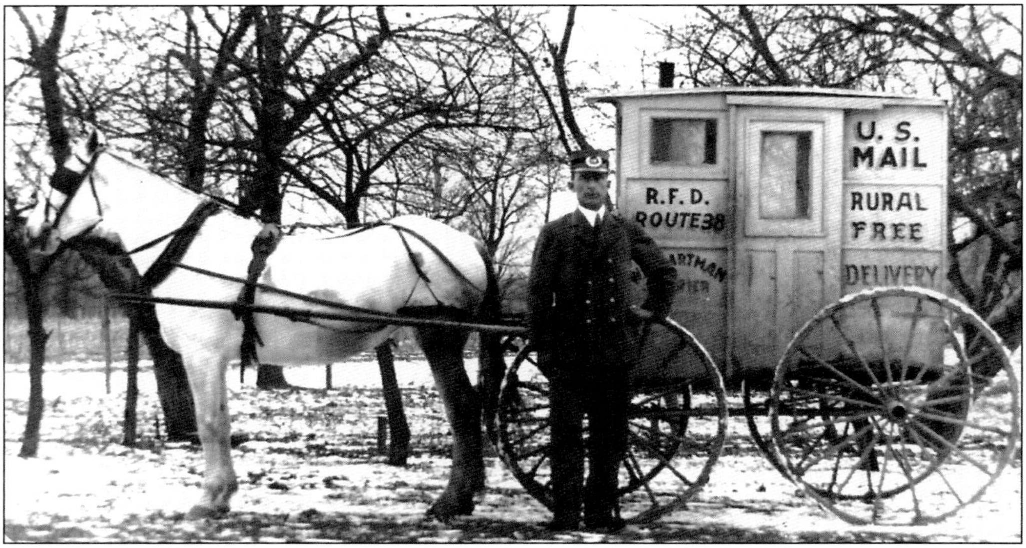

WALTER HARTMAN, MAILMAN. This is Walter Hartman, the U.S. mail carrier for Route 38, Union City. Hartman lived in rural Wayne Township and was known to be a mail carrier in 1908. (Union City Public Library.)

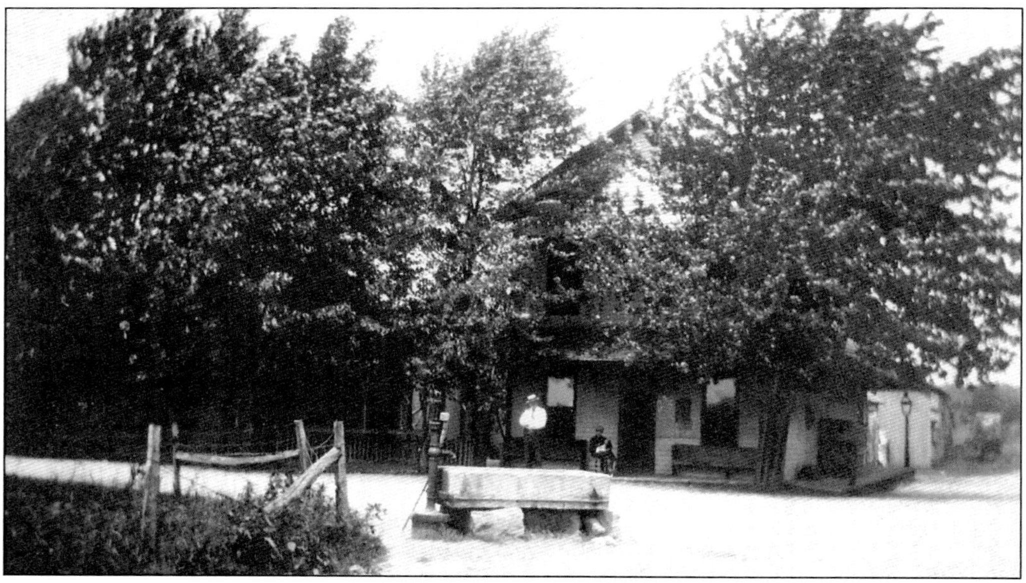

BARTONIA STORE. Bartonia Store, at the northwest corner of Greenville Pike and Arba Pike, was likely erected sometime after 1891, when a previous store burned. For a time, the Knights of the Golden Eagle (KGE) used the upper room for their lodge hall until 1916. The structure currently houses a restaurant. (Linda L. Black.)

BARTONIA METHODIST EPISCOPAL CHURCH. Bartonia Methodist Episcopal Church was organized in 1848. Edward Barton, the founder of the village, donated a lot to the congregation south of the only intersection in the village. A church was built there about 1850. The building shown here was erected in 1887 on the same site and dedicated on December 18. It was remodeled in 1925. An addition was made in 1958. (Linda L. Black.)

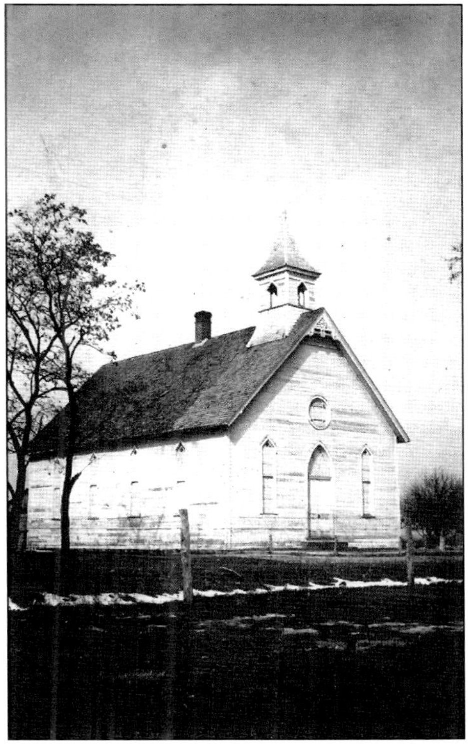

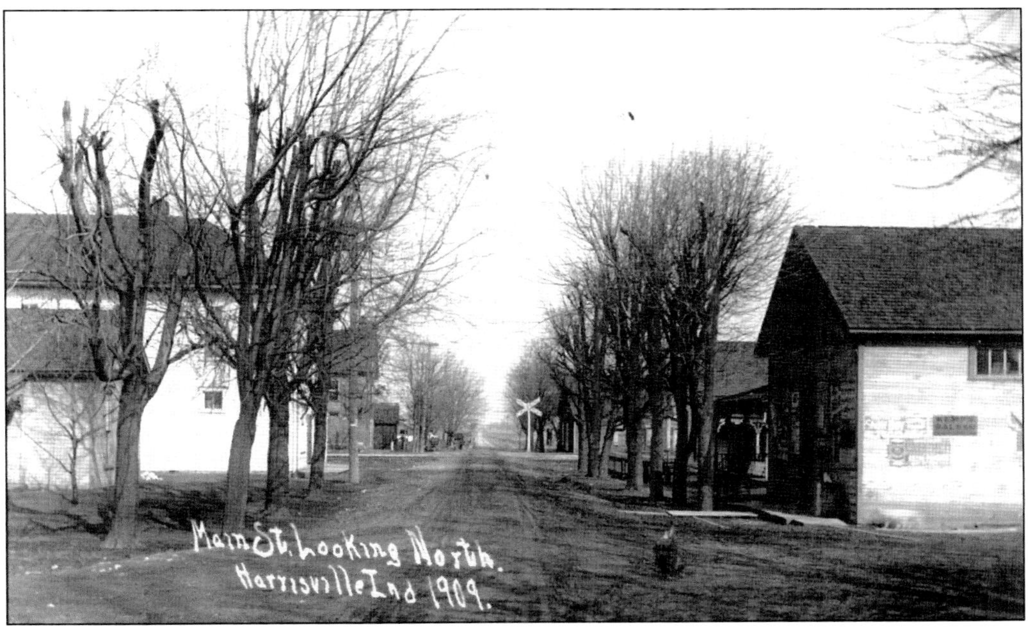

HARRISVILLE MAIN STREET. This view looks north on Main Street. The crossing of the Big Four Railroad is visible in the distance. At left is the storekeeper's house and KGE hall. At right is a store building. The buildings on the left are extant. (Gregory P. Hinshaw.)

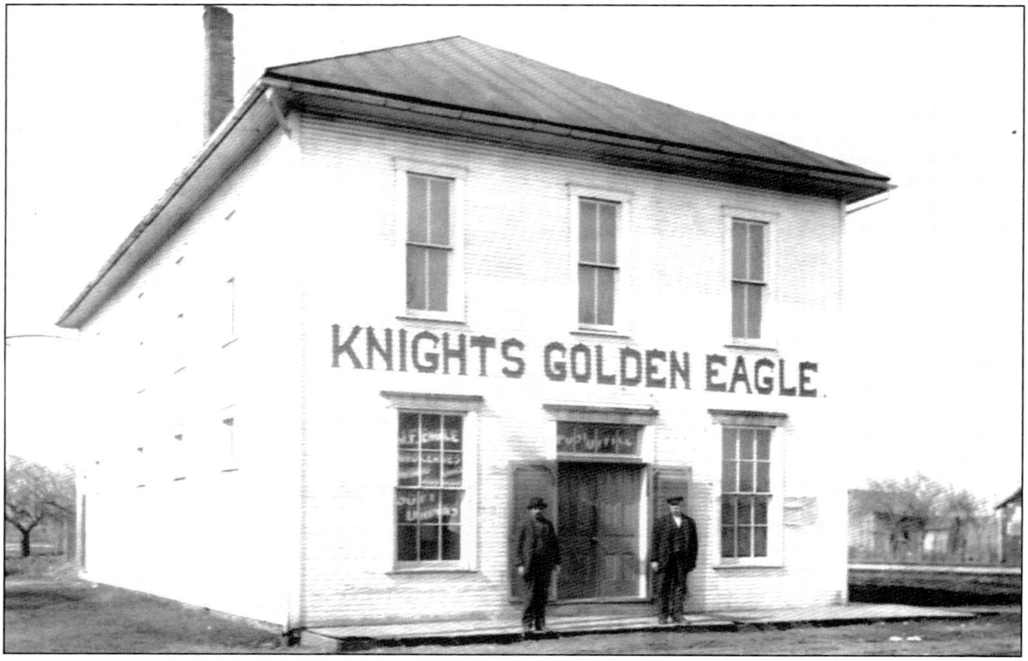

HARRISVILLE KGE HALL. The KGE, an organization with ritual based on the Crusaders, organized in Harrisville in 1894. Built in 1902, this structure is said to have been the first KGE hall erected in the state. The lower floor housed a store and the post office. The man shown at left is Luther E. Coats, the village's postmaster in 1909–1910. The local lodge disbanded in 1952. (Esther Karns.)

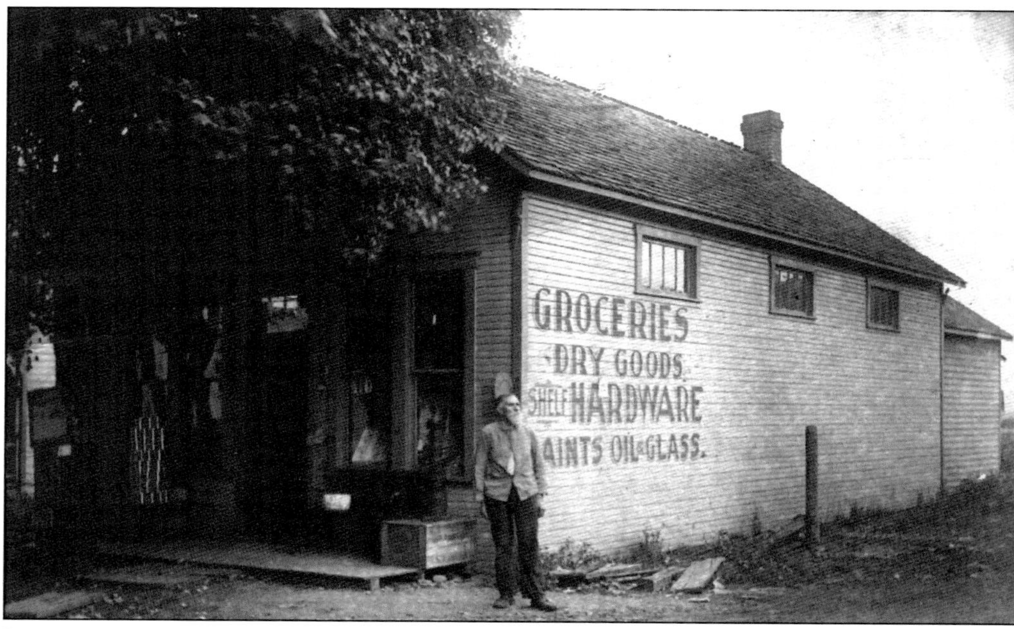

HARRISVILLE GROCERY STORE. The grocery and general store located on the east side of Main Street in Harrisville is shown here. This building has been razed. (Gregory P. Hinshaw.)

HARRISVILLE CHRISTIAN CHURCH. Harrisville Christian Church was organized in 1865. A church building was erected in 1866. In 1899–1900, the structure depicted here was erected on South Street based on plans by Hampton Gettinger and dedicated on February 4, 1900. The belfry has been removed, and a large brick addition was built in 1978–1979. (Gregory P. Hinshaw.)

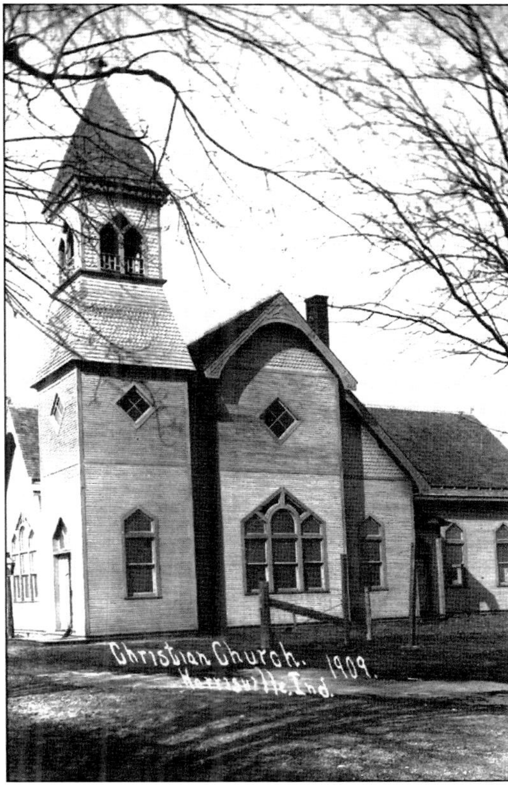

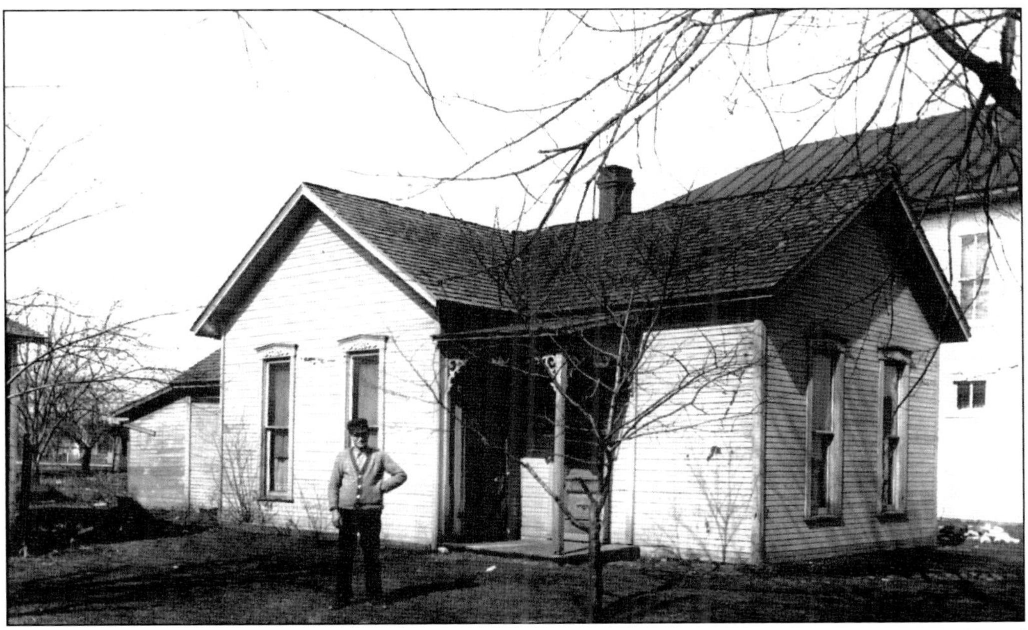

HARRISVILLE STOREKEEPER'S RESIDENCE. This residence stands south of the KGE hall and general store on Main Street. At the time of this photograph, it was occupied by the family of Luther E. Coats, storekeeper and postmaster in 1909–1910. (Gregory P. Hinshaw.)

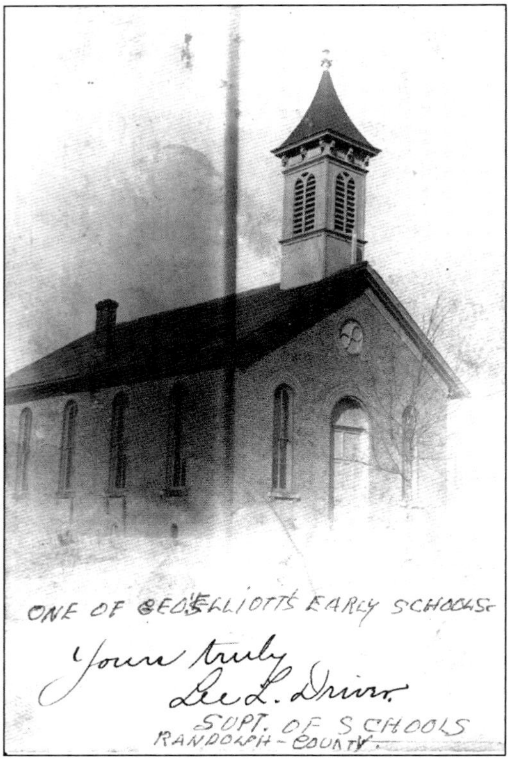

No. 9 School. No. 9 School, Wayne Township, was informally known as both Chenoweth School and Harter School. It was erected in 1883 at the southwest corner of Highway 227 and County Road 250 S. It closed in 1912, and students were sent to the new Wayne School in the fall. The building was sold in 1914. It is still extant although vacant. The card bears the signature of Lee L. Driver. (Gregory P. Hinshaw.)

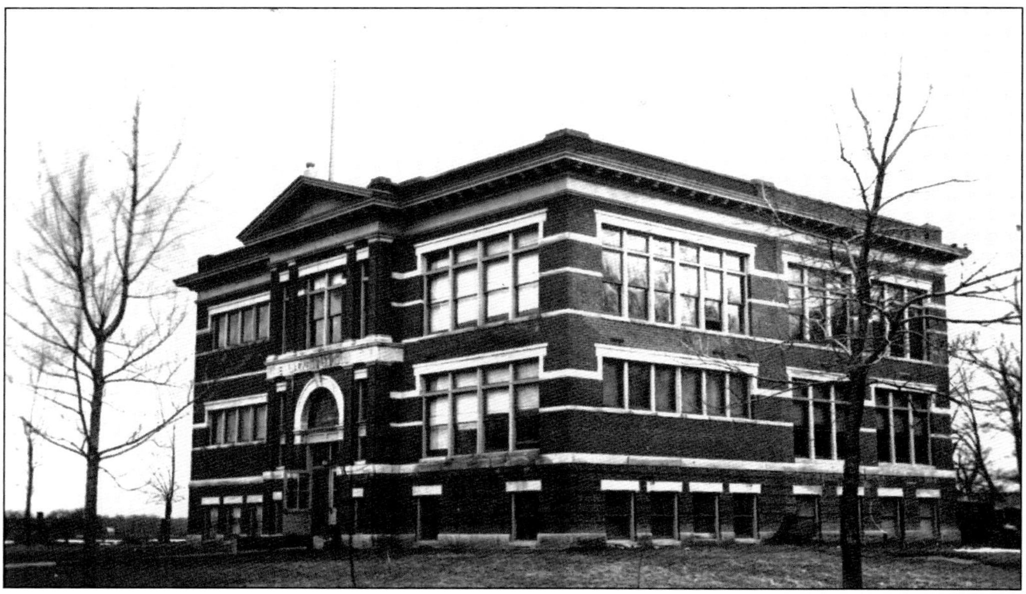

Jackson School. Jackson School was erected in 1910 at the center of Jackson Township on present-day County Road 700 N between 600 E and 700 E. It was dedicated on December 2, 1910. An addition was constructed in 1915. High school students were transferred to Saratoga ("Ward-Jackson") in the fall of 1958. The building housed elementary students until the spring of 1962. It was destroyed by a fire on October 29, 1989. (Randolph County Historical Society.)

Three

FARMLAND AND VICINITY

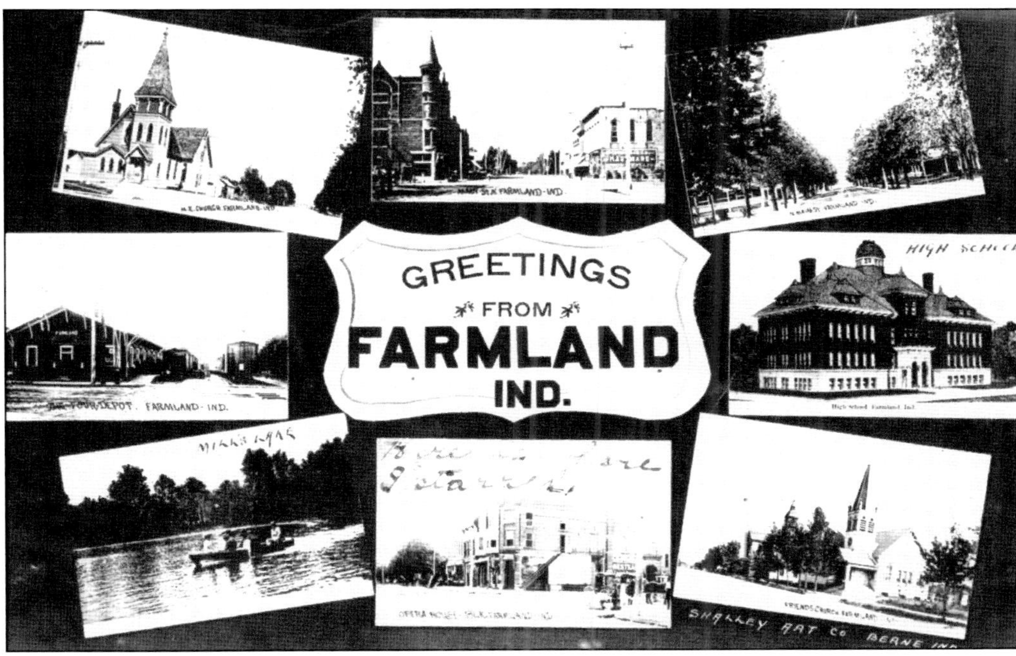

GREETINGS FROM FARMLAND. The Shalley Art Company of Berne, Indiana, produced many of these cards, including at least two versions for Farmland. This card shows, clockwise from the upper left, the Methodist Episcopal church, a view north on Main Street, a view south on Main Street, Farmland High School, the Friends church, the opera house block, Mills Lake, and the Big Four depot. (Harold Watson.)

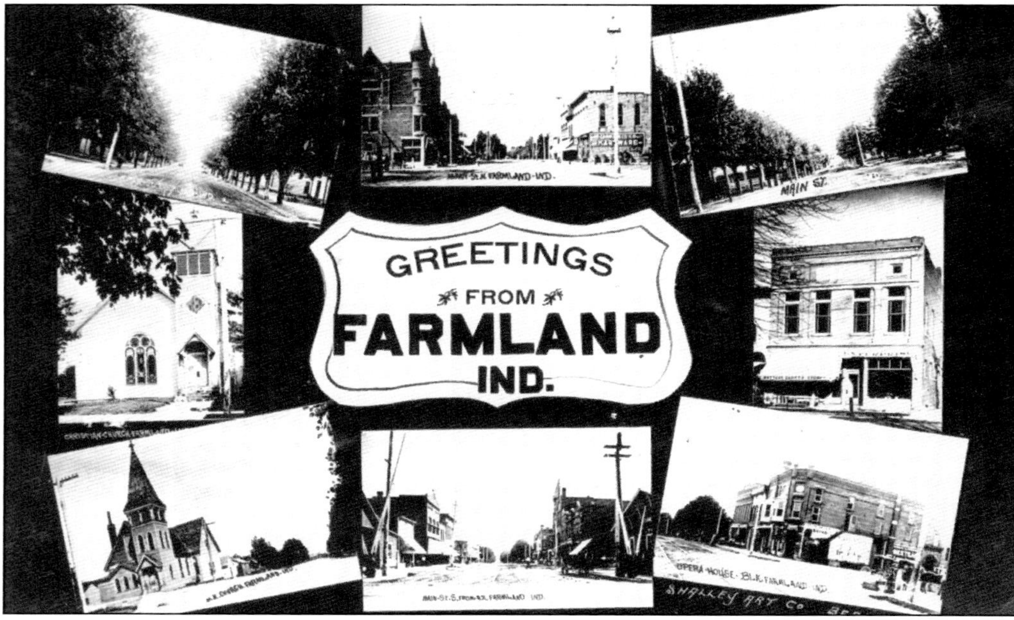

GREETINGS FROM FARMLAND, VERSION TWO. Another version of the Shalley Art Company's card shows, clockwise from the upper left, a view south on Main Street, a view north on Main Street, another view south on Main Street, the Knights of Pythias building, the opera house block, a view south on Main Street from north of the railroad, the Methodist Episcopal church, and the Christian church. (Judy Wilson Wright.)

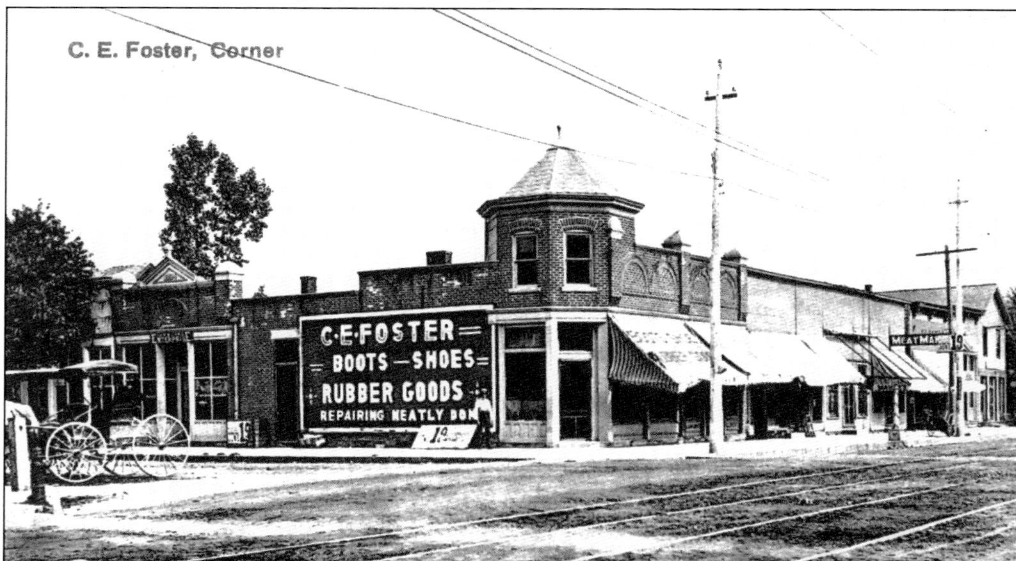

C. E. FOSTER CORNER. The C. E. Foster Corner stands at the southeast corner of Main and Henry Streets. The building was constructed in 1895. The buildings to the right, all frame, no longer survive. The first set was replaced by a new building in 1961. The next two survived until 1991. Macy Hall, the last building, with a gabled front, was erected in 1866. It was razed in the 1950s. (Steve Longnecker.)

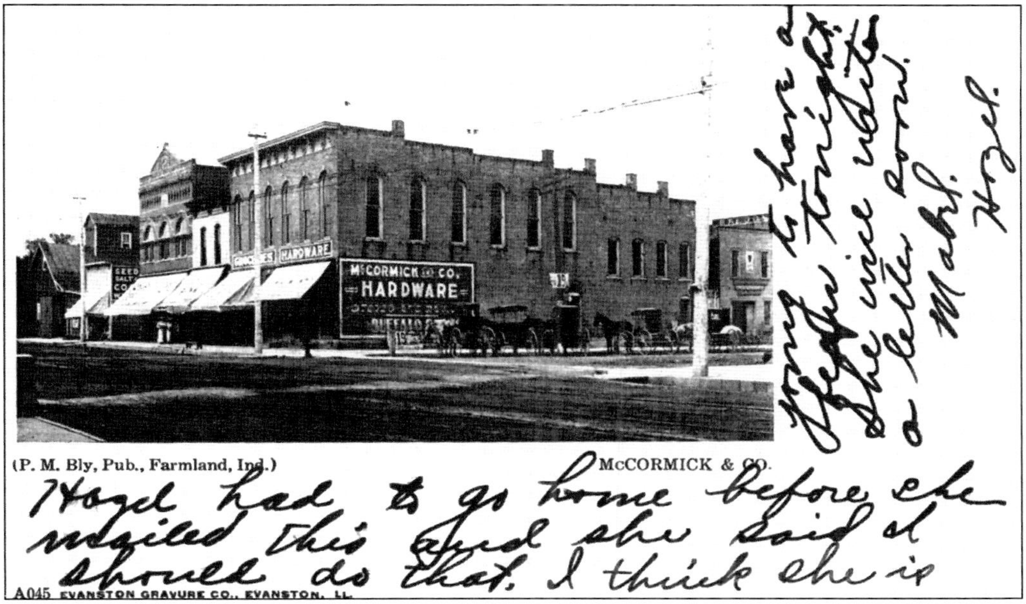

McCormick and Company. The Dennis Thornburg Block was erected in 1867 at the northeast corner of Main and Henry Streets. The first building to the left, the L. A. Gable Building, was erected in 1879 or 1880. The next building is the Clayton Block, completed in 1899. To the north are a small feed building and the Goodrich Elevator, removed in 1919 and replaced by a new structure. (Steve Longnecker.)

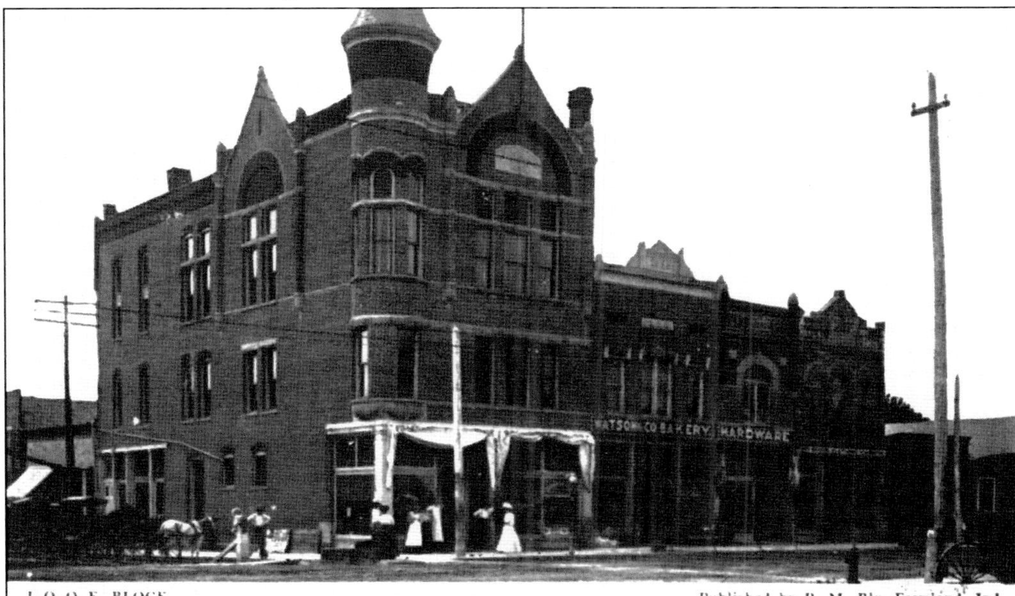

IOOF Block. The IOOF block, located at the northwest corner of Main and Henry Streets, is probably Farmland's most picturesque block. These buildings were built in 1898 following a devastating fire on November 29, 1897. They are, from left, the IOOF building, the Masonic building, the Wood Building, and the Clayton Building. The small building at the right was used as a feed store and was razed in the 1970s. (Gregory P. Hinshaw.)

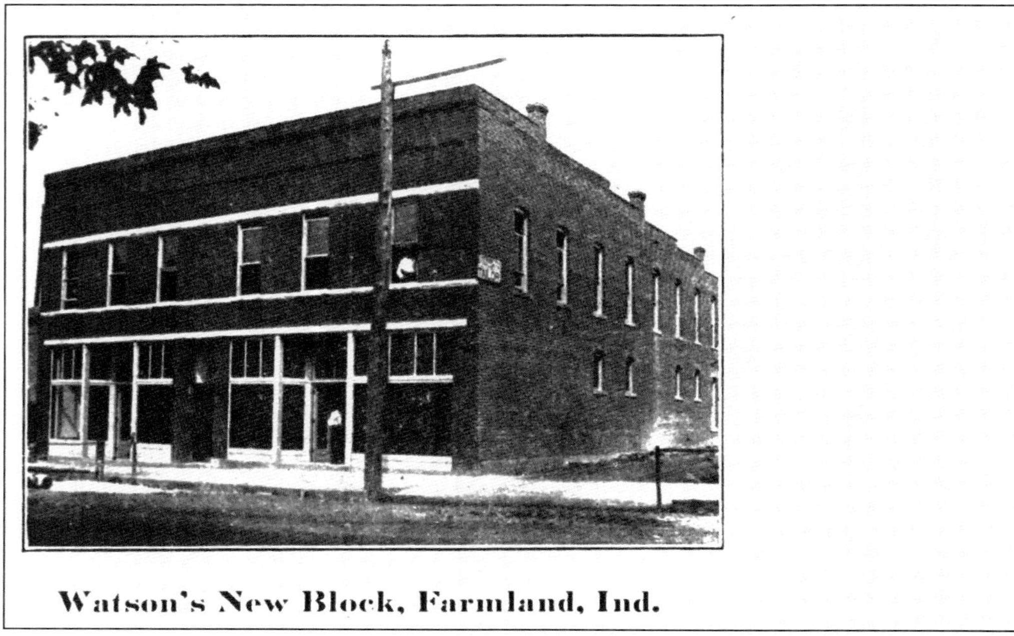

Watson's New Block. Watson's Block stands on the north side of West Henry Street. The building was erected in 1908 by G. B. Watson. The view shows Luther Thornburg, a mortician and furniture dealer, looking from an upstairs window of his business. (Judy Wilson Wright.)

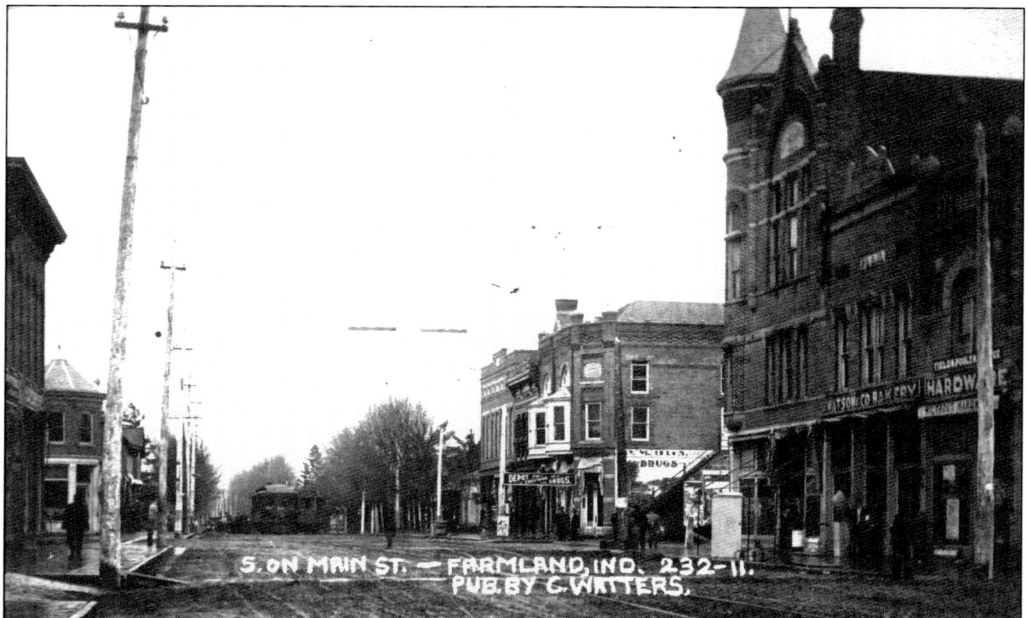

South on Main Street. This view looks at the west side of Main Street from just south of the railroad. Across the street is the opera house block, including the Red Men's hall, erected in 1898; the Farmland State Bank, erected in 1888–1889; and the opera house, erected in 1889. At right is the IOOF block. Two cars of the Indiana Union Traction Company can be seen meeting in the background. (Judy Wilson Wright.)

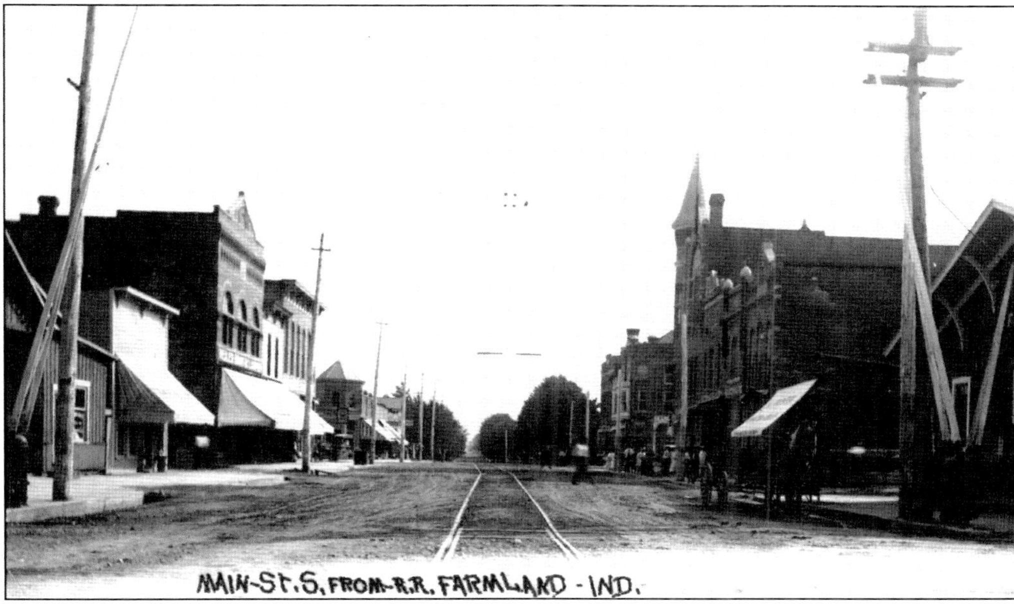

MAIN STREET SOUTH FROM THE RAILROAD. This image shows Main Street from just north of the Big Four Railroad. The interurban tracks run down the middle of the street. At left are the Goodrich Brothers Elevator, the Clayton Block, the Gable Building, the Thornburg Block, and the Kramer Building. At right are the depot, removed in 1921, the Clayton Building, the Wood Building, the Masonic building, the IOOF block, and the opera house. (Gregory P. Hinshaw.)

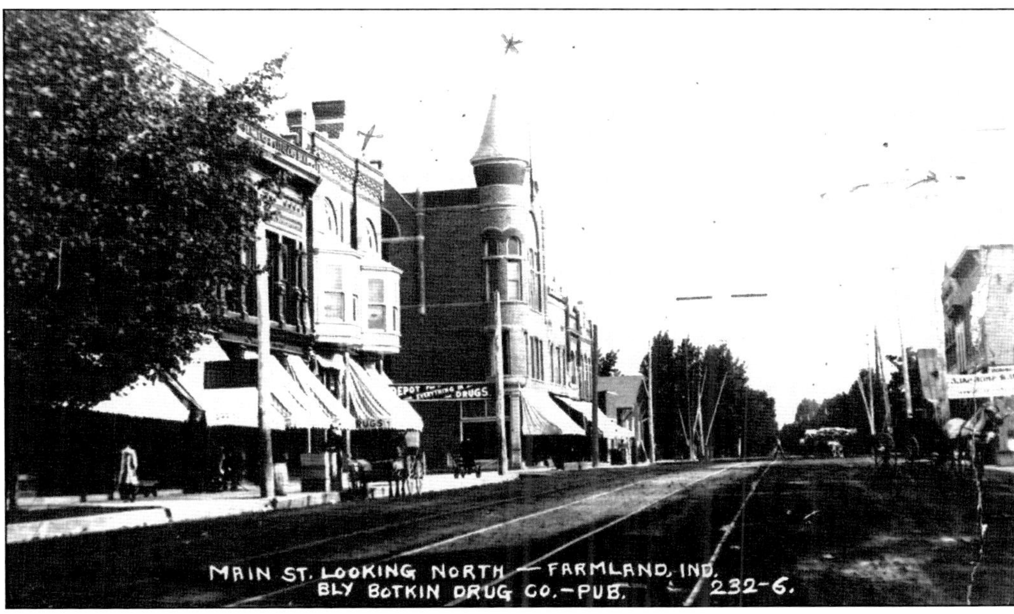

MAIN STREET LOOKING NORTH. This view depicts the west side of Main Street looking north from south of downtown. At left are the Red Men's hall, Farmland State Bank, opera house, IOOF hall, Masonic building, Wood Building, and Clayton Building. A small feed store and the depot can be seen in the distance. (Judy Wilson Wright.)

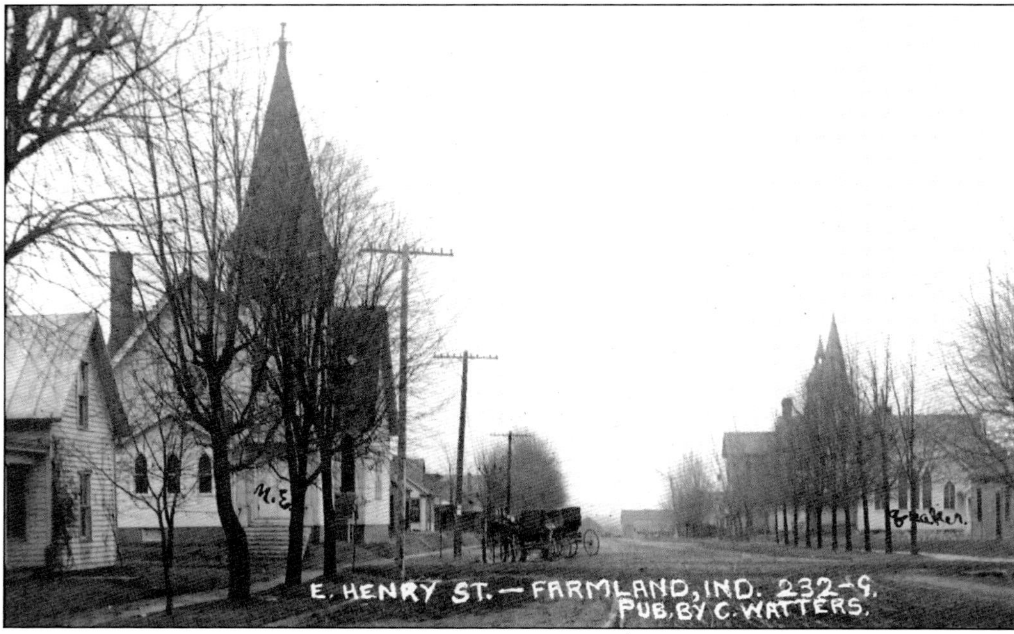

East Henry Street. At left is the Methodist Episcopal church, erected in 1896–1897. At right is the Friends church, erected in 1903. The old public school stands just beyond the Friends church. (Gregory P. Hinshaw.)

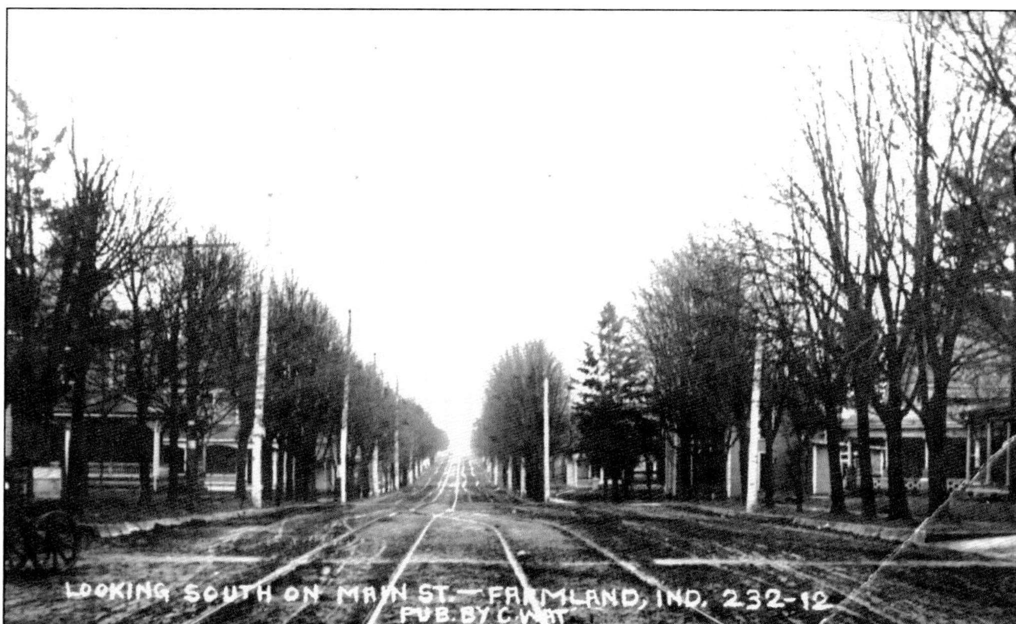

Looking South on Main Street. This view looks south on Main Street from downtown. The double-tracked section of the lines of the Indiana Union Traction Company is visible in the foreground. (Gregory P. Hinshaw.)

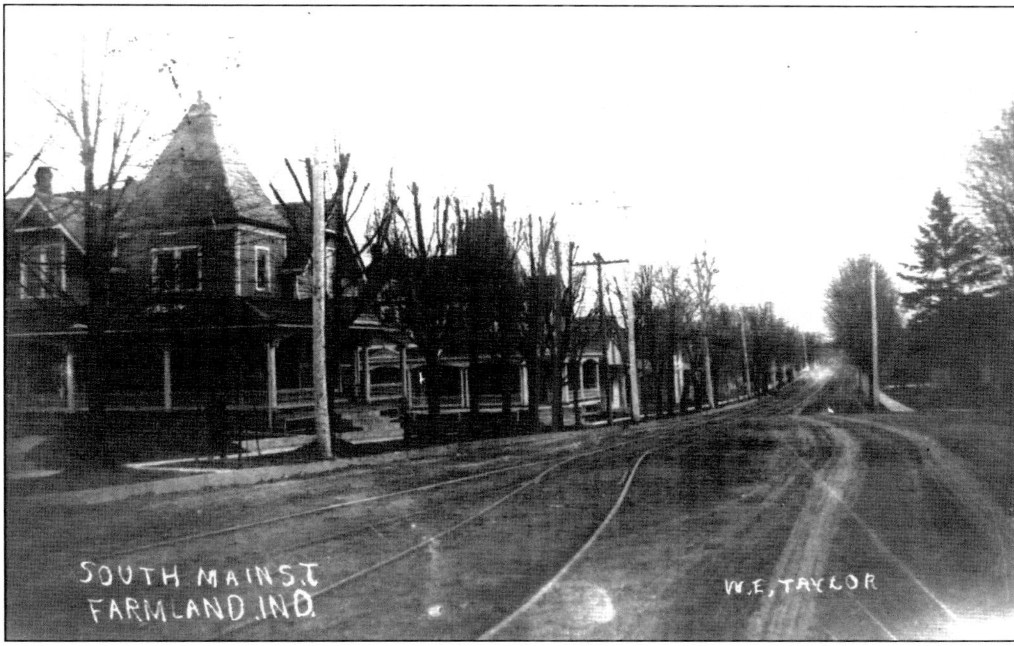

SOUTH MAIN STREET. This view also looks south on Main Street from downtown, looking at the east side of the street. The two residences shown, on the east side of Main Street just south of the business district, remain extant and in nearly original condition. (Harold Watson.)

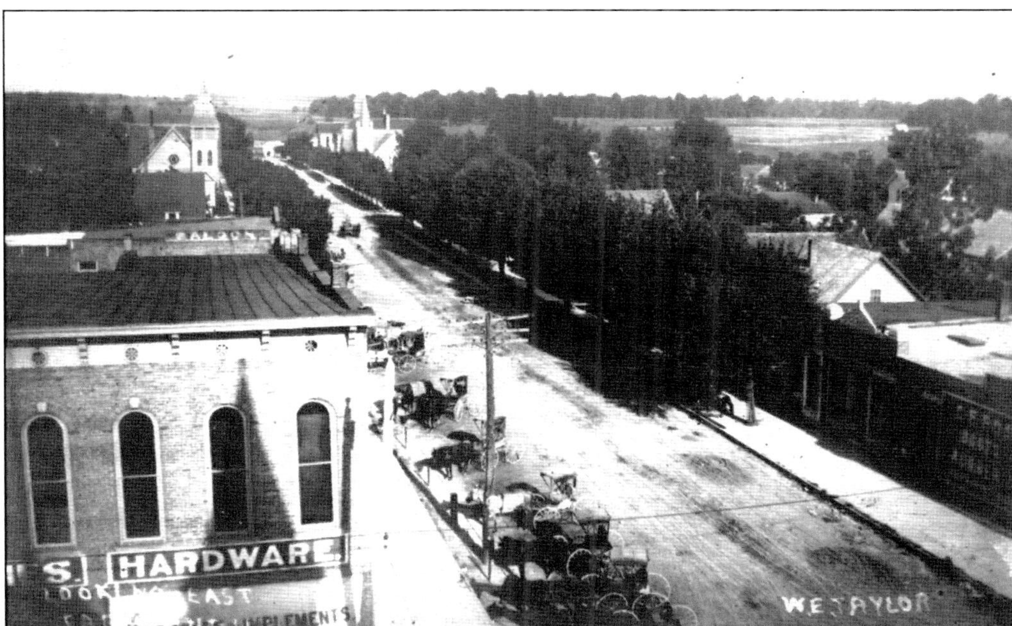

LOOKING EAST. This photograph was taken from the tower of the IOOF hall, looking east on Henry Street. The building in the foreground is the Dennis Thornburg Block, while the Methodist Episcopal church, Friends church, and old public school can be seen in the distance. (Harold Watson.)

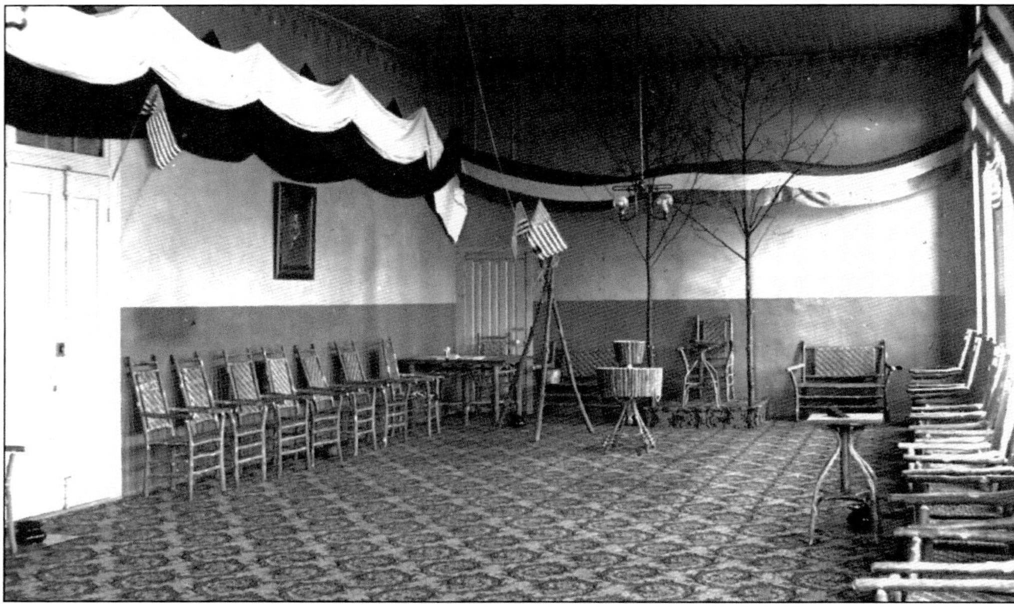

Modern Woodmen of America Hall. The Modern Woodmen of America is a fraternal benefits society with a ritual based on "forest freedom." Farmland's William McKinley Camp, No. 10357, was organized in 1901. It met in several locations. This room was thought to be in the upstairs of the Dennis Thornburg Block. The local camp was dissolved in 1964. (Gregory P. Hinshaw.)

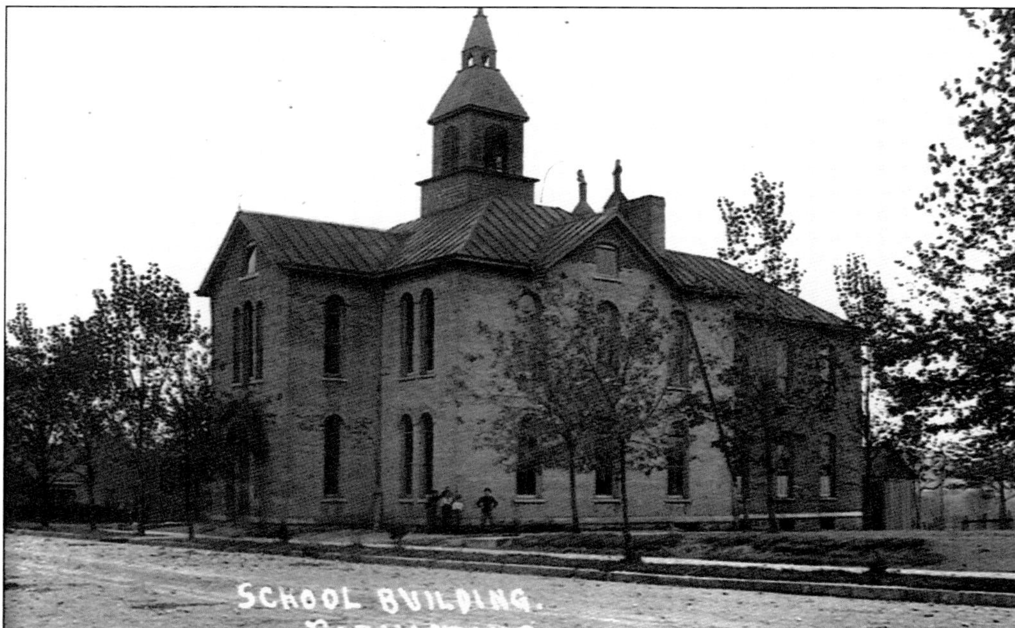

Public School. This building stood on the south side of East Henry Street, east of Plum Street. It was built in 1868–1869 and was enlarged in 1890. The building was used until 1909. It was sold in 1913 and was razed in May 1926. (Helen Maxine Wright.)

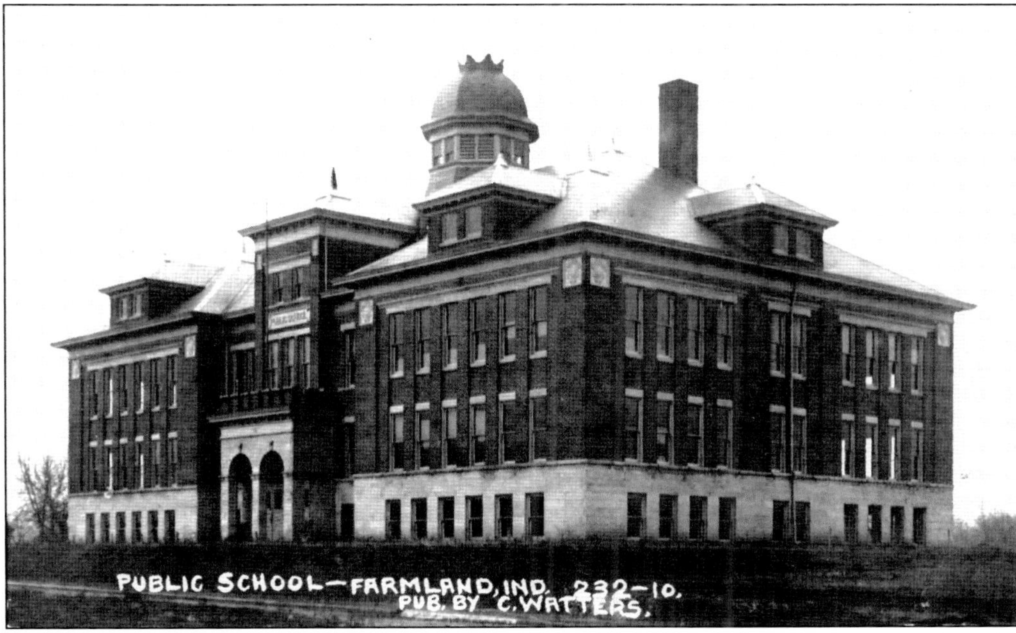

PUBLIC SCHOOL. This building stood on the east side of North Morris Street, south of Pursley Street. It was erected in 1908–1909 and dedicated on November 24, 1909. A gymnasium was added in 1940–1941. High school students were sent to Monroe Central High School in the fall of 1963. Elementary students were transferred to the new Monroe Central Elementary School in 1983. The building was razed in the spring of 1984. (Gregory P. Hinshaw.)

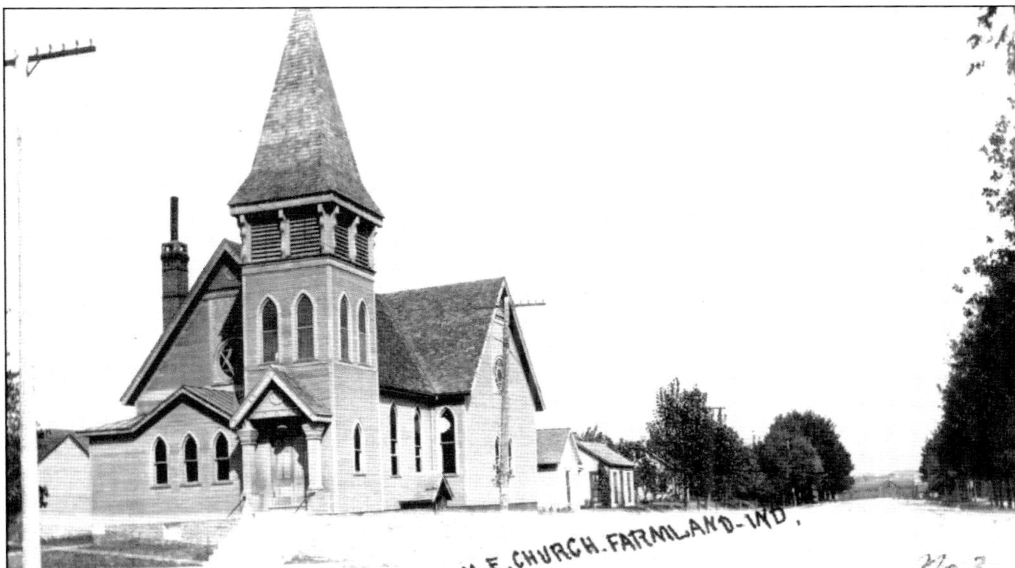

METHODIST EPISCOPAL CHURCH. A class of the Methodist Episcopal Church was organized in Farmland in 1856. Services were held in schoolhouses until a building was constructed at Henry and Plum Streets in 1866–1867. The structure depicted here was erected in 1896–1897. The structure was used with only minor alterations until it was destroyed by fire on September 1, 1953. A new building was built on North Morris Street. (Gregory P. Hinshaw.)

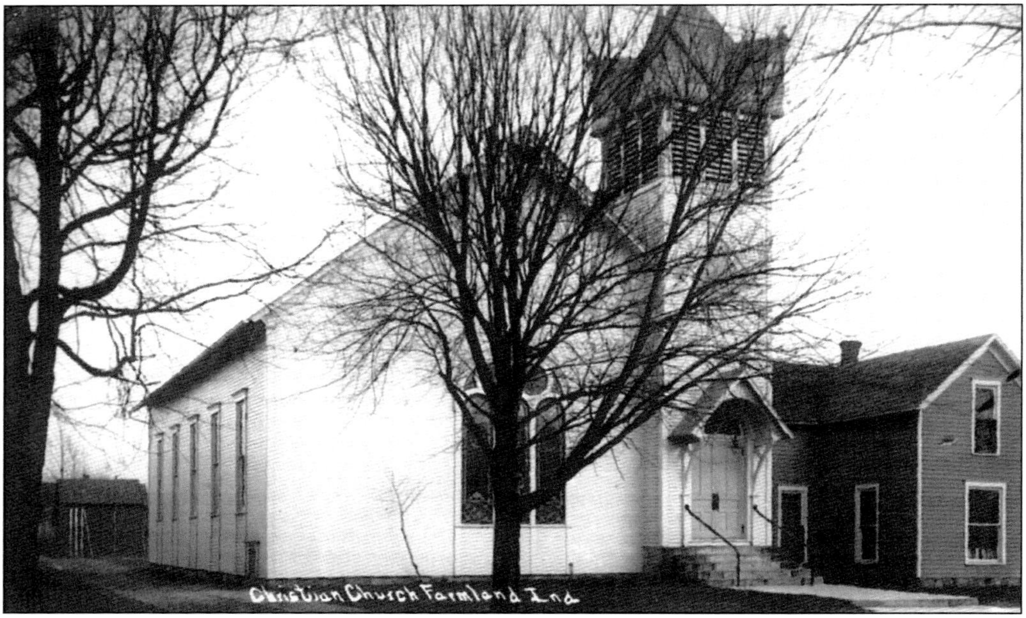

CHRISTIAN CHURCH. The Christian Church was organized in Farmland in 1856. Services were held in a schoolhouse on Angling Road until the building depicted here was completed on North Main Street in 1888. The building was remodeled in 1904. The structure was enlarged in 1925, and an annex was added to the rear of the building between 1968 and 1971. (Edna Modisett.)

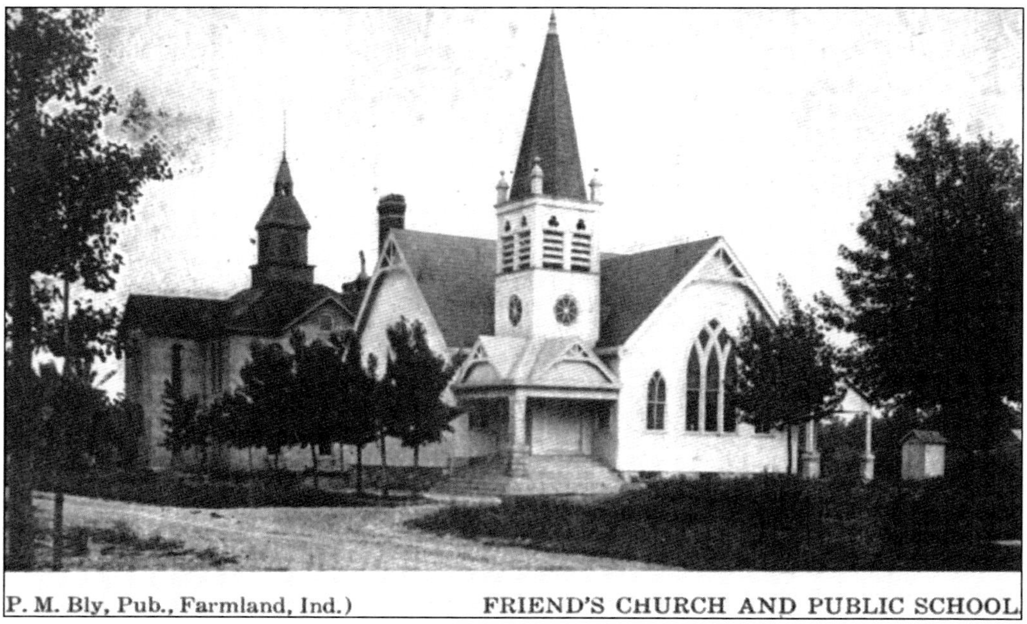

FRIENDS CHURCH AND PUBLIC SCHOOL. Regular Friends services were held in Farmland beginning in 1878. Official organization came in 1882. Two structures served the congregation until the building shown here was erected in 1903. It was enlarged in 1906, 1915, and between 1981 and 1983. The building was used until 2001, when a new structure was occupied. The 1869 public school can also be seen in this view. (Gregory P. Hinshaw.)

D. H. MORRIS, MAIL CARRIER. There are multiple varieties of these cards, sold by vendors to mail carriers as Christmas greeting cards for rural patrons. They were not addressed and were delivered without postage. This card depicts David H. Morris, a Farmland carrier who lived on East Jackson Street. In the background is the IOOF building, where the post office was located until 1958. (Randolph County Historical Society.)

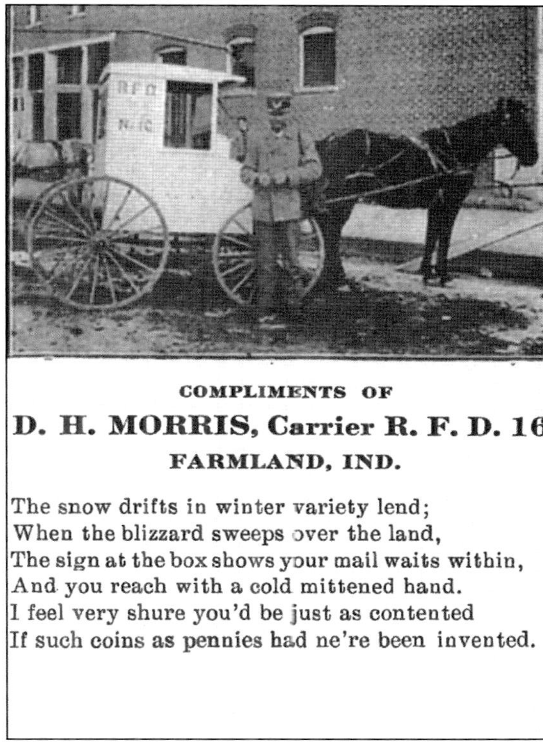

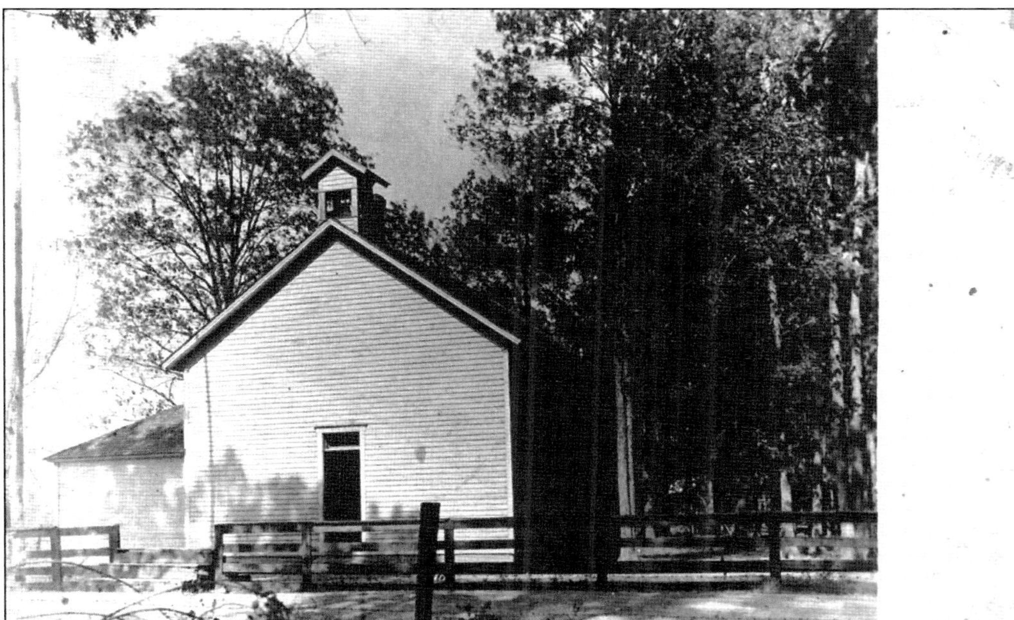

HICKORY GROVE SCHOOL. Hickory Grove School, Monroe Township, No. 2, stood on the north side of County Road 400 N, west of 800 W. The property was secured in 1880. The frame building depicted here was erected between 1898 and 1904. The school closed in the spring of 1913. The building is no longer in existence. (Janice Harvey.)

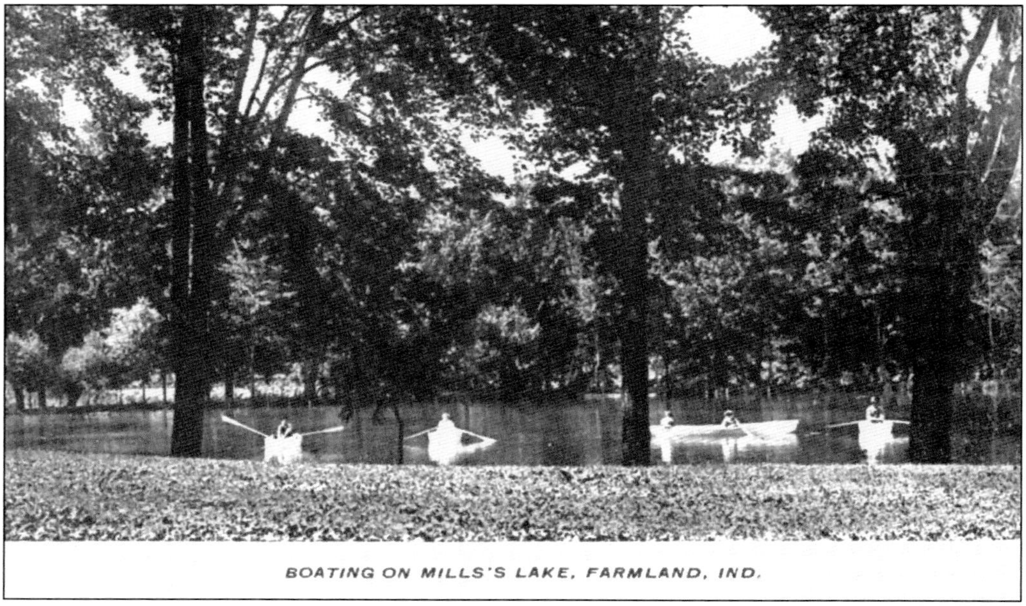

BOATING ON MILLS LAKE. Mills Lake, located southeast of Farmland in Stoney Creek Township, was created by damming White River at Sparrow Creek in the 1890s. The park included a bear pit and a dance hall. The park declined in the 1920s and finally ended about 1935. (Steve Longnecker.)

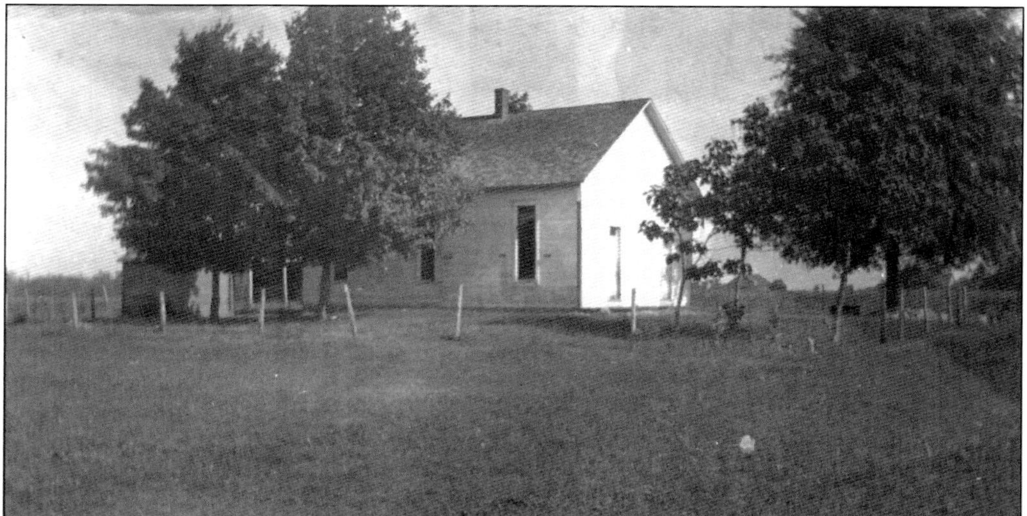

POPLAR RUN FRIENDS CHURCH. Poplar Run Friends Church was located in Stoney Creek Township, at County Roads 900 W and 300 S. The congregation, established in 1841, was first served by a log building. A frame meetinghouse was erected in 1856. The structure depicted here was erected in 1883. The building was totally remodeled in 1911 and in 1963. The congregation was discontinued in 1979. A Baptist congregation has used the structure since 1980. (Gregory P. Hinshaw.)

HUBBARD SCHOOL. Hubbard School, Stoney Creek Township, No. 5, stood three miles south of Farmland on the west side of Highway 1. The school closed in 1914 due to insufficient attendance and was sold in 1917. It was moved a short distance to the south, where it is used as a residence. (Judy Wilson Wright.)

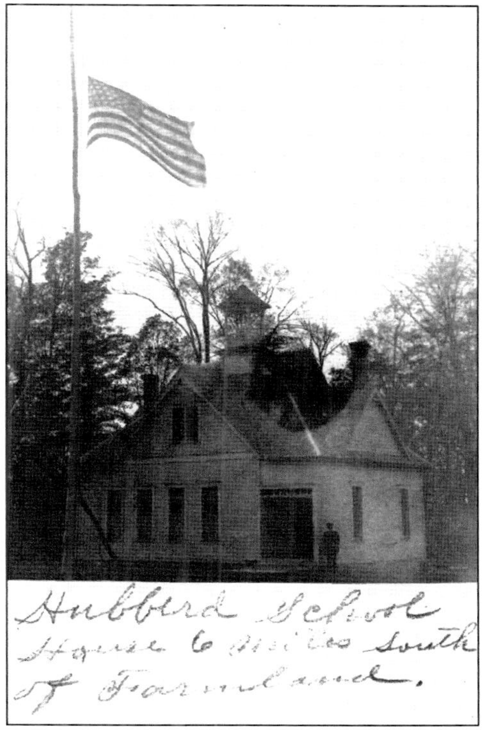

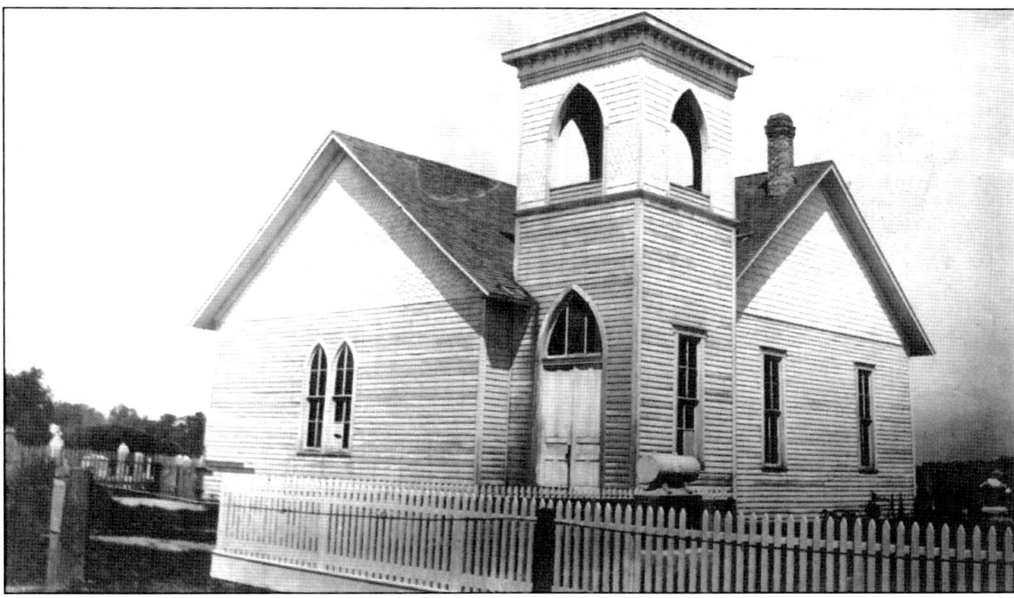

HOPEWELL METHODIST PROTESTANT CHURCH, BEFORE 1913. Hopewell Methodist Protestant Church stood northeast of Farmland on County Road 550 N in Green Township. The congregation was established sometime before 1845. A frame church was erected in 1853. A new church was built about 1877. The building was extensively remodeled in 1900, as shown here. The building burned in 1913. A new building was erected in 1914–1915 and served until the congregation was discontinued in 1992. (Harold Watson.)

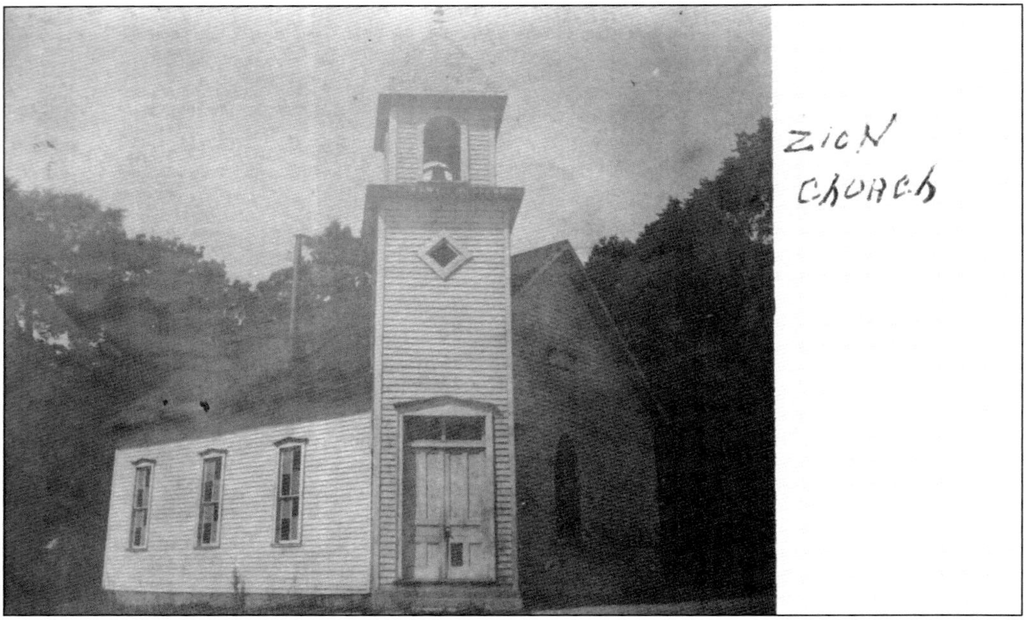

ZION UNITED BRETHREN CHURCH. Zion United Brethren Church stood five miles north and one mile west of Farmland on Highway 1 in Green Township. The congregation organized about 1860. Services were held in a schoolhouse until 1875, when the structure depicted here was erected. When the denomination split in 1889, Zion joined the "Old Constitution," or "Radical," United Brethren. The church disbanded in 1928. The structure was razed about 1939. (Harold Watson.)

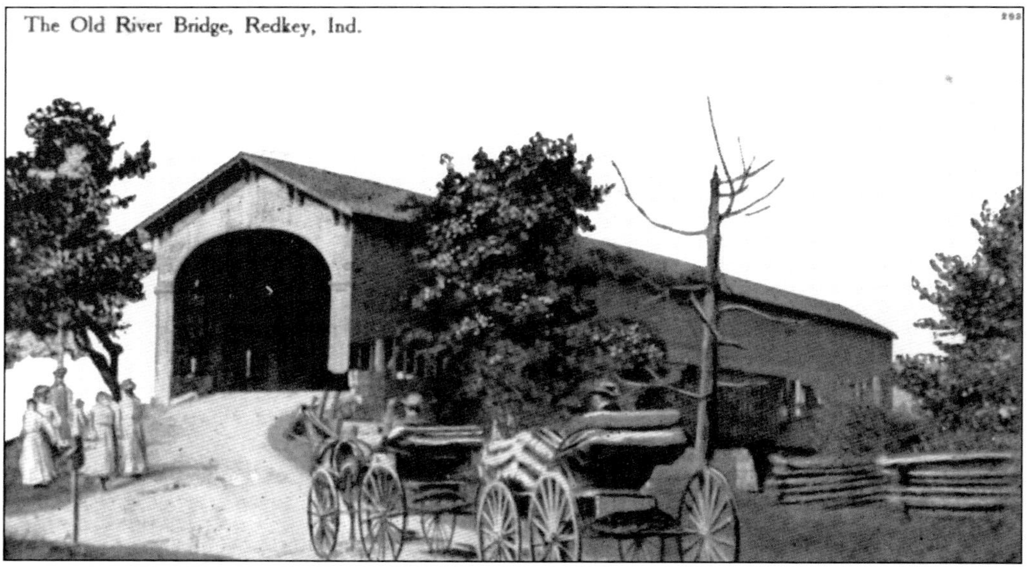

OLD RIVER BRIDGE. This postcard shows the Steubenville Covered Bridge, which crossed the Mississinewa River on present-day Highway 1 in Green Township, several miles south of Redkey. The bridge was erected in 1883 by the Kennedy Brothers of Rush County. It was 140 feet long, 16 feet wide, and 14 feet high. It was replaced by a new two-span bridge in 1941. (Gregory P. Hinshaw.)

Four

Parker City and Vicinity

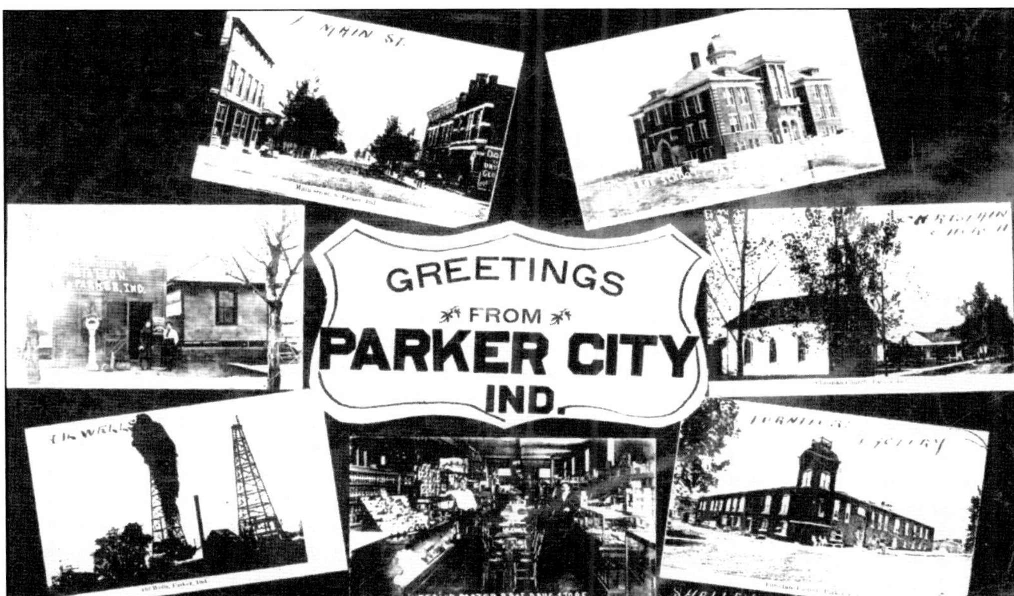

Greetings from Parker City. This Shalley Art Company composite shows, clockwise from upper left, Main Street looking south, Monroe School, the Christian church, the Vaught Brothers Furniture Factory, the interior of the Porter Brothers Drug Store, oil wells, and the station of the Indiana Union Traction Company. (Gregory P. Hinshaw.)

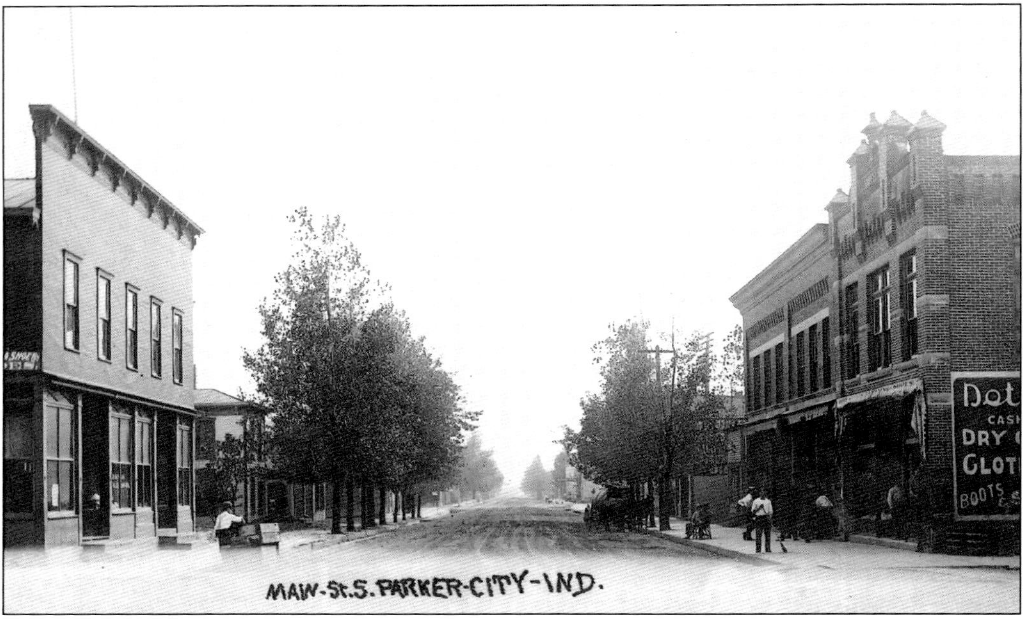

MAIN STREET SOUTH. This view looks south on Main Street from Howard Street. The building at left was removed about 1938 and was the site of the Parking Banking Company after 1959. The buildings at right are still extant, although altered in appearance. (Randolph County Historical Society.)

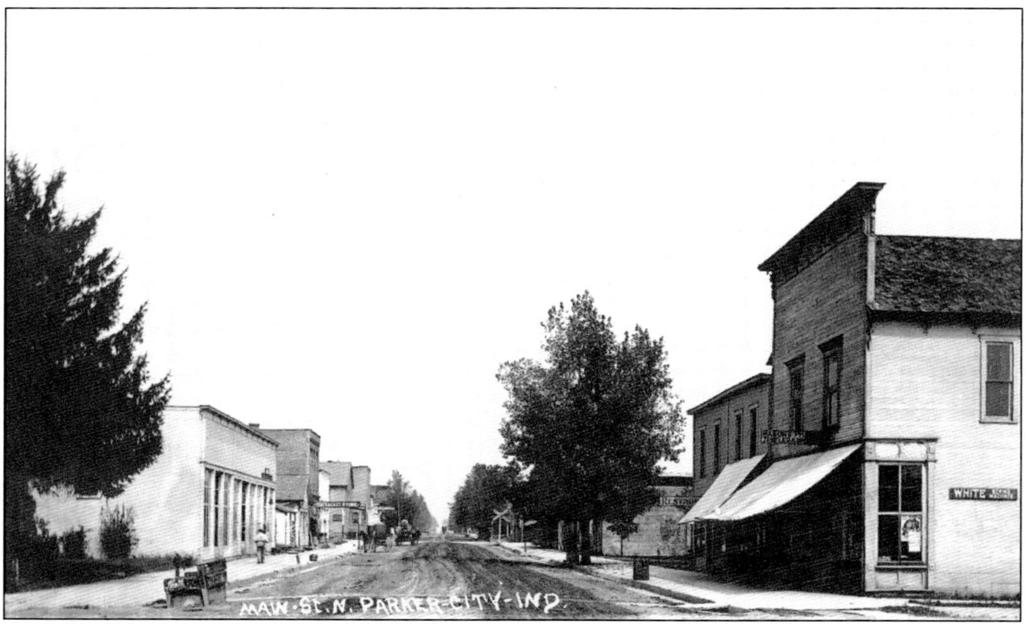

MAIN STREET NORTH FROM WASHINGTON STREET. This view looks north on Main Street from Washington Street. The crossing of the Big Four Railroad can be seen in the distance. None of the buildings depicted here, except for the two-story brick block south of the railroad, are extant. The Knapp Building, at left in the foreground, was erected in 1907 by Frank Hyer and Joe Meeks and was razed in 1968. (Randolph County Historical Society.)

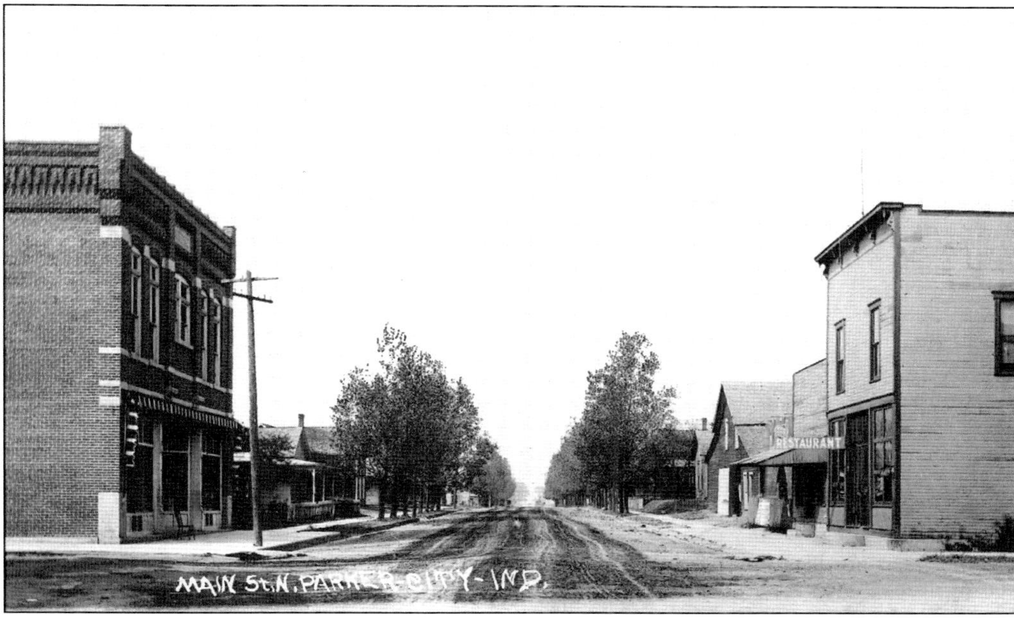

Main Street North from Howard Street. This view looks north on Main Street from Howard Street. At left is the IOOF hall, built in 1906. The buildings on the right were removed about 1926 for the construction of the Wood-Morgan Garage building. (Randolph County Historical Society.)

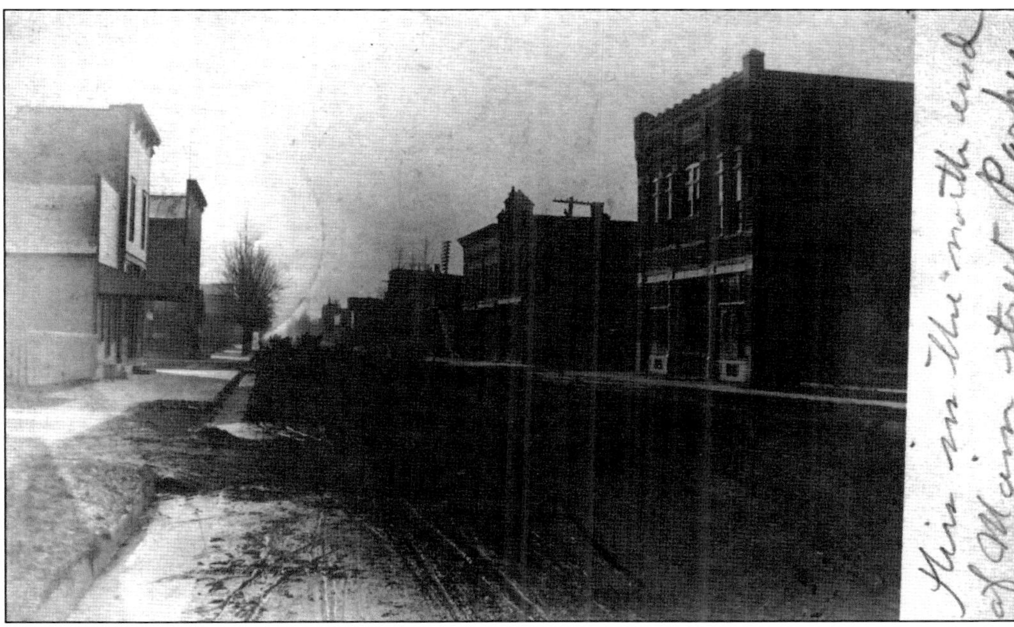

Main Street Looking South. This view looks south on Main Street from just north of Howard Street. At the right is the IOOF hall and Porter Brothers Drug Store. (Gregory P. Hinshaw.)

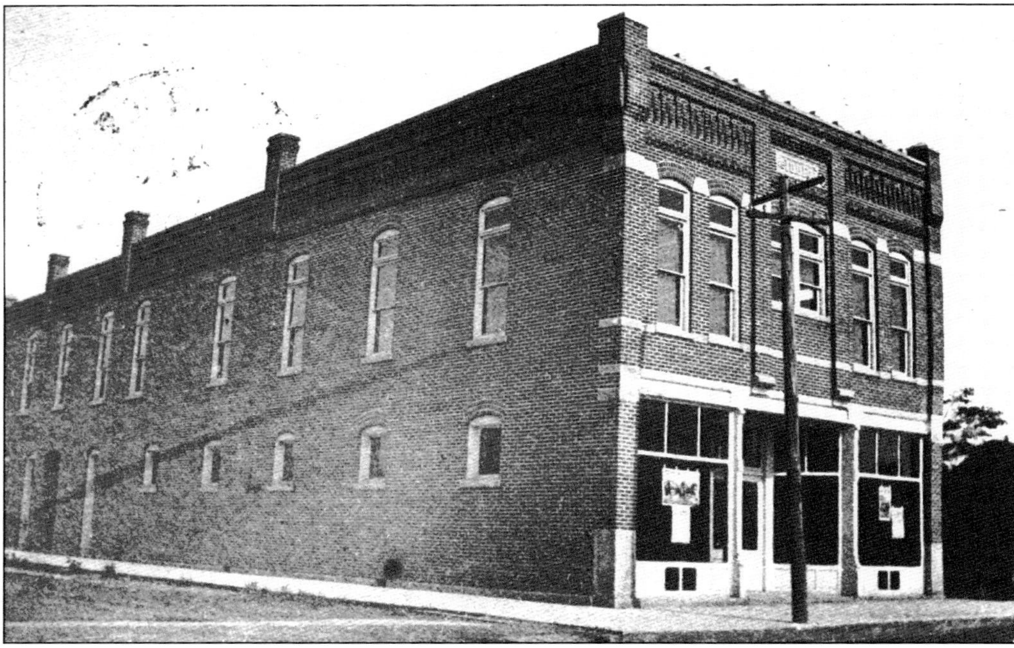

IOOF Hall. This building is the IOOF hall, erected in 1906 at the northwest corner of Main and Howard Streets. The Masonic Lodge purchased the building in 1923. It has used the upper floor in the years since. (Gregory P. Hinshaw.)

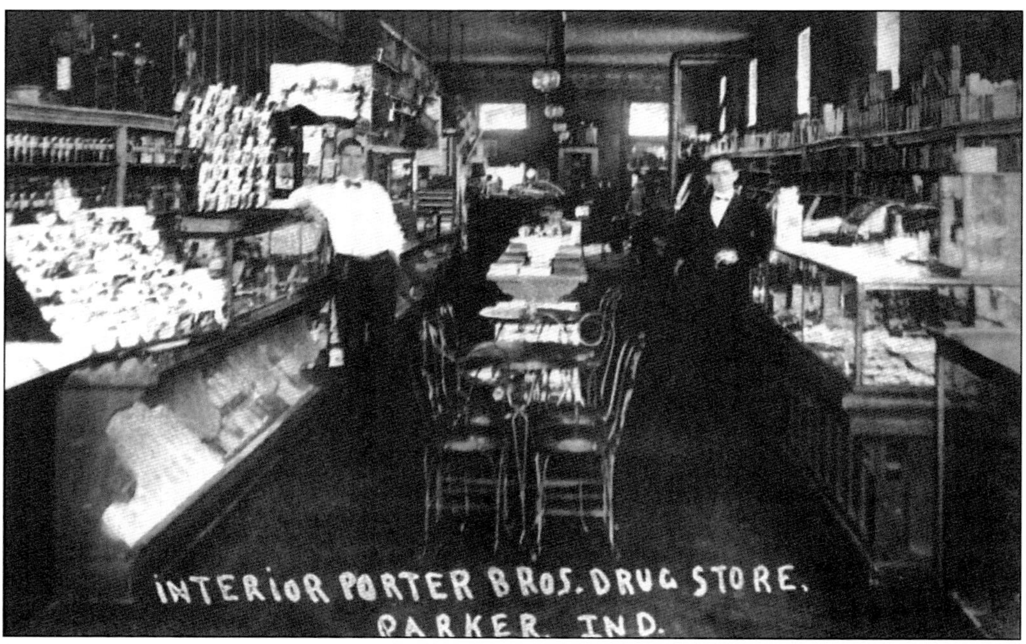

Interior of Porter Brothers Drug Store. This store, operated by F. B. Porter, was located at the southwest corner of Main and Howard Streets. (Randolph County Historical Society.)

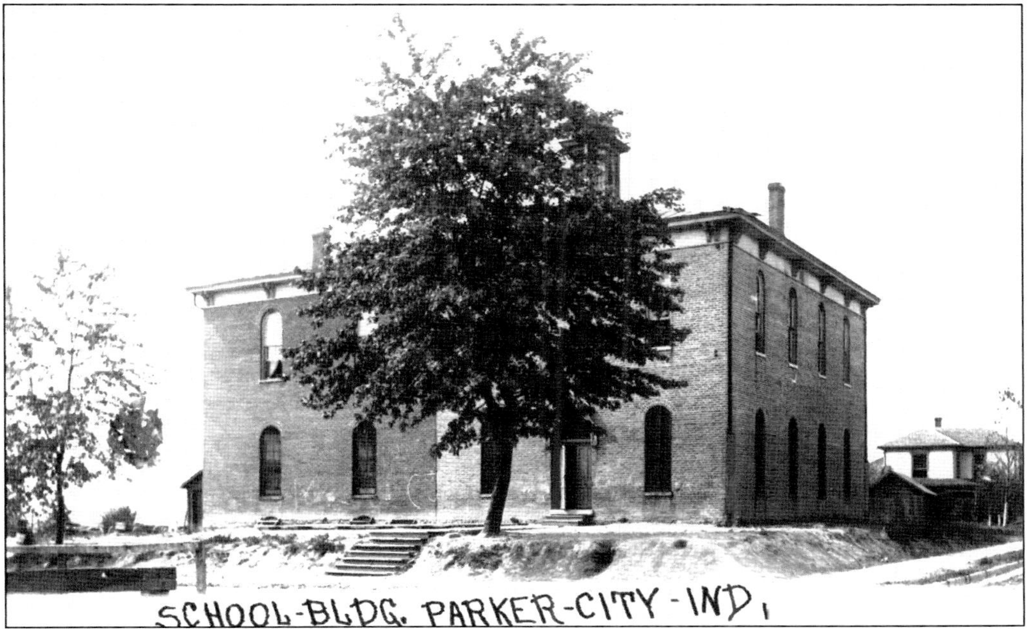

SCHOOL BUILDING. This building stood at the southwest corner of Franklin and Washington Streets. It was built in 1875 and enlarged in 1895 and 1903. In 1909, the town school board was abolished and control of the school passed to the Monroe Township trustee, who built a new school north of town. This building was sold in 1919 and remained on the site for many years. (Gregory P. Hinshaw.)

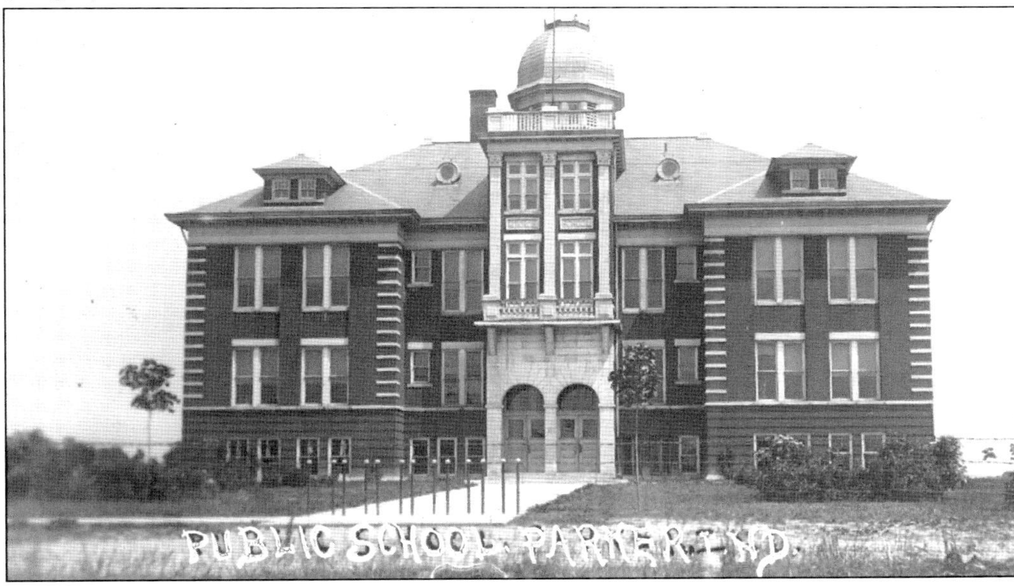

PUBLIC SCHOOL. Originally known as Monroe School, this building was constructed north of town in 1909–1910 and dedicated on May 4, 1910. A gymnasium was added to the rear of the building in 1925. High school students were sent to Monroe Central High School in the fall of 1963, and elementary students were sent to Monroe Central Elementary School in 1983. The building was razed in the spring of 1984. (Gregory P. Hinshaw.)

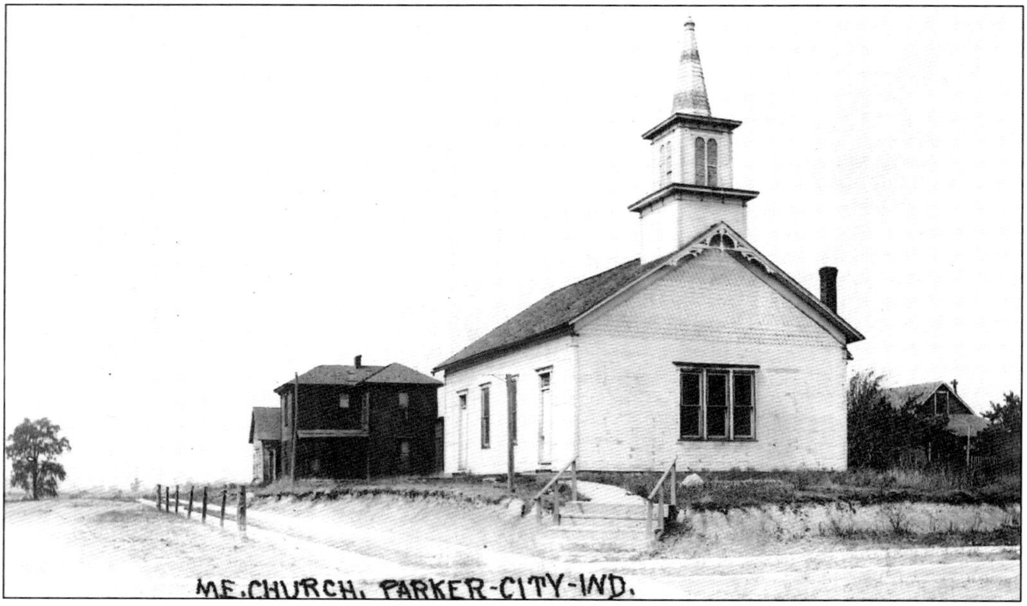

Methodist Episcopal Church, Before 1910. A class of the Methodist Episcopal Church was organized in Morristown about 1851. The building shown here was erected in 1872 on the northwest corner of Washington and Franklin Streets. It was remodeled, as depicted here, in 1898. The building was completely overhauled in 1910. (Randolph County Historical Society.)

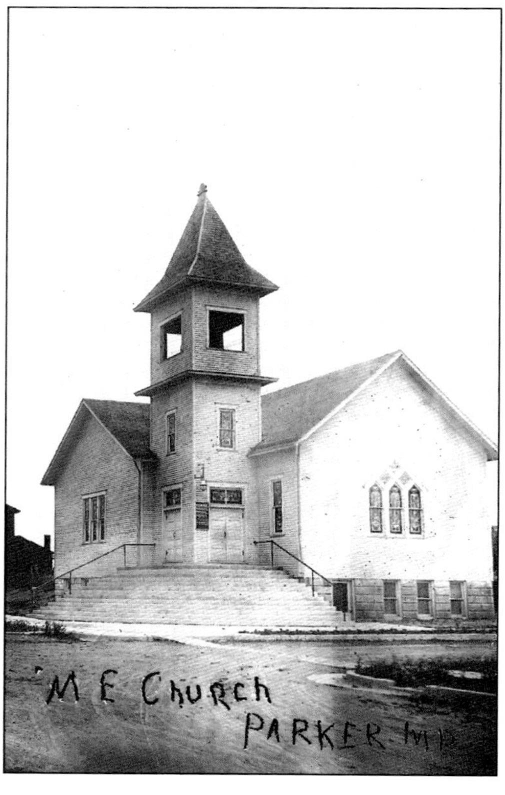

Methodist Episcopal Church After 1910. The 1872 church was completely remodeled and enlarged in 1910 and rededicated on December 18, 1910. The building was used until 1940, when a new brick church was completed at the corner of Main and Washington Streets. This building was razed soon after. (Randolph County Historical Society.)

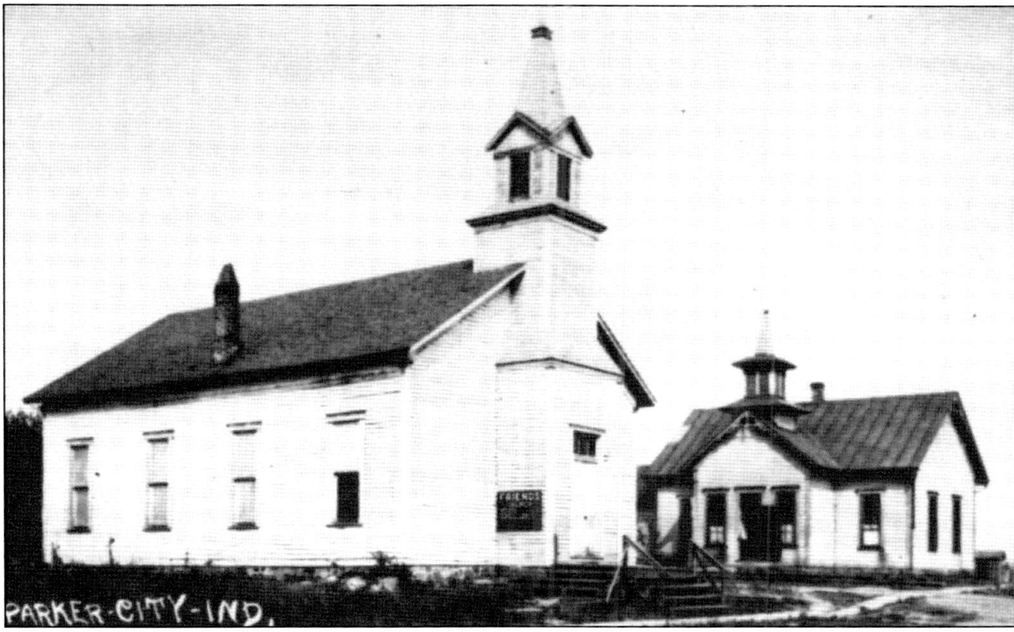

FRIENDS CHURCH AND PRIMARY SCHOOL. This building, at the northwest corner of Howard and Fulton Streets, was erected by the New Light Christian Church in 1873–1874. It was sold to the Friends Church in 1880. The spire was removed many years ago, and the belfry was removed in 2002. The building at the right is the primary school, completed in late 1888. It has been used as a residence for more than a century. (Randolph County Historical Society.)

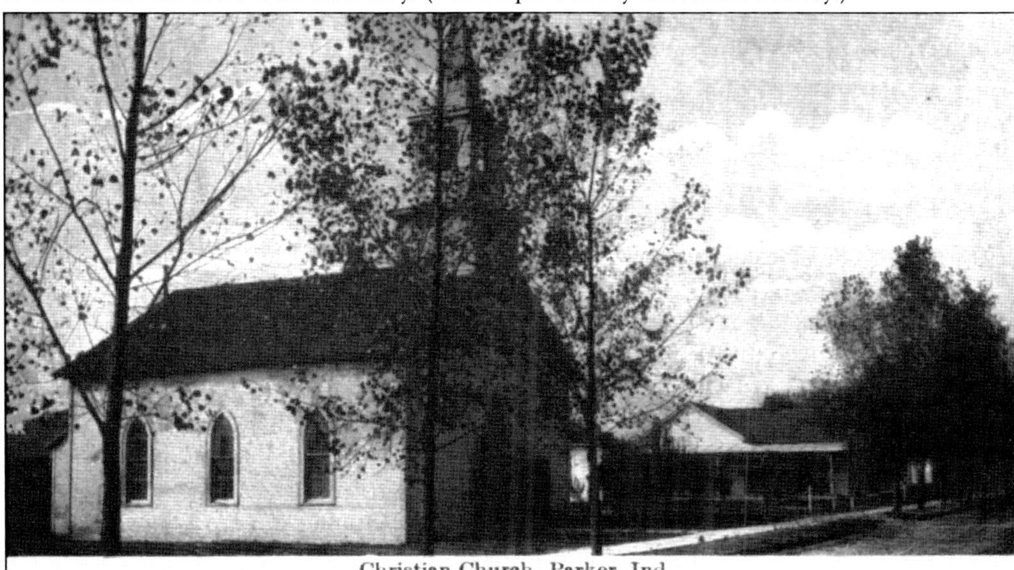

CHRISTIAN CHURCH. The Disciples of Christ organized in Parker in 1886 and moved a church from "Mud Valley," a mile west of town, to a site on South Main Street in 1891. By 1903, the church was defunct but was reorganized in 1905, and the building was remodeled in 1910. The building was sold to Church of the Nazarene in 1918. They have used it with minimal alterations in the years since. (Gregory P. Hinshaw.)

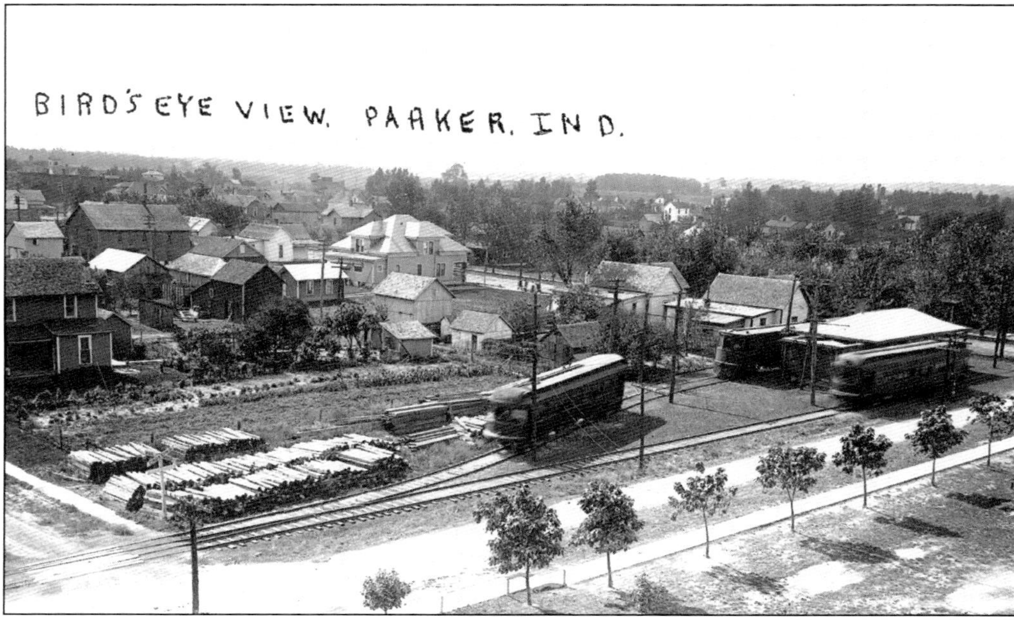

Bird's-Eye View. This view looks southwest from the tower of the Monroe School. In the foreground is the station of the Indiana Union Traction Company. The structure was remodeled many years ago to serve as an ice-cream shop. (Jane Lyle.)

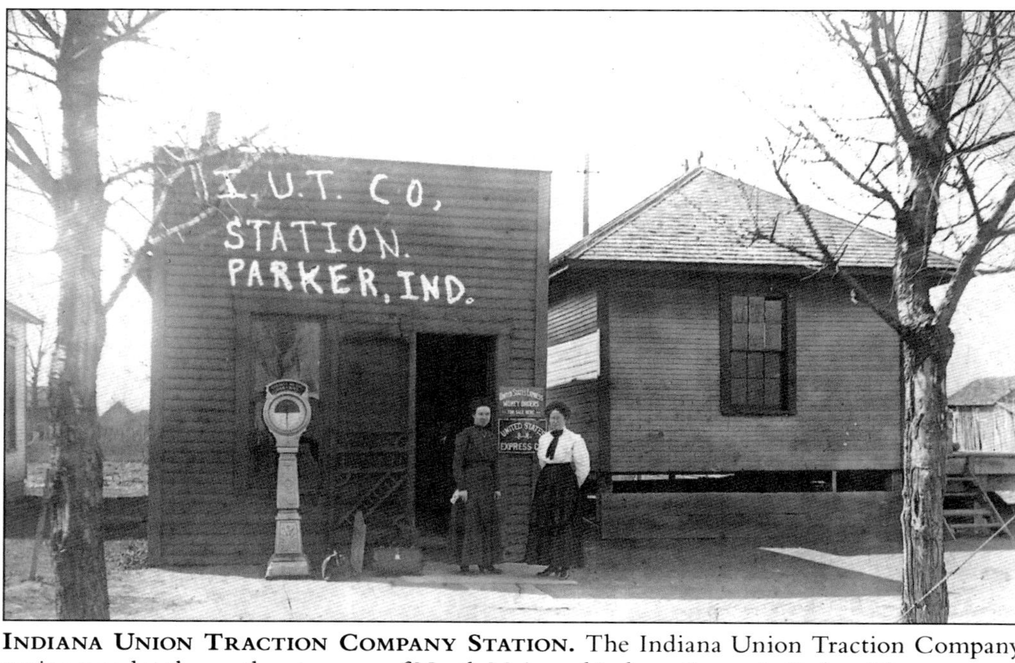

Indiana Union Traction Company Station. The Indiana Union Traction Company station stood at the southeast corner of North Main and Jackson Streets in Parker. The structure, although altered significantly, remains today. (Randolph County Historical Society.)

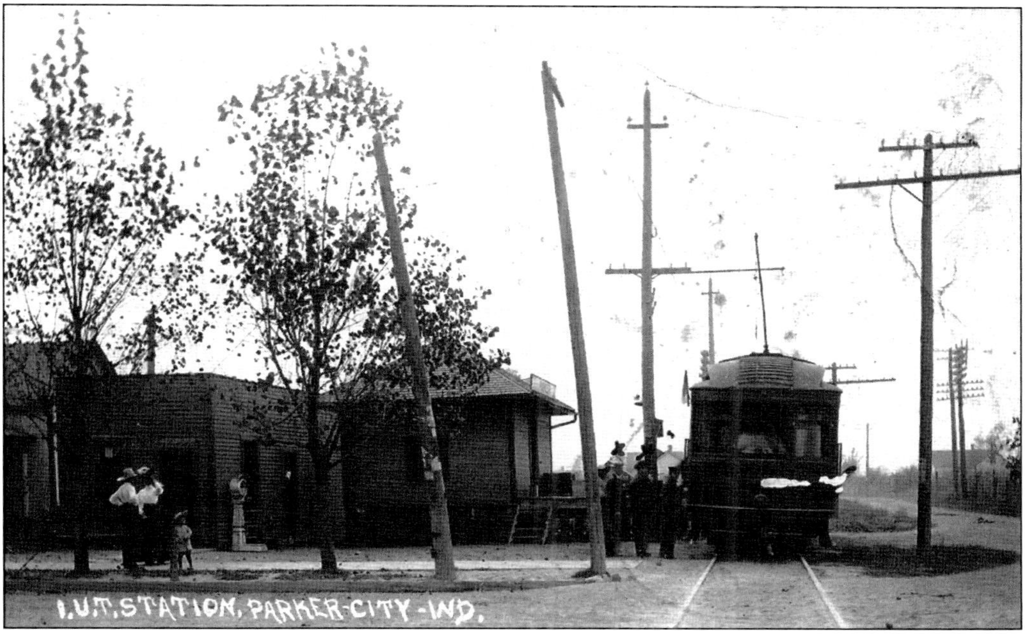

INDIANA UNION TRACTION COMPANY STATION AND PASSENGERS. Here passengers wait to board a car of the Indiana Union Traction Company. (Max Harter.)

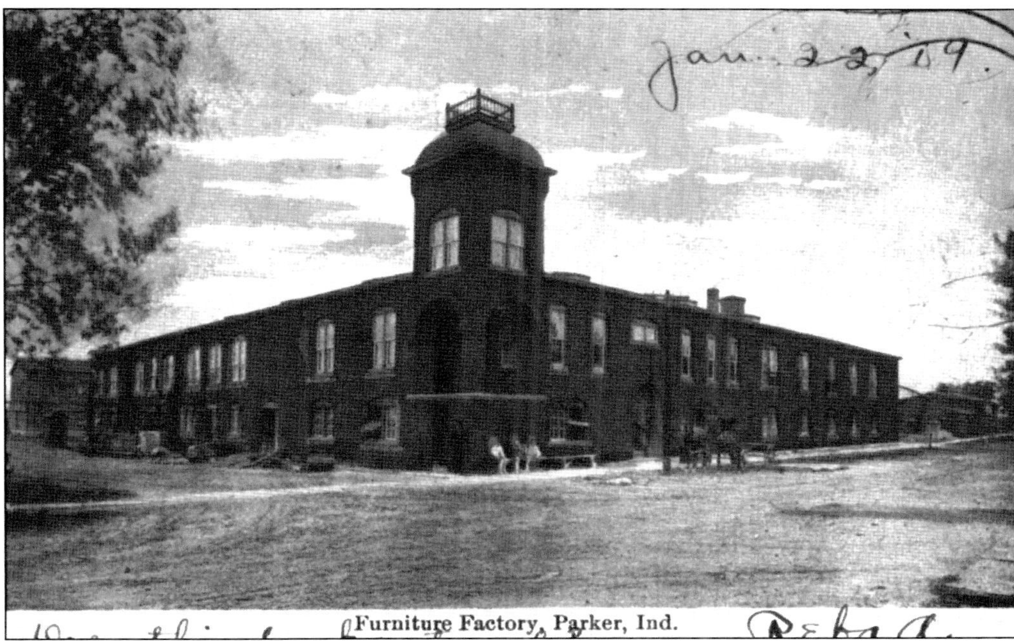

FURNITURE FACTORY. H. C. Vaught and Sons Furniture Factory stood on the southwest corner of Fourth and Howard Streets on the west side of Parker. The company's grounds included two city blocks. The company, organized in 1893, specialized in church furniture. The building burned and was rebuilt in 1901. It was sold in 1909 and again in 1914, after which it was no longer operational. (Tom McKee.)

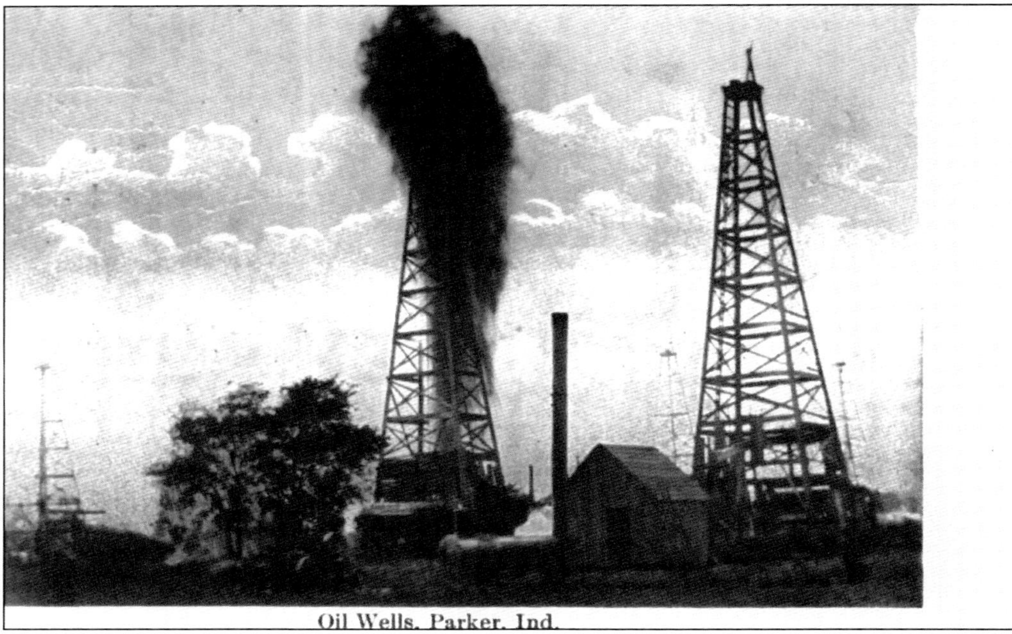

OIL WELLS. Oil was discovered near Parker in 1902. The ensuing boom quadrupled Parker's population to over 2,000 people. Many local landowners received royalty incomes of thousands of dollars a month. The boom was short-lived. (Harold Watson.)

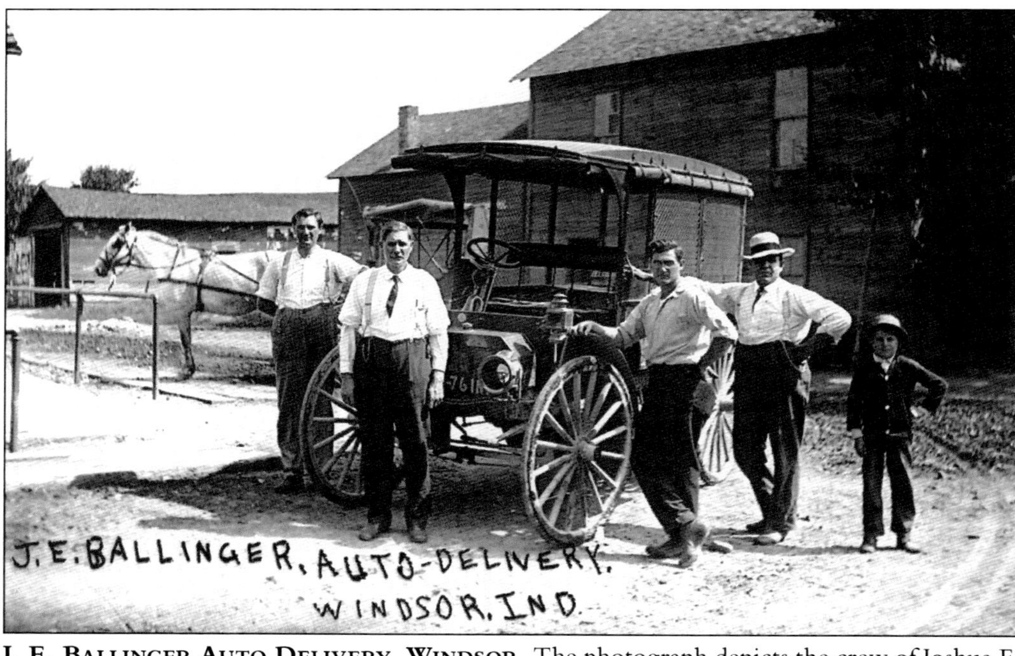

J. E. BALLINGER AUTO DELIVERY, WINDSOR. The photograph depicts the crew of Joshua E. Ballinger, a storekeeper in Windsor, a village in Stoney Creek Township, south of Parker. Ballinger also operated a delivery truck for a time. He is pictured here with members of his family. (Jeffrey Koenker.)

Five

Ridgeville, Saratoga, and Vicinity

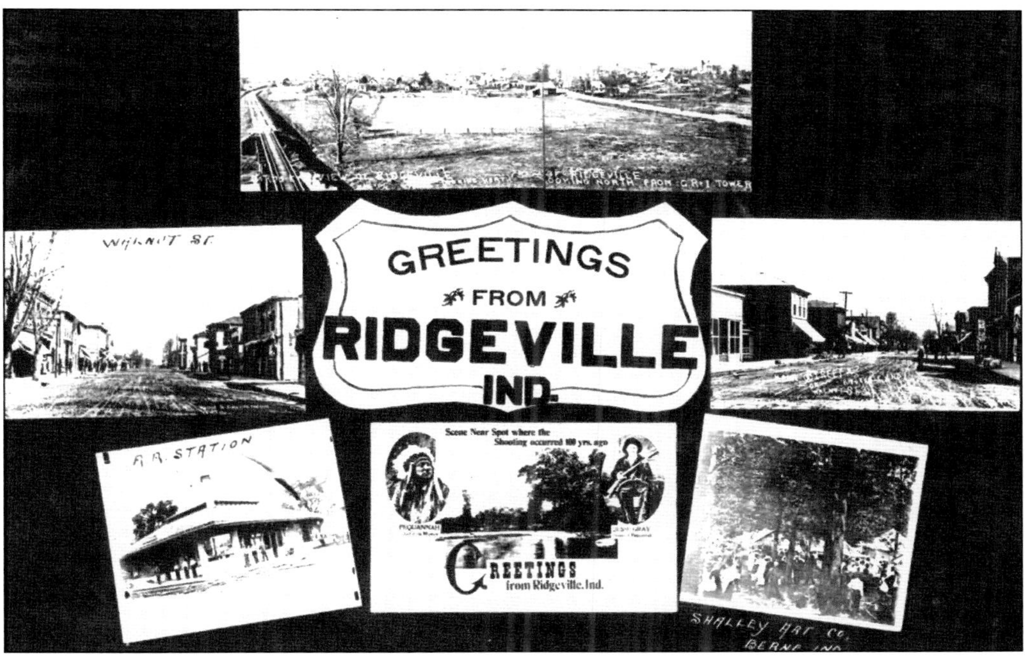

Greetings from Ridgeville. This Shalley Art Company composite shows, clockwise from the top, a bird's-eye view looking north from the Grand Rapids and Indiana Railroad tower, Walnut Street, an outdoor gathering, Pequannah and Jesse Gray, the railroad station, and Walnut Street. (Judy Wilson Wright.)

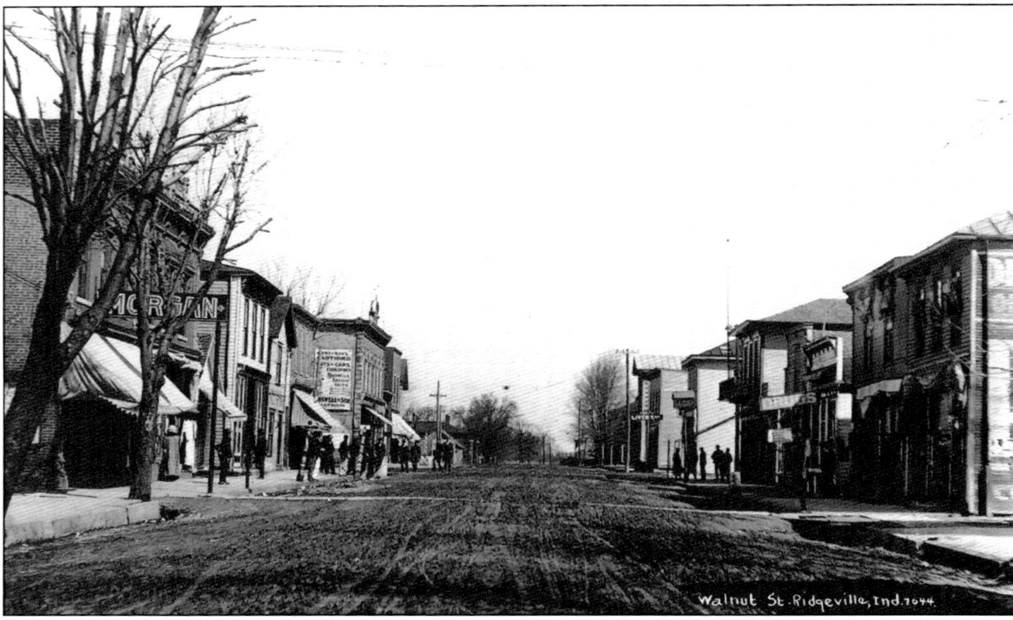

RIDGEVILLE'S WALNUT STREET LOOKING NORTH FROM FIRST, 1908. Nearly all the buildings depicted here are gone. The brick building with the large cornice at left is the Shiffer Block, erected in 1879 at Walnut and Second Streets. The building at right with the balcony is the Lemaux-Pettyjohn Grocery. The Ridgeville State Bank used the gabled front building on the right at the far end of the street. A new facade was placed on the building in 1911. (Jane Lyle.)

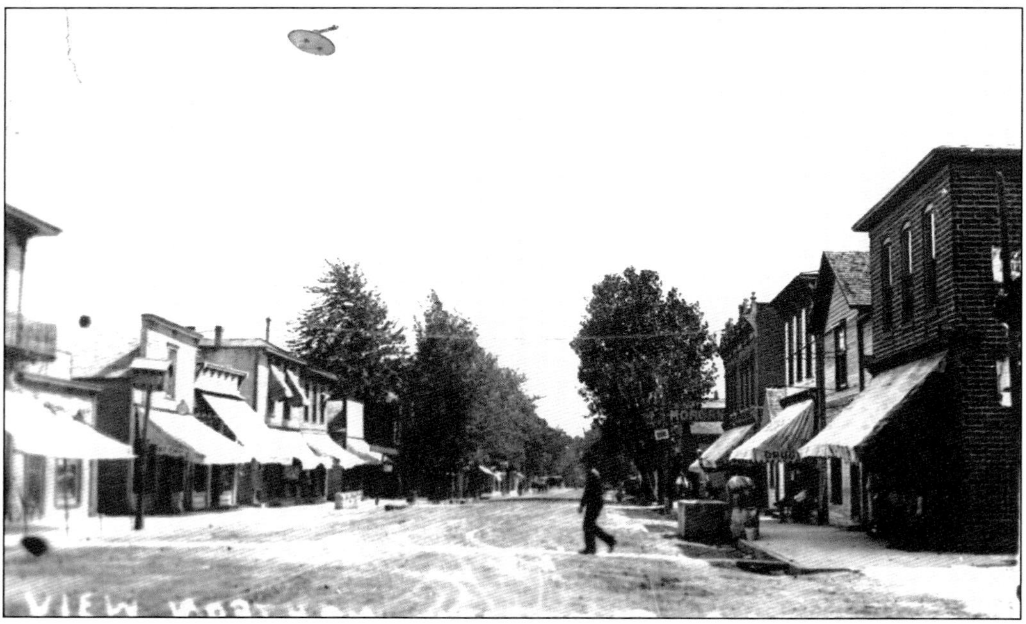

RIDGEVILLE'S WALNUT STREET, LOOKING SOUTH. Virtually none of the structures depicted in this view are extant. Some of the structures on the left were replaced by the IOOF hall in 1913. The First National Bank had not yet been constructed on the right side of the street in 1909. (Randolph County Historical Society.)

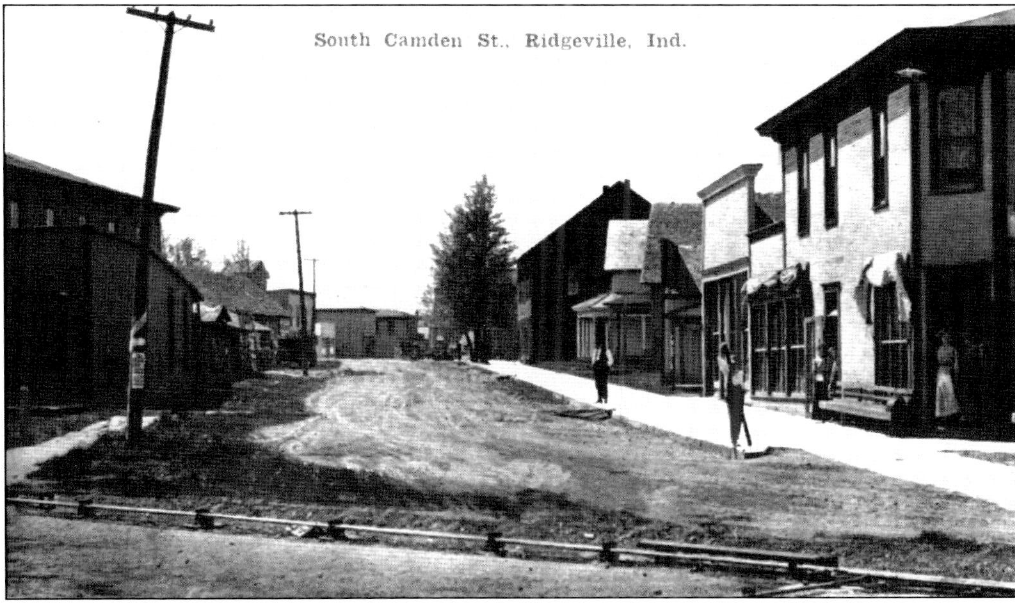

SOUTH CAMDEN STREET, RIDGEVILLE. This view looks south on Camden Street just south of the town's depot and the crossing of the Panhandle and Grand Rapids and Indiana Railroads. None of these buildings remain today. (Gregory P. Hinshaw.)

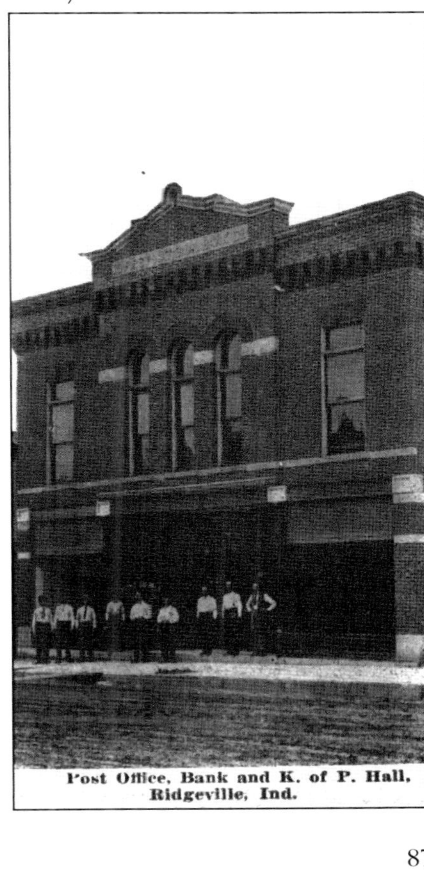

POST OFFICE AND BANK, RIDGEVILLE. The First National Bank was erected in 1909. The town's post office moved into the building shortly thereafter. The Knights of Pythias moved to the IOOF hall in 1919 and disbanded in 1923. The National Bank merged with the Ridgeville State Bank in 1929. Shown are the town's four mail carriers on the left, two post office clerks in the middle, and three bank employees on the right. (Gregory P. Hinshaw.)

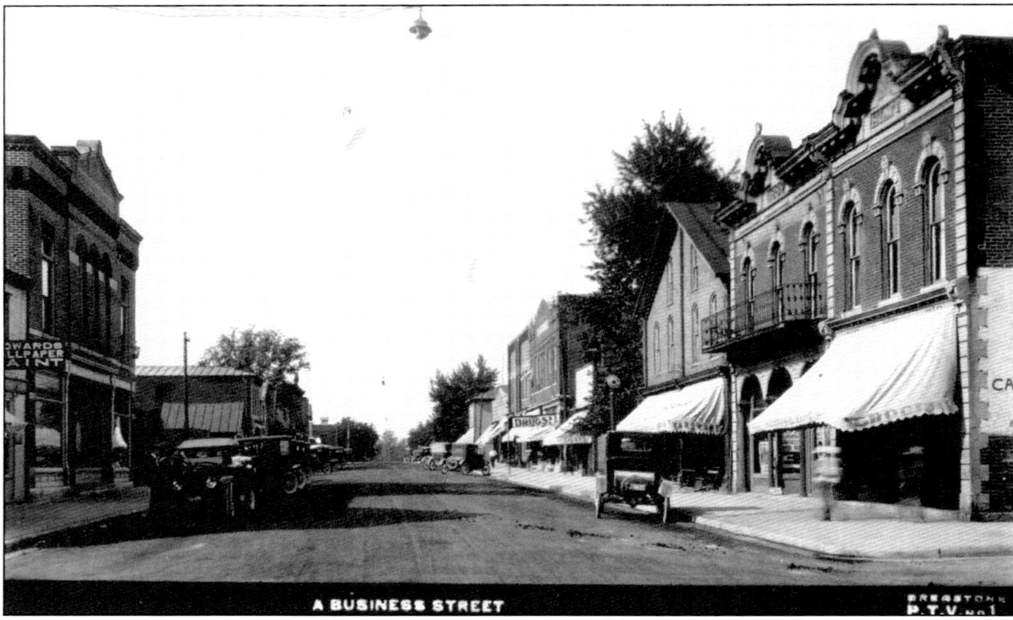

A BUSINESS STREET (WALNUT STREET), RIDGEVILLE. This real-photo view looks to the north, where the tower of the city building, built in 1919–1920, can be seen. At the right is Addington's Grocery, housed in the Hiatt Building, built in 1882 and razed in 1975. Farther down the street on the right is the IOOF block, built in 1913–1914. At the left is the First National Bank building, built in 1909. (Randolph County Historical Society.)

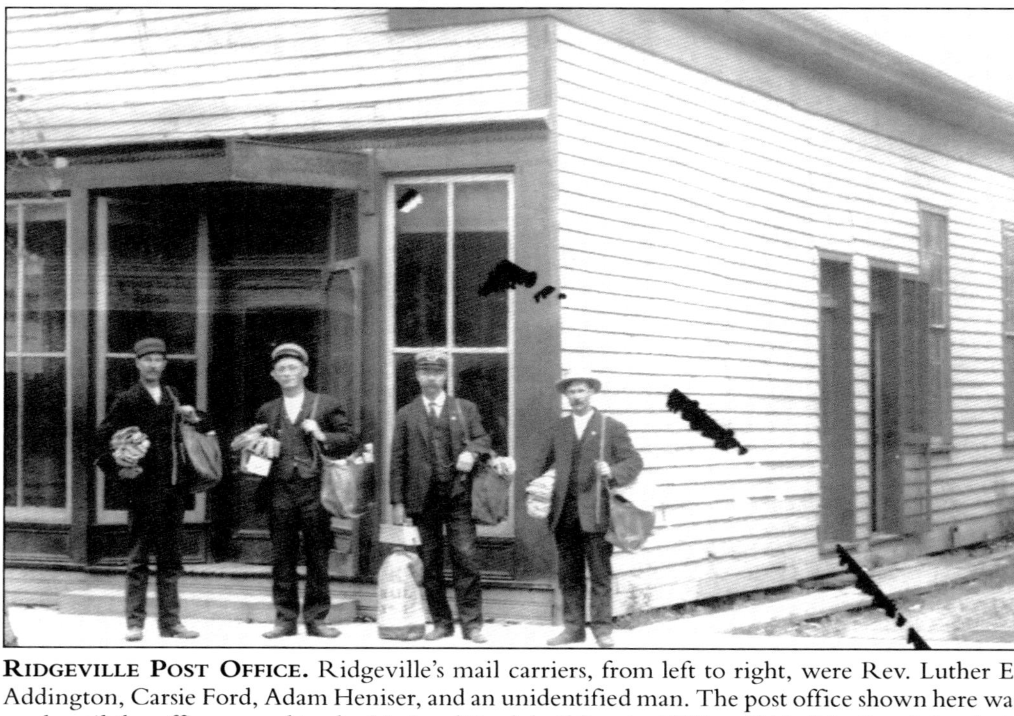

RIDGEVILLE POST OFFICE. Ridgeville's mail carriers, from left to right, were Rev. Luther E. Addington, Carsie Ford, Adam Heniser, and an unidentified man. The post office shown here was used until the office moved to the National Bank building in 1909 or 1910. (Marilyn Schaefer.)

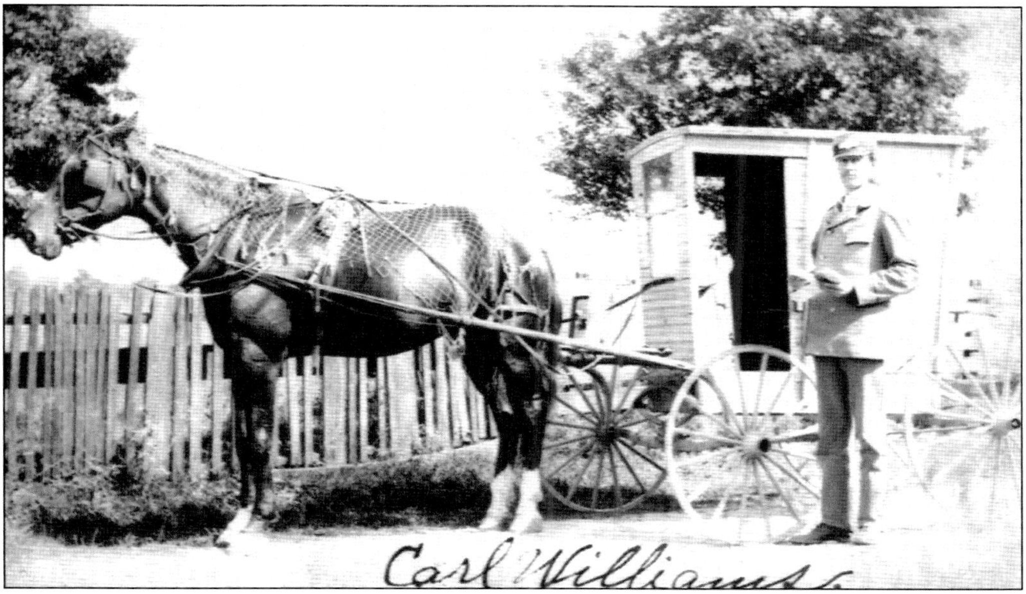

LUTHER E. ADDINGTON AND MAIL WAGON. Rev. Luther E. Addington, a Quaker minister, also served as a rural mail carrier on a Ridgeville rural route as early as 1902. In 1913, he became the first minister of any denomination in Randolph County to own an automobile, used to deliver mail. He was removed as a mail carrier for political reasons in 1915. (Marilyn Schaefer.)

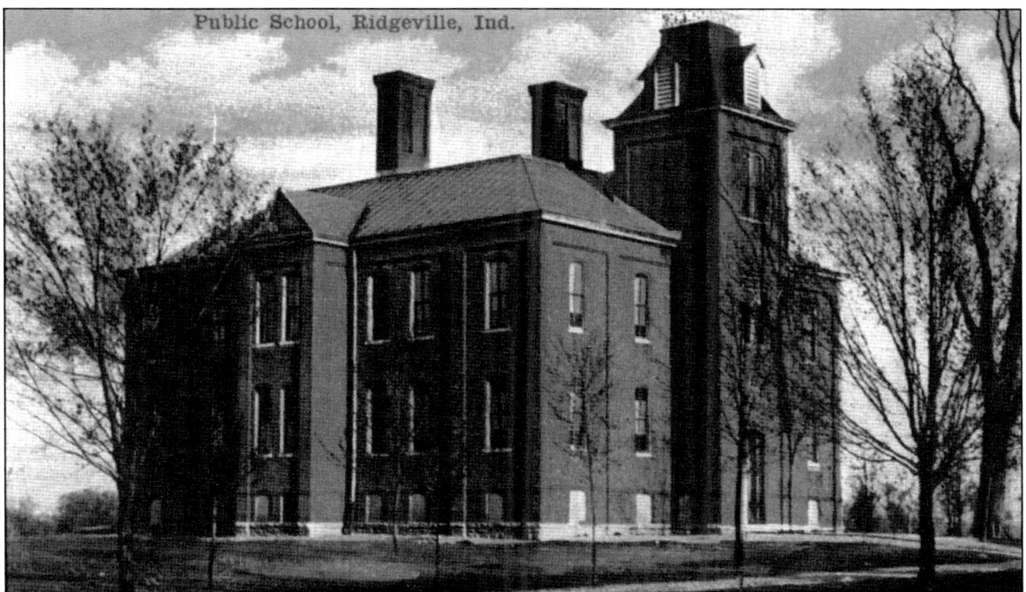

RIDGEVILLE PUBLIC SCHOOL. This structure, constructed in 1893 on Sheridan Street just north of East Main Street, replaced a building on the same site, which burned in 1892. The town's school board was dissolved in 1920, and control passed to Franklin Township. The building was condemned and razed in 1922 in preparation for the construction of a new school on the site in 1923–1924. The last school building was razed in October 1982. (Gregory P. Hinshaw.)

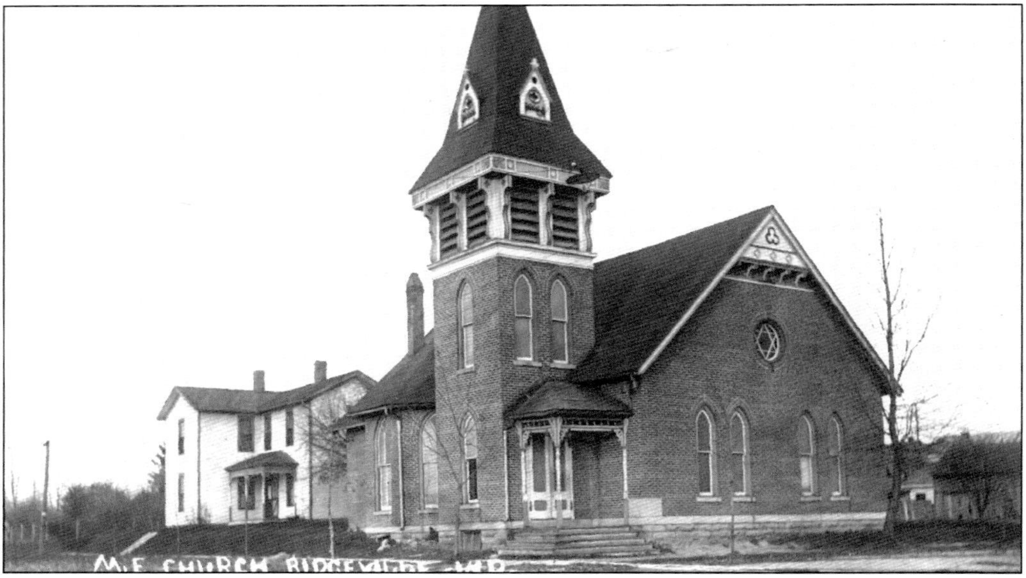

Ridgeville Methodist Episcopal Church. A Methodist Episcopal class was organized in Ridgeville in 1858, and a building was erected at First and Race Streets soon after. In 1888, a new building was erected. The building was remodeled in 1903. The spire was removed in 1953, and an addition was made to the rear of the church in 1959. In 1968, this church became known as Bethel United Methodist Church. The congregation disbanded in 2008. (Gregory P. Hinshaw.)

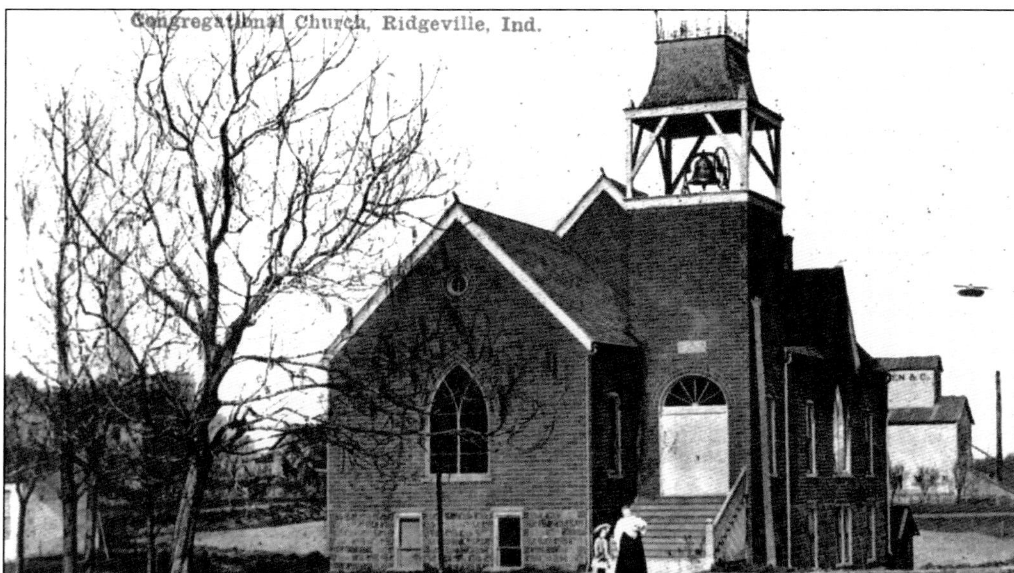

Ridgeville Congregational Church. A Congregational Church was organized in Ridgeville in 1892, and services were held in the college building. The structure shown here was erected on Sheridan Street at First Street in 1903. The congregation disbanded in about 1947, and in 1948, the structure was sold to the Masons, who used it until they disbanded in 1998. The building is now vacant. (Gregory P. Hinshaw.)

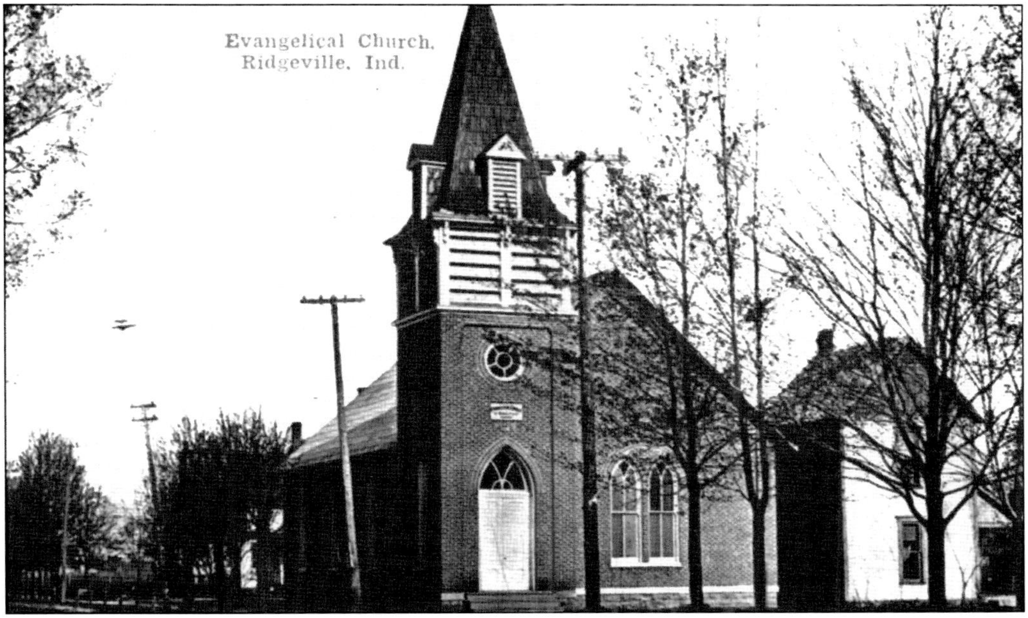

Ridgeville Evangelical Church. The structure depicted here, located at the southeast corner of Portland and First Streets, was erected in 1888 as the Free Will Baptist Church and dedicated in December. The Evangelical Association organized a congregation in Ridgeville in 1907 and purchased the building in 1908. The congregation became known as Calvary United Methodist Church in 1968. (Gregory P. Hinshaw.)

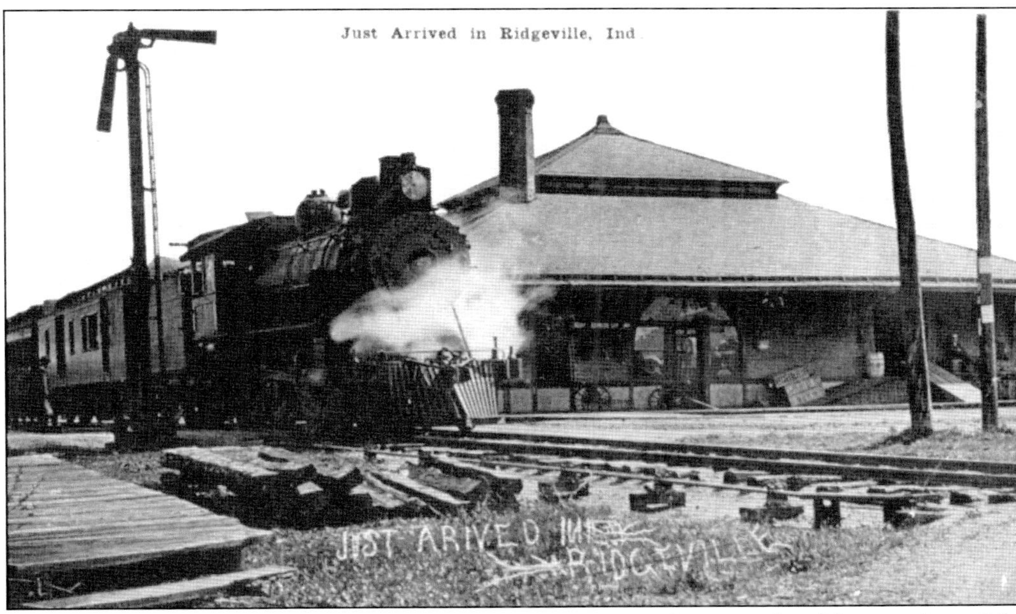

Just Arrived in Ridgeville. This depot was located on the east side of the crossing of the Panhandle and Grand Rapids and Indiana Railroads. It was built in 1889–1890. The building was used until the completion of a new depot in 1913. (Gregory P. Hinshaw.)

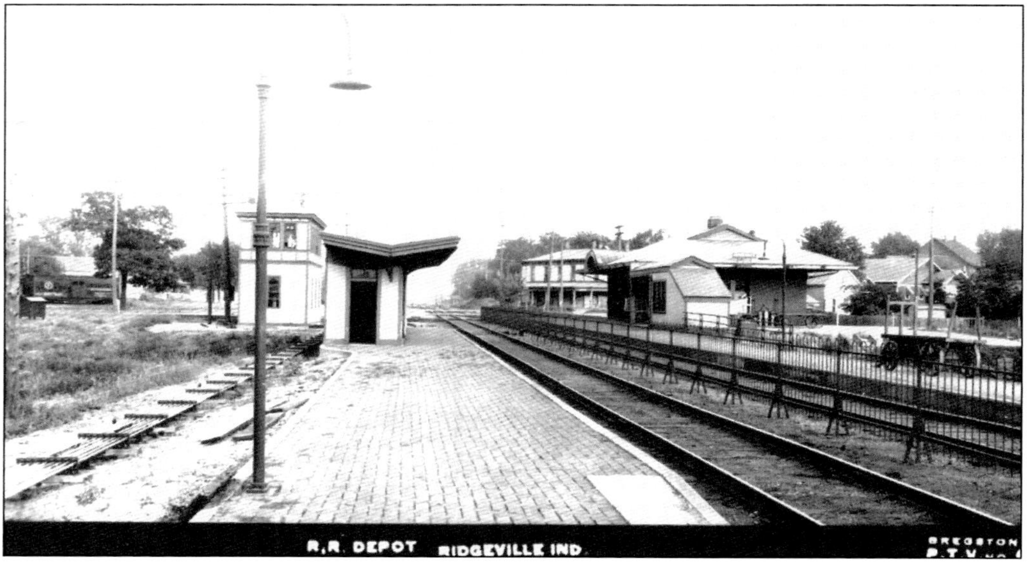

RIDGEVILLE RAILROAD DEPOT. Union Depot at Ridgeville was built in 1912 and served passengers of both the Pittsburgh, Cincinnati, Chicago, and St. Louis Railroad (Panhandle) and Grand Rapids and Indiana Railroad. This view is looking northwest and depicts a signal tower and entrance to a pedestrian underpass. The depot was razed in 1983. The Grand Rapids and Indiana line was abandoned in 1975. The Panhandle line was abandoned in 1993. (Randolph County Historical Society.)

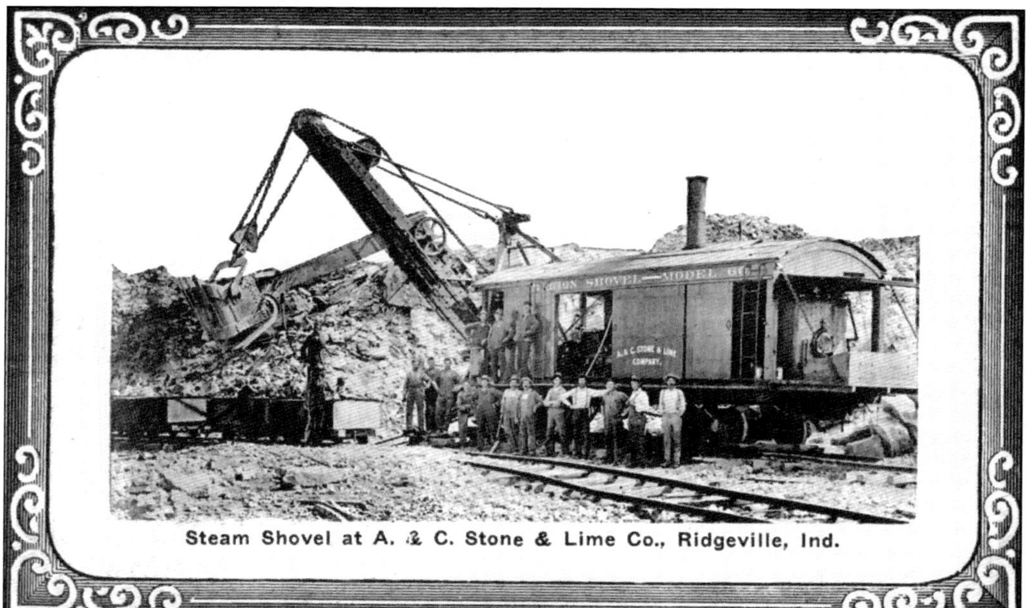

STEAM SHOVEL AT A. AND C. STONE AND LIME COMPANY. The A. and C. Stone and Lime Company operated a stone quarry just east of Ridgeville on present-day County Road 850 N in Ward Township. The quarry had access to the Panhandle Railroad. The quarry was allowed to fill with water in 1941 and became known as Limestone Lake. (Randolph County Historical Society.)

JOSEPH LAY BRUSH AND BROOM, RIDGEVILLE. The Joseph Lay Brush and Broom Factory was located in the former Ridgeville College building on College Street in the east side of town. Construction began in 1867 and was completed in the 1870s. Originally owned by the Free Will Baptists, it was sold to the Congregationalists in 1891 and closed in 1901. The Lay Company acquired the building in 1902. The building was razed in 1932. (Gregory P. Hinshaw.)

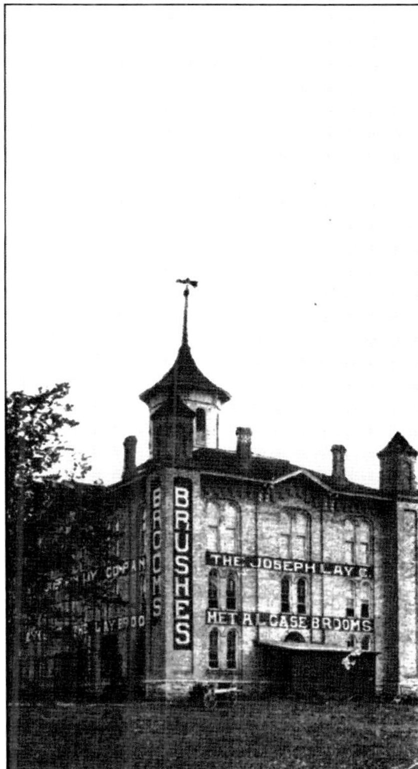

Broom Factory, Ridgeville, Ind.

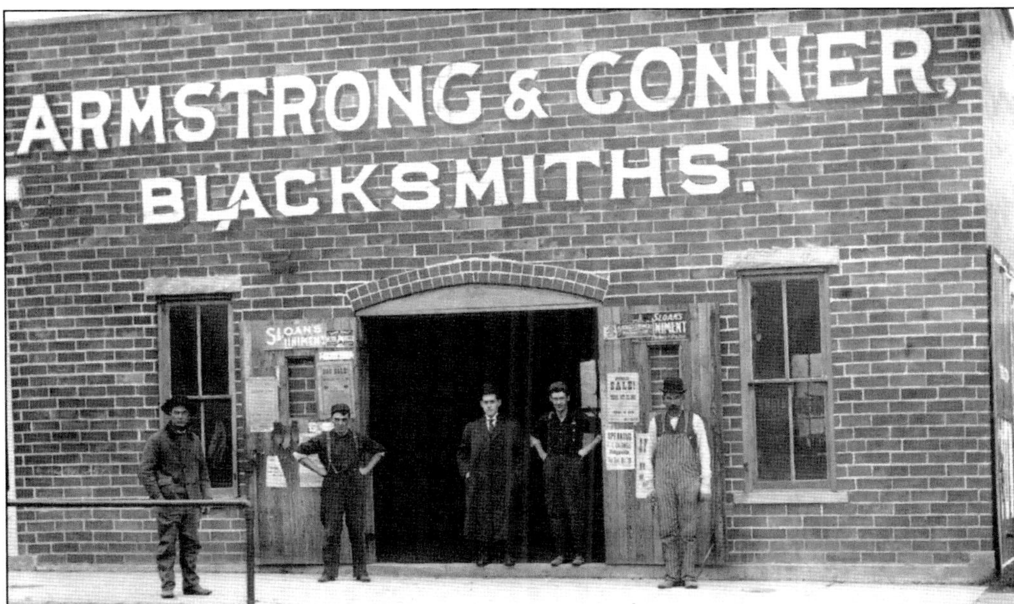

ARMSTRONG AND CONNER BLACKSMITHS, RIDGEVILLE. This blacksmith shop was located in Ridgeville. Its exact location is unknown. (Jane Lyle.)

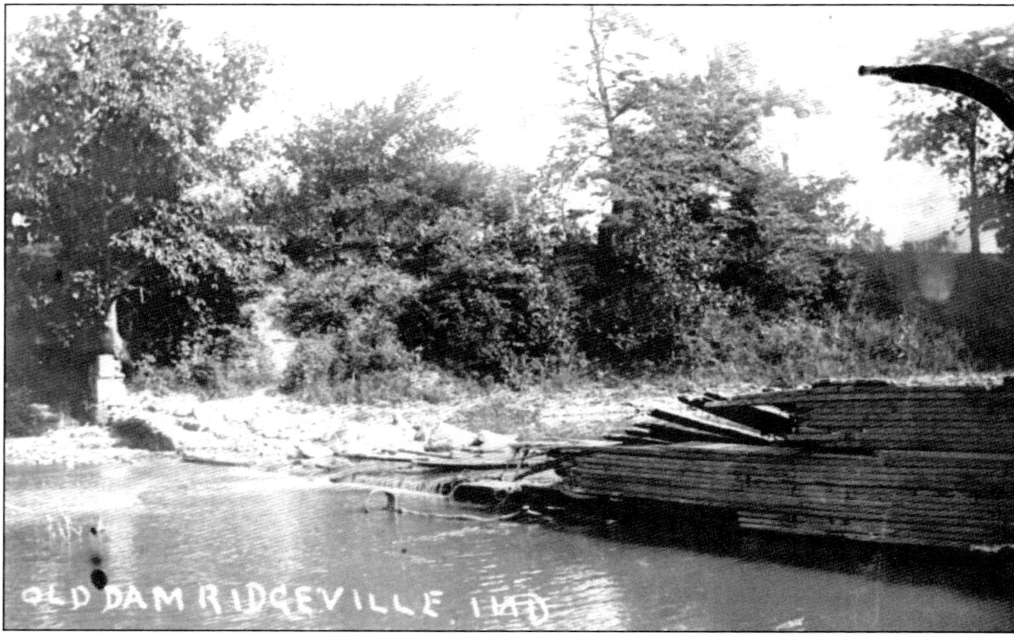

OLD DAM. The date of the construction of Lake Pequannah, or Pequanaha, is not known. The lake was located at the southeast corner of Ridgeville and was created by damming the Mississinewa River. In 1895, a new dam, probably the one shown here, was constructed, and the lake was dramatically enlarged. A new masonry dam was constructed in 1913. (Minnetrista Cultural Center.)

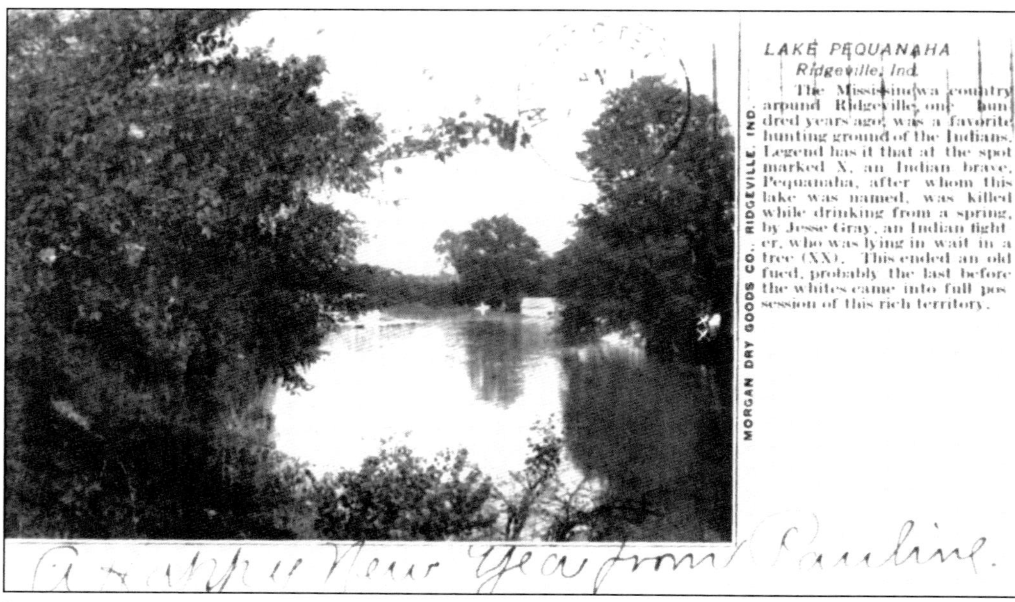

LAKE PEQUANAHA. Lake Pequanaha was named for a Miami Indian marksman shot near the site by Jesse Gray, a pioneer settler, in about 1820. The site of the killing is shown here. (Gregory P. Hinshaw.)

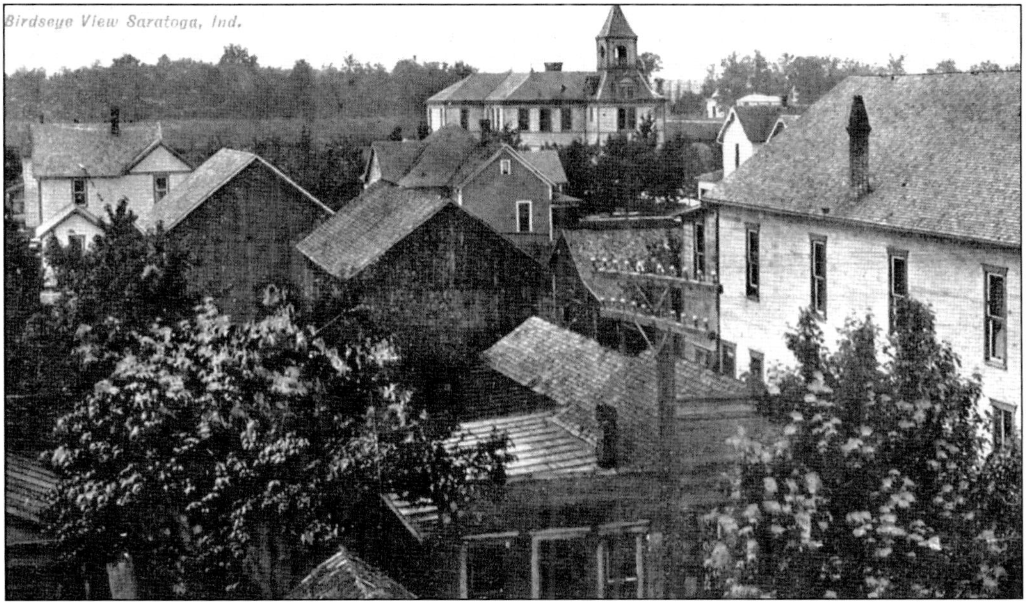

SARATOGA, BIRD'S-EYE VIEW SOUTHWEST. This view looks southwest from Main Street. The frame schoolhouse can be seen in the background. The buildings in the foreground stood on the south side of Main Street. (Max Harter.)

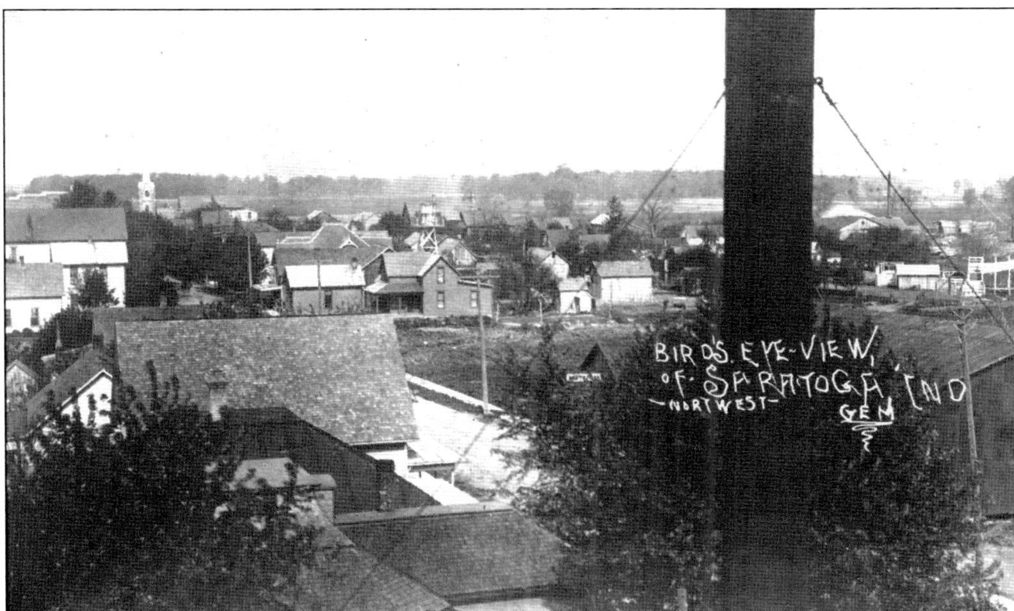

SARATOGA, BIRD'S-EYE VIEW NORTHWEST. This view looks west northwest from the elevator, located on the south side of Main Street at the railroad. The business buildings of the town are at the left, while the tower of the United Brethren Church is visible in the background. (Lowell and Anna Fraze.)

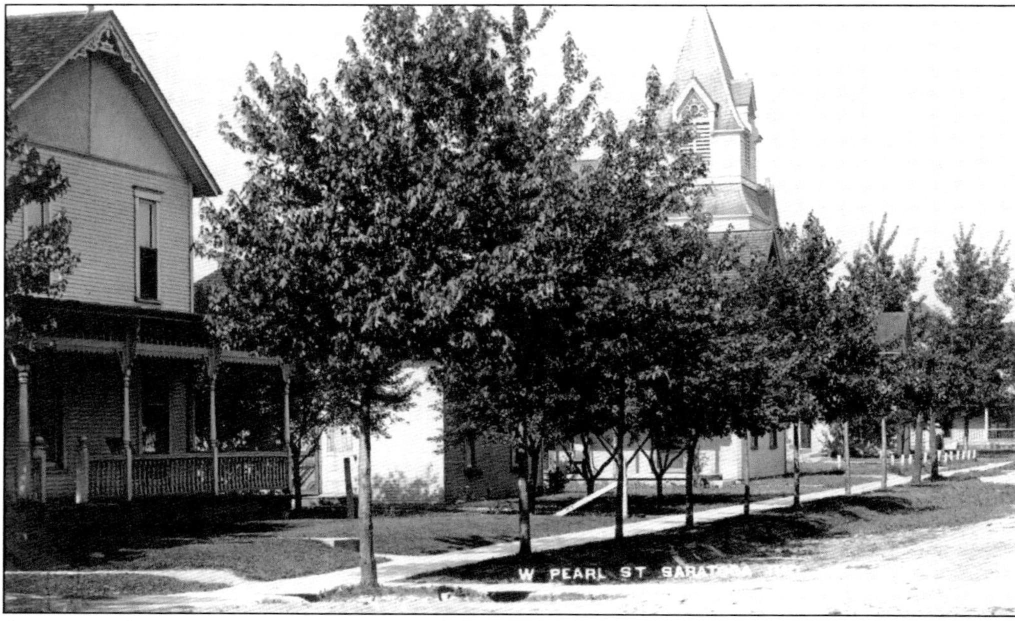

Saratoga's West Pearl Street. This view, looking west, shows the south side of Pearl Street. The Methodist Episcopal church, erected in 1903, is shown. (Gregory P. Hinshaw.)

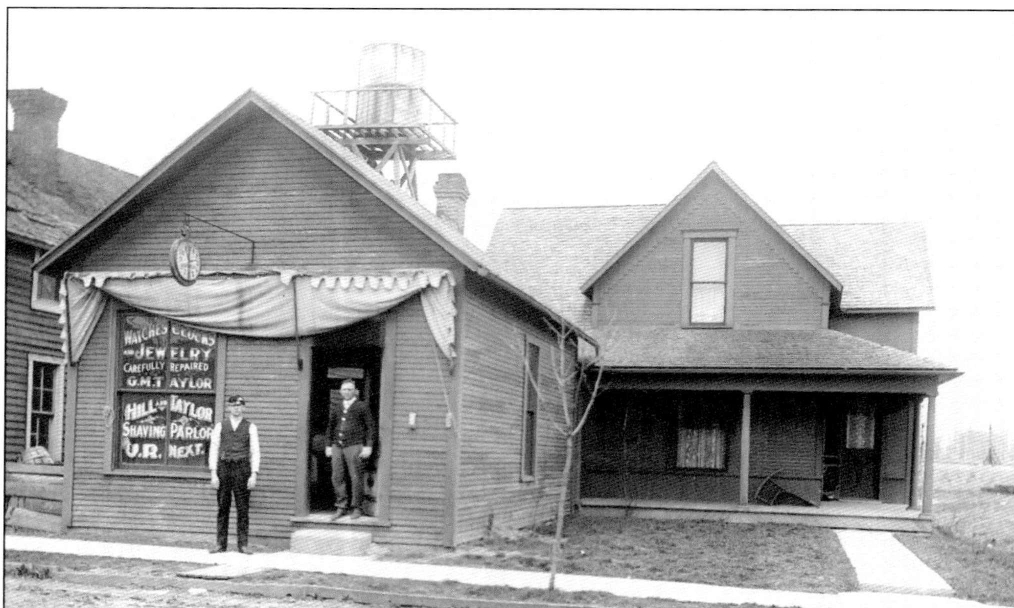

G. M. Taylor Watches and Jewelry and Hill and Taylor's Barber Shop, Saratoga. Located on Main Street, the establishment was owned by George M. Taylor and Robert Hill. (Jane Lyle.)

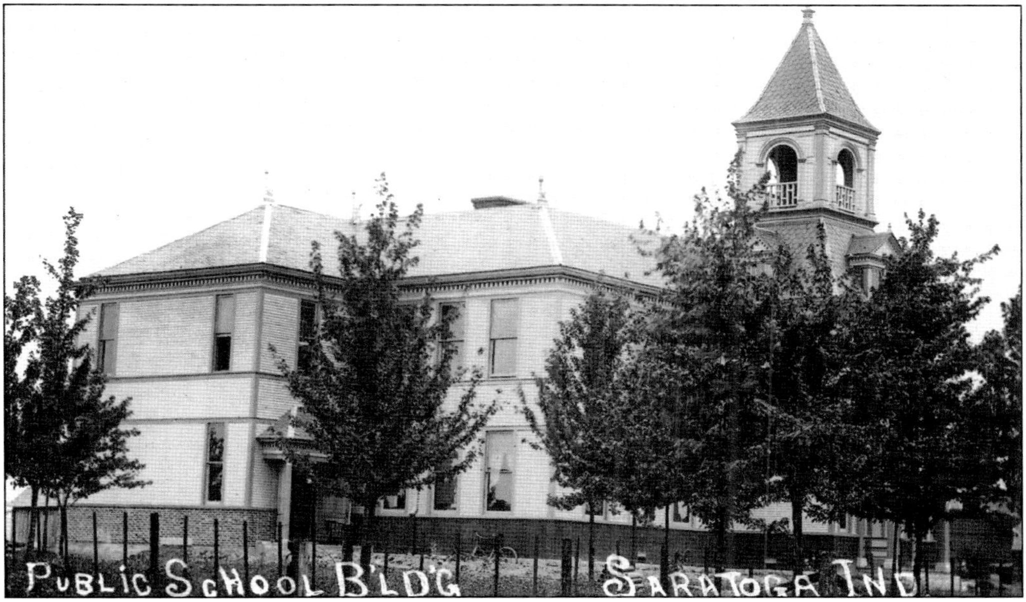

SARATOGA PUBLIC SCHOOL BUILDING. This frame school building was erected on the south side of Pearl Street, east of Barber Street, in 1898. An addition was made to the rear of the building in 1908, as shown here. Another addition was made in 1915. The building was razed to make way for a new building on the site, erected in 1926–1927. The last building was razed in the fall of 1982. (Jane Lyle.)

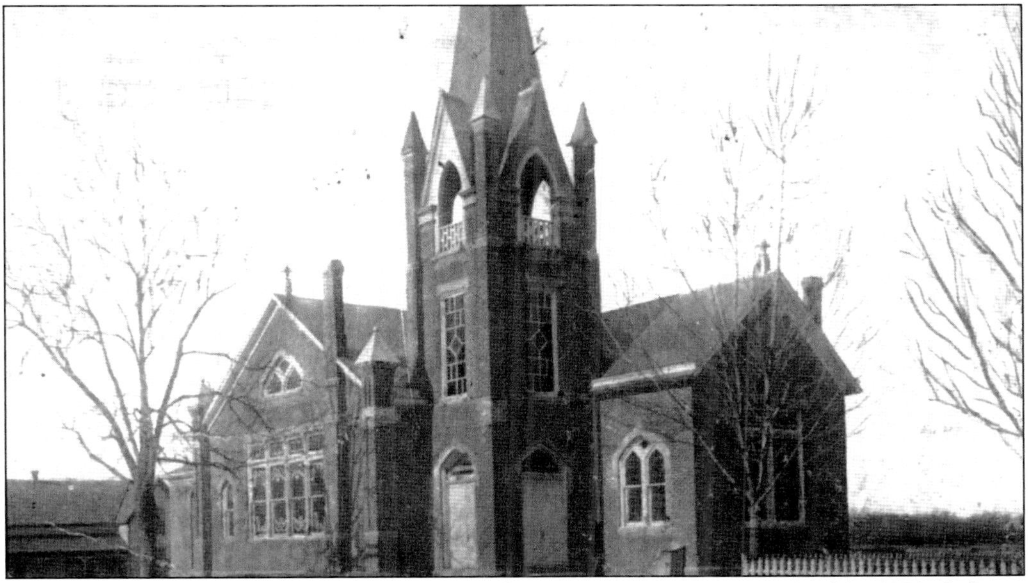

SARATOGA UNITED BRETHREN CHURCH. This congregation was organized in 1871. A frame building was constructed in 1873, enlarged in 1893, and enlarged again in 1908, taking the appearance that it has here. In 1968, Saratoga's Methodist and Evangelical United Brethren Churches merged in the Evangelical United Brethren building. The tower was removed in 1980, and an addition was completed. This is the only former United Brethren congregation in existence in Randolph County. (Gregory P. Hinshaw.)

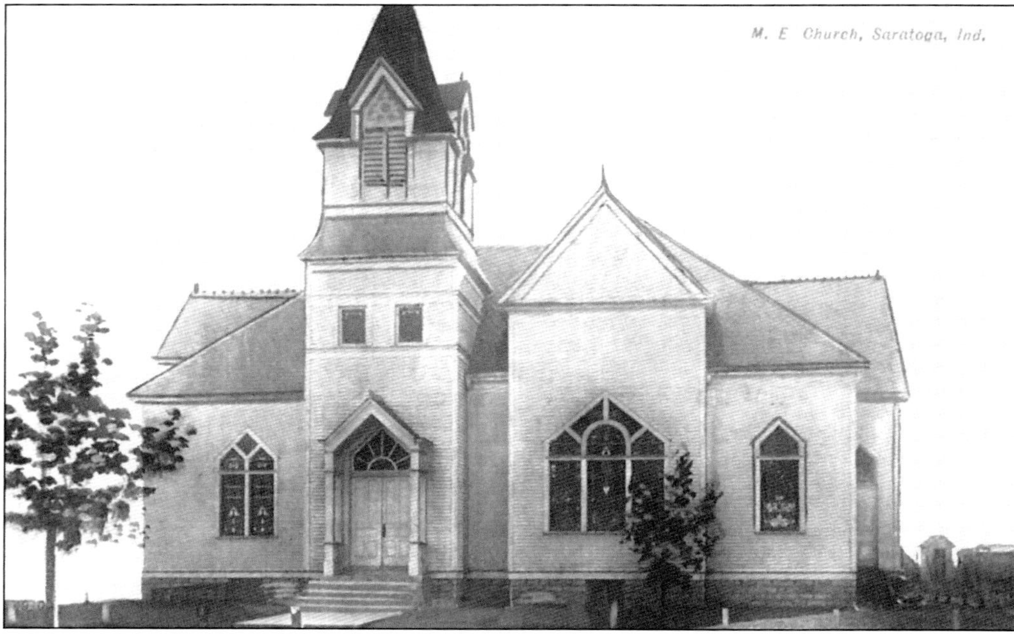

SARATOGA METHODIST EPISCOPAL CHURCH. Prospect Methodist Episcopal Church was organized in 1836 north of Saratoga. In 1878, the congregation moved into town and built a church on Main Street. In 1903, a new church building was erected on the south side of Pearl Street, just east of Barber Street, and dedicated on June 7, 1903. The congregation merged with the United Brethren Church in 1968, and the Methodist Episcopal church was razed in 1971. (Randolph County Historical Society.)

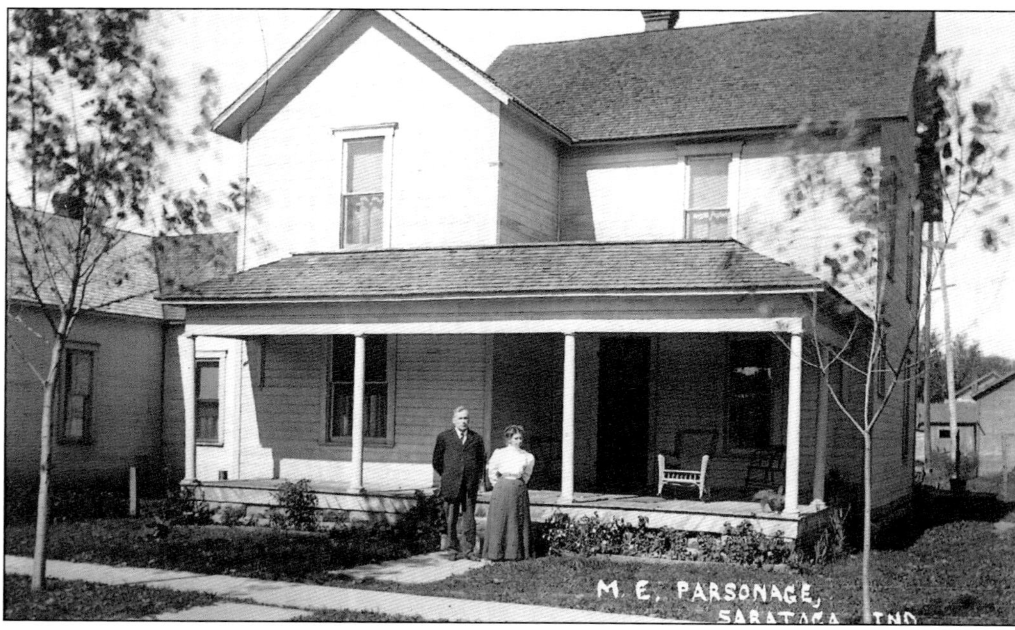

SARATOGA METHODIST EPISCOPAL PARSONAGE. The parsonage of the Saratoga Methodist Episcopal Church was erected in 1905. (Jane Lyle.)

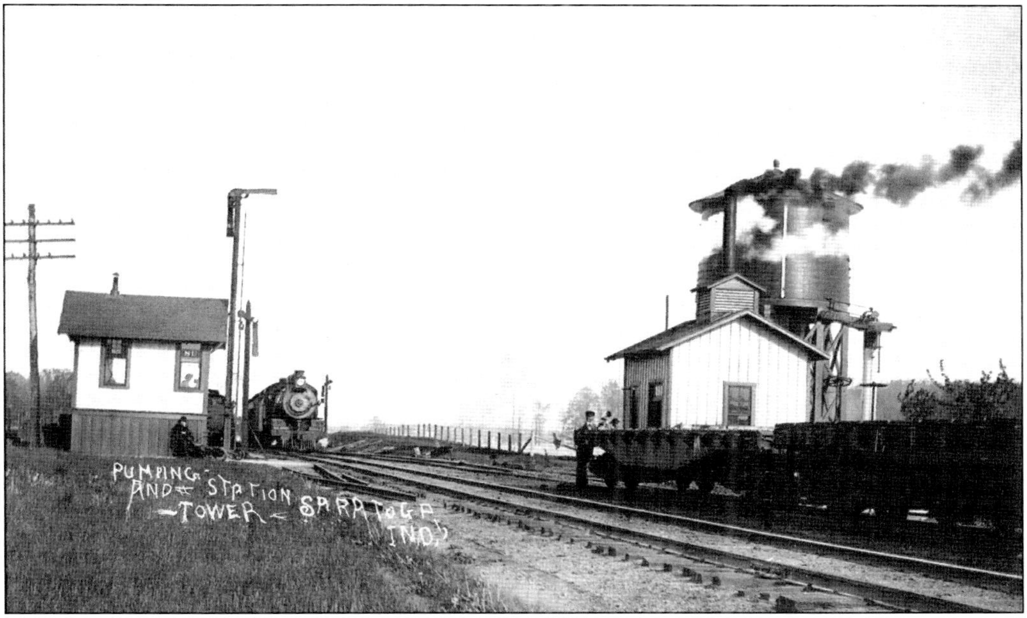

SARATOGA PUMPING STATION AND DEPOT. Situated along the Pittsburgh, Cincinnati, Chicago, and St. Louis Railroad, the pumping station and tower were operated for many years by Lincoln McKee. (Jane Lyle.)

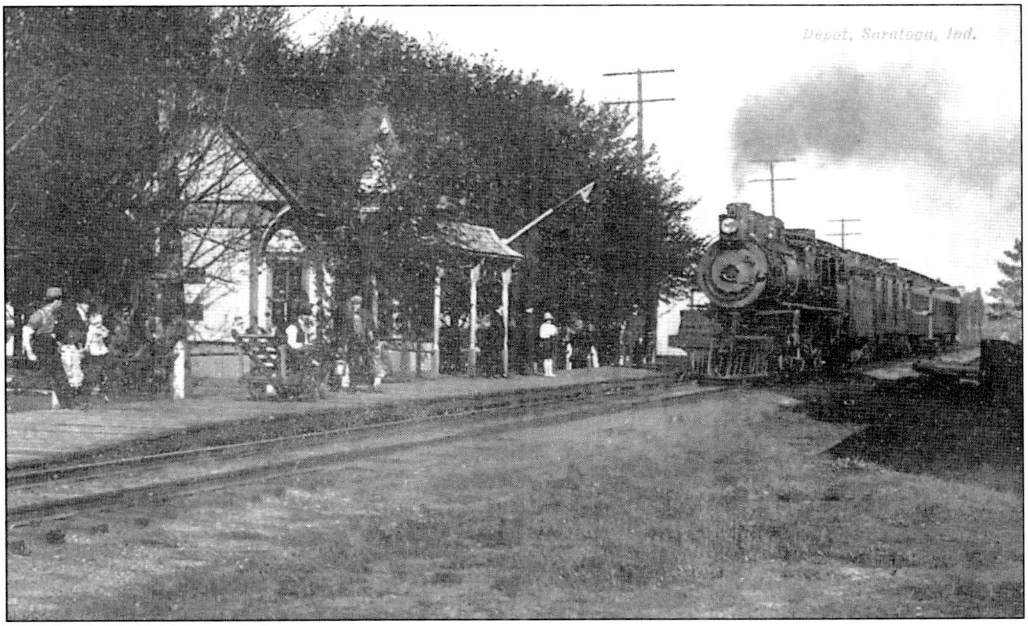

SARATOGA DEPOT. This structure was located east of the east crossing on the south side of Main Street. It was erected in 1891. The depot was moved to the north side of the street in 1910. A new depot was constructed in 1911. (Jane Lyle.)

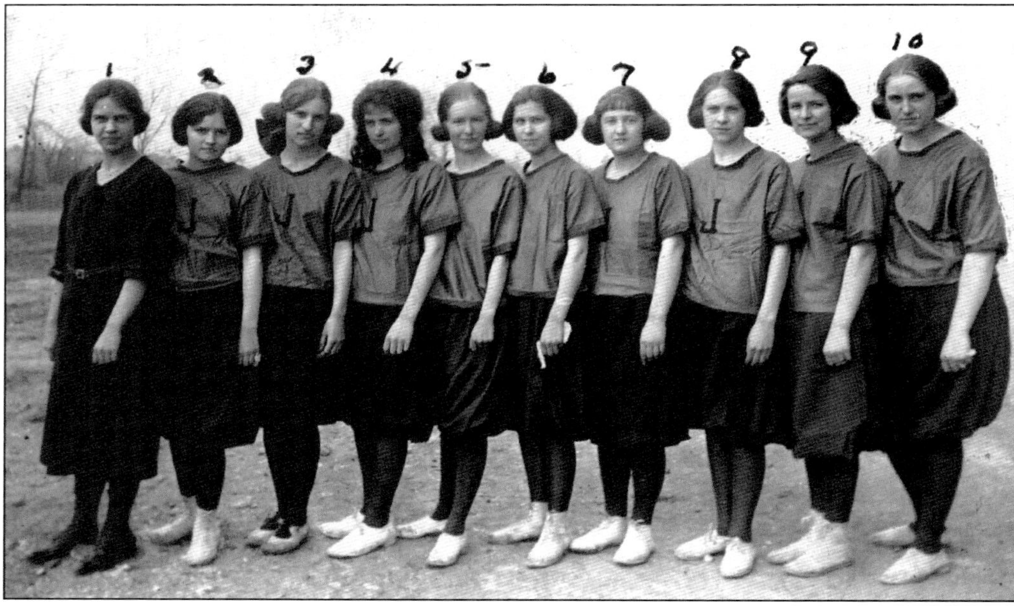

GIRLS' BASKETBALL TEAM, JEFFERSON HIGH SCHOOL. Jefferson School, located eight miles north of Winchester, was constructed in 1910–1911. This real-photo postcard depicts the Jefferson girls' basketball team about 1915. Seen here are, from left to right, Mary Henderson, coach; Esther Spillers; Constance Myers; Anna Sipe; Doris Odle; Hazel Miller, forward; Freeda R., guard; Elizabeth Furrow; Lois Collins, and Beulah Myers, center. (Randolph County Historical Society.)

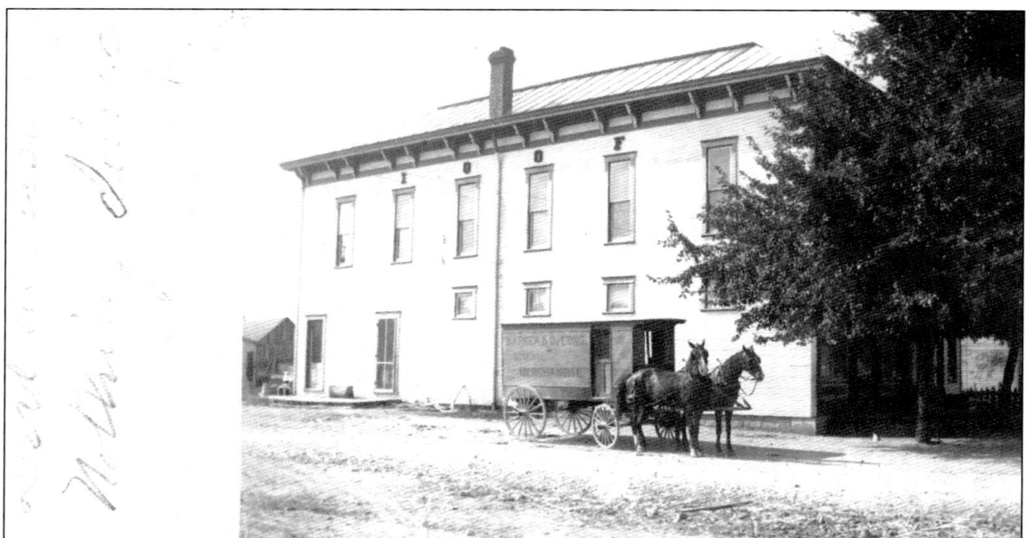

IOOF HALL, DEERFIELD. The IOOF hall in Deerfield stood at the northwest corner of U.S. Highway 27 and State Road 28. The building was dedicated on November 26, 1892. In the foreground is the huckster wagon of Albert DeLong and Frank Harker, who owned a general store that operated in the building. The lodge disbanded in 1936, the store finally closed in 1942, and the structure was razed in 1963. (Gregory P. Hinshaw.)

Six

Lynn and Vicinity

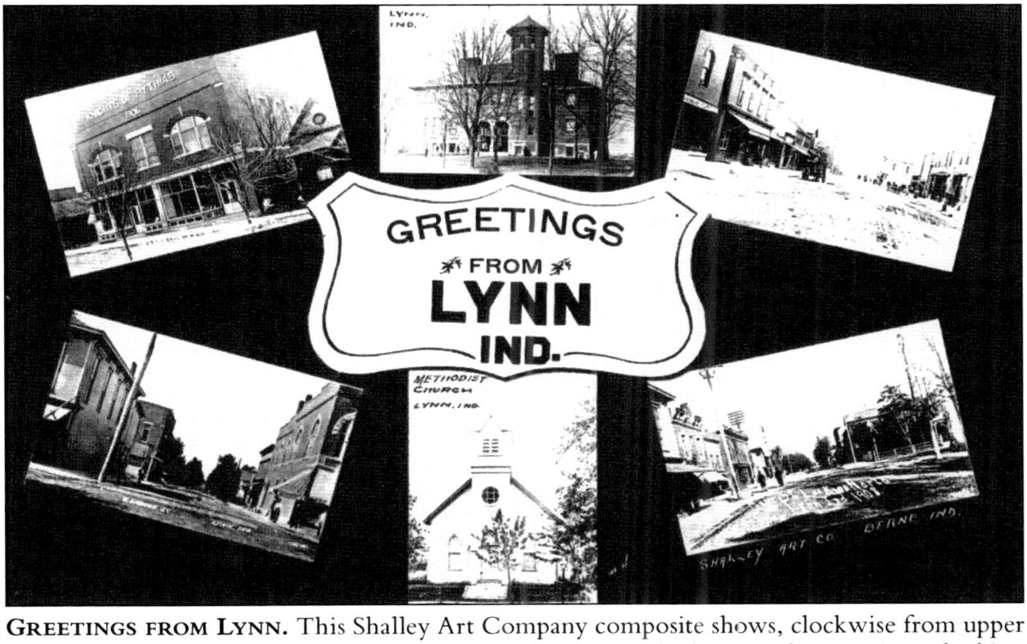

Greetings from Lynn. This Shalley Art Company composite shows, clockwise from upper left, the Knights of Pythias hall, the public school, Main Street looking south, Main Street looking north, the Methodist church, and Church Street looking west. (Gregory P. Hinshaw.)

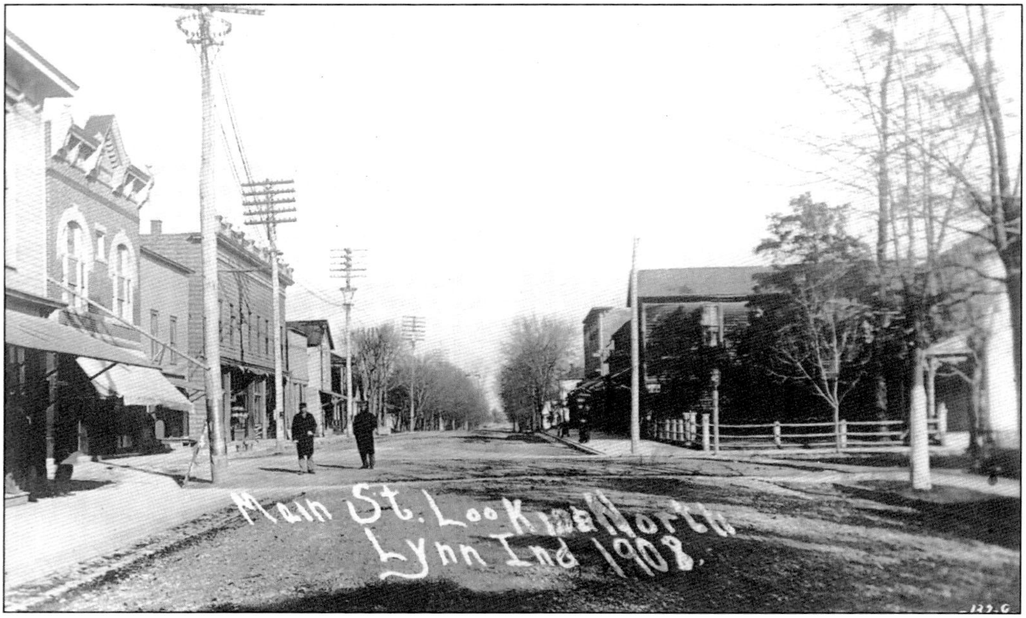

Main Street Looking North. This view looks north on Main Street from just south of Church Street. At left are the Masonic block, erected in 1905, and the "Cement Block," erected in 1904. The small structure between the two was razed in 1964 for an expansion of the bank. (Jane Lyle.)

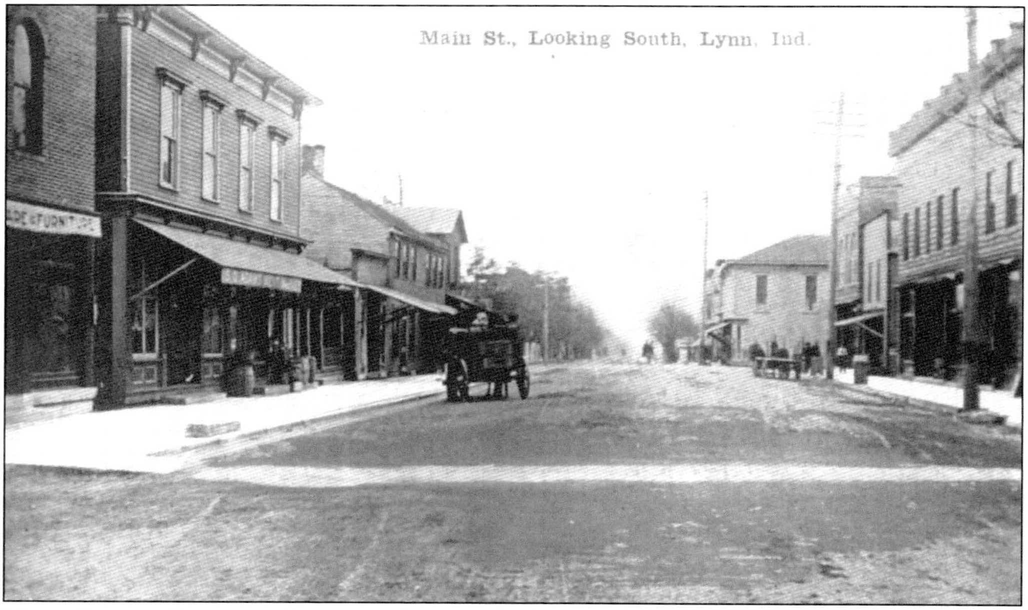

Main Street Looking South. This view looks south on Main Street from Sherman Street. The Cement Block and Masonic block are on the right. The first two buildings at left were razed in 1941 to make room for the public library. The other buildings at left were razed in the early 1950s. The IOOF building, with the hipped roof, at the southwest corner of Main and Church Streets, was razed in 1979. (Gregory P. Hinshaw.)

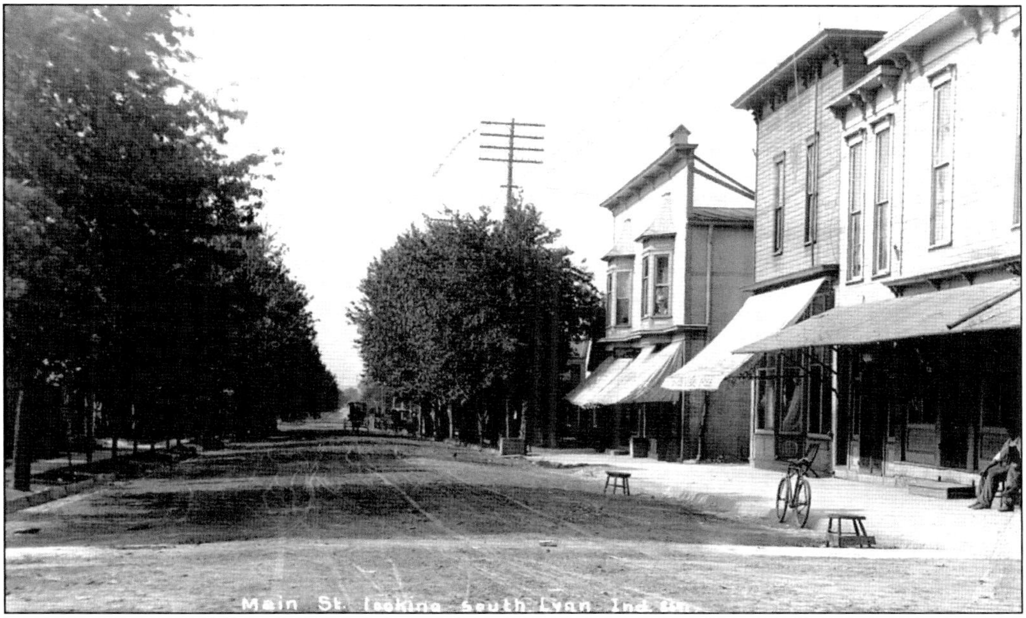

Main Street Looking South from Church Street. This view depicts the west side of Main Street, looking south from Church Street. The first building, the IOOF hall, was erected in about 1880 and razed in 1979. The large building with the bay windows was the Hinshaw Block, erected by E. J. and W. E. Hinshaw in 1897. The small stools along the street were used by bicyclists to "mount their wheels." These buildings were razed in 1979. (Judy Wilson Wright.)

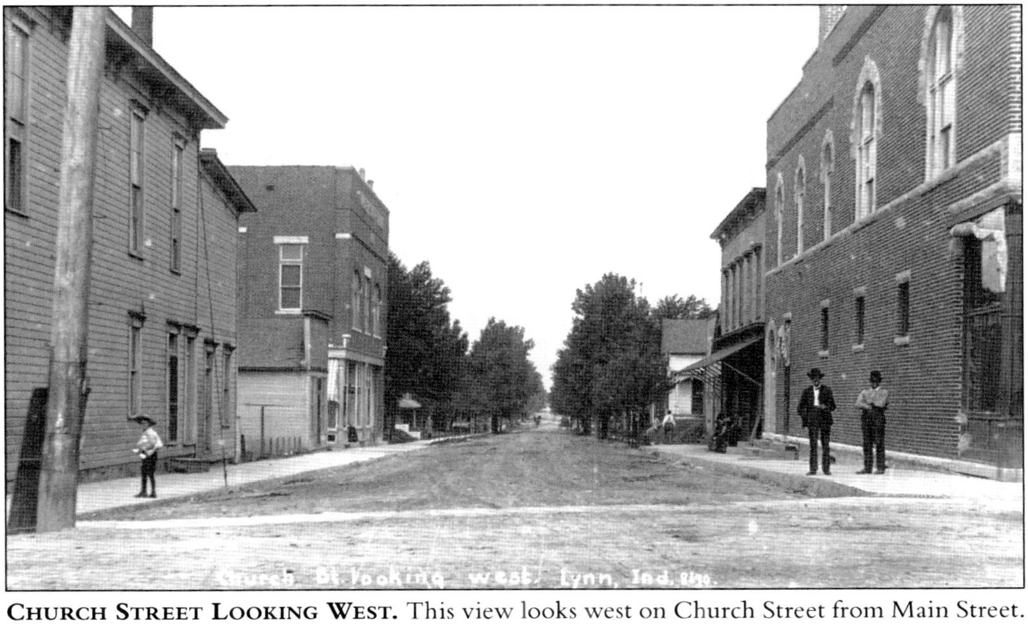

Church Street Looking West. This view looks west on Church Street from Main Street. At right are the Masonic block, Chenoweth's old store, and the office of the Lynn Herald. The frame building on the left is the IOOF hall, and the brick building on the left is the Knights of Pythias hall. (Judy Wilson Wright.)

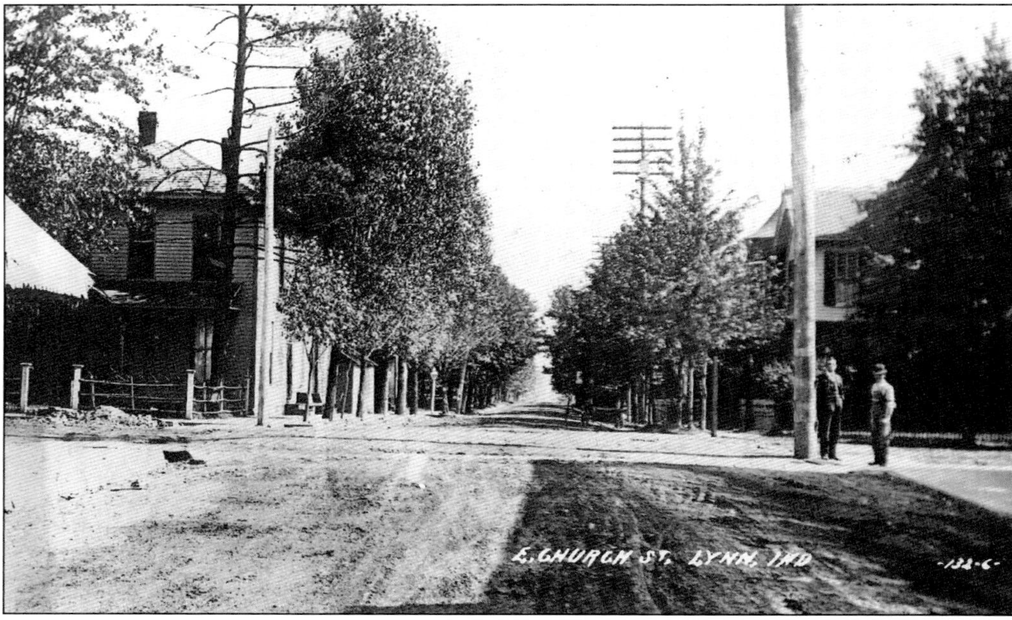

East Church Street, 1909. This view looks east on Church Street from just west of Main Street. At right is the home of Dr. J. S. Blair, razed in 1969 to make room for a new city building. At left is the Nichols House, a hotel run by Henry D. Nichols. It was razed in 1922 to make way for a filling station. (Thomas Keesling.)

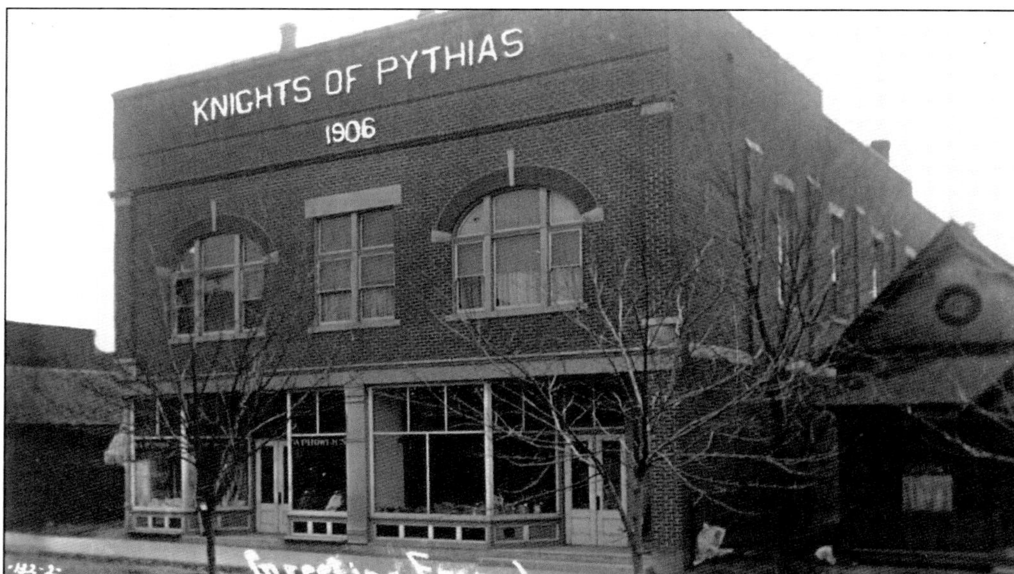

Knights of Pythias Hall. The Knights of Pythias hall was erected on the south side of Church Street, just west of Main Street, in 1906–1907 and dedicated on May 23. The local lodge was instituted in 1884. It was the last of the Pythian Lodges in Randolph County, surrendering its charter in 1966. The building was destroyed by the tornado of March 10, 1986. (Gregory P. Hinshaw.)

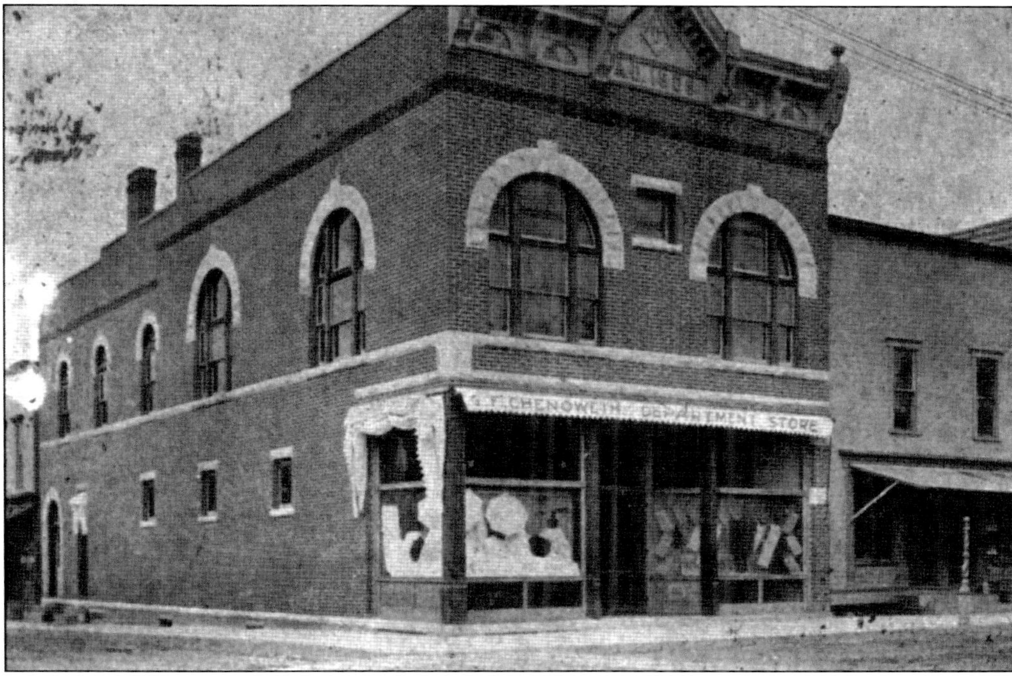

MASONIC BLOCK. This building was erected at the northwest corner of Main and Church Streets in 1905. Chenoweth's Department Store was long located on the ground floor. The Masonic Lodge moved to new quarters in 1975. The building remains extant and is the only old brick commercial building left in Lynn. (Gregory P. Hinshaw.)

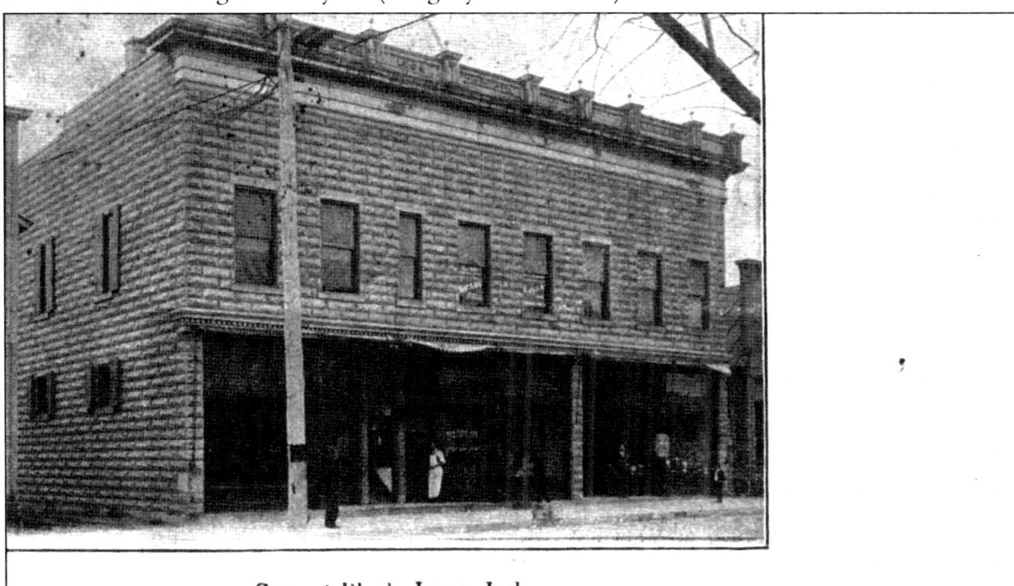

CEMENT BLOCK. The Cement Block was erected in 1904 by C. R. Carter and the Citizens Banking Company on the west side of Main Street, north of the Masonic block. The building to the south was razed in 1964 for expansion of the bank. Having undergone several changes of name, the bank still uses the structure. (Tom Harshman.)

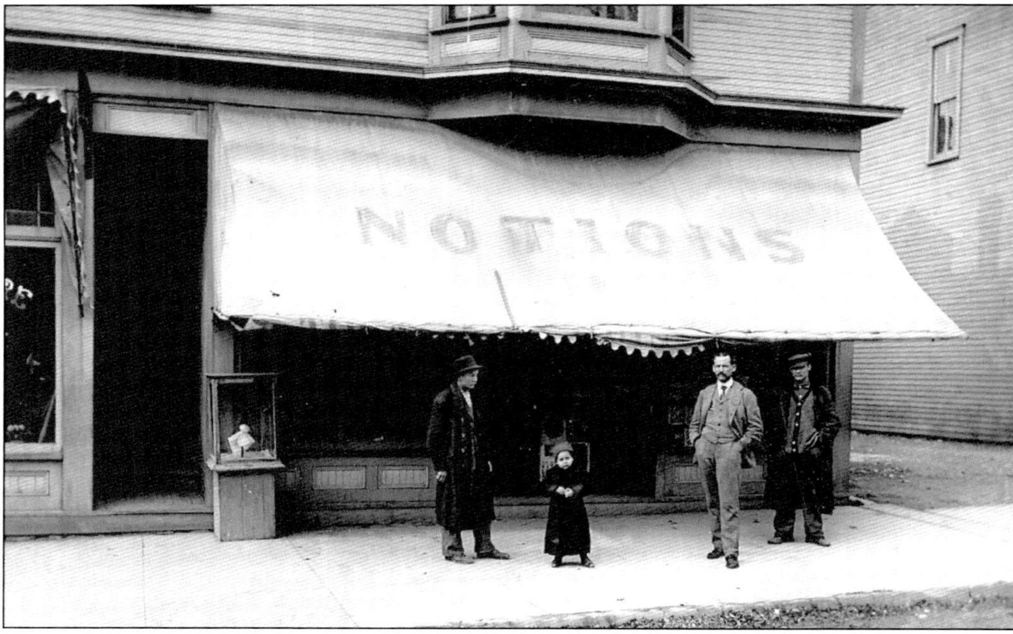

Notions Store. This store was located in the Hinshaw Block on the west side of South Main Street, south of Church Street. It was likely the general store of Elkanah J. Hinshaw. (Washington Township Public Library.)

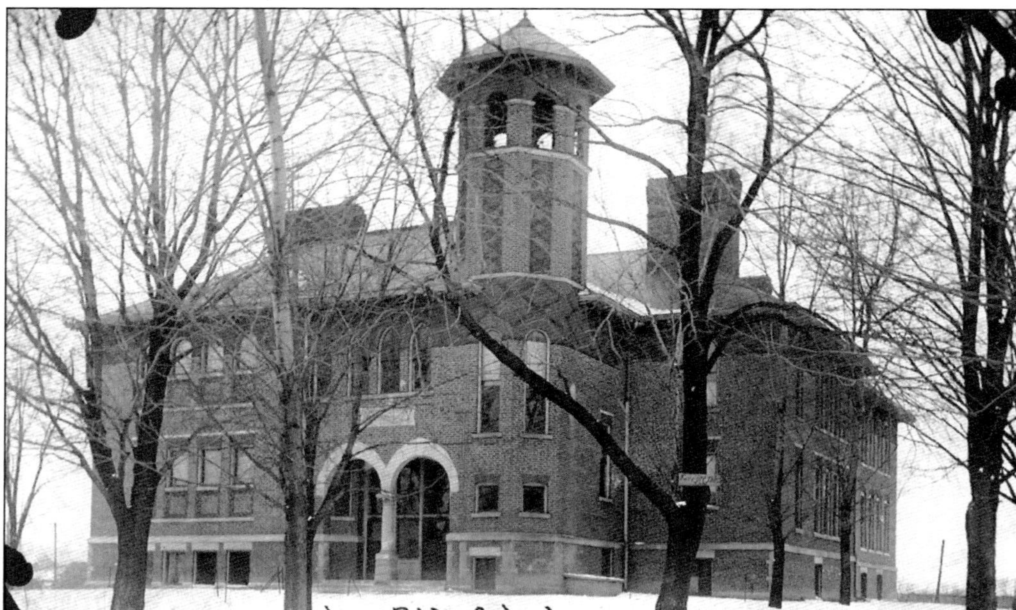

Lynn Public School. This building was erected on Sherman Street in 1902. An addition, to the north, was erected in 1909. In 1928–1929, a gymnasium was added to the front, and the tower was removed. In 1954–1955, an addition was made to the west. High school students were transferred to Randolph Southern High School, on the north side of town, in January 1976. The tornado of March 10, 1986, destroyed the building. (Tom Harshman.)

METHODIST EPISCOPAL CHURCH. A Methodist Episcopal class was organized in Lynn in about 1854, and a building was constructed on East Church Street in about 1854. The building shown here was constructed on the same site in 1886. The congregation merged with the Spartanburg United Methodist Church in 1972, and the building was sold to the Masonic Lodge, which remodeled it from 1973 to 1975 and used it until disbanding in 1982. (Max Harter.)

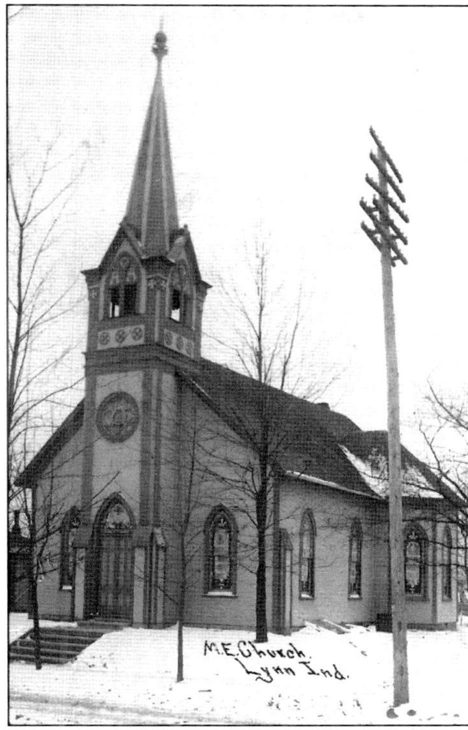

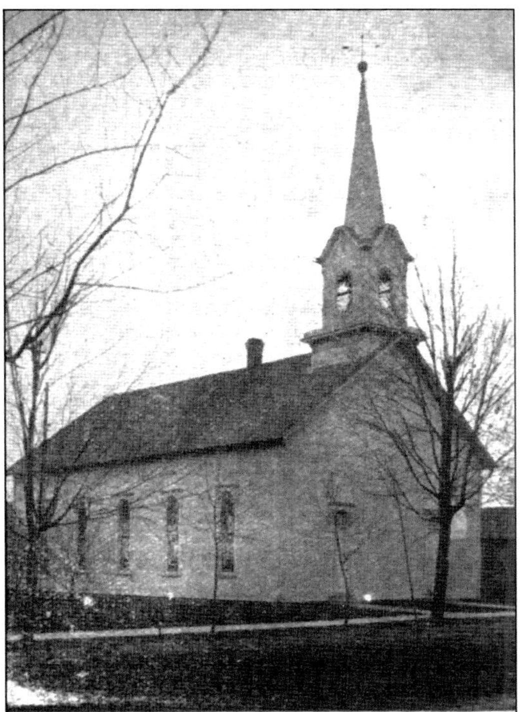

First Church of Christ, Lynn, Ind.

FIRST CHURCH OF CHRIST. The Church of Christ was organized in 1886. A church was erected on the north side of West Church Street that year and dedicated on July 25. The church split over the use of musical instruments in 1895. The building was enlarged in 1914 and 1957. The old structure was removed, and a new sanctuary was dedicated on November 1, 1970. (Gregory P. Hinshaw.)

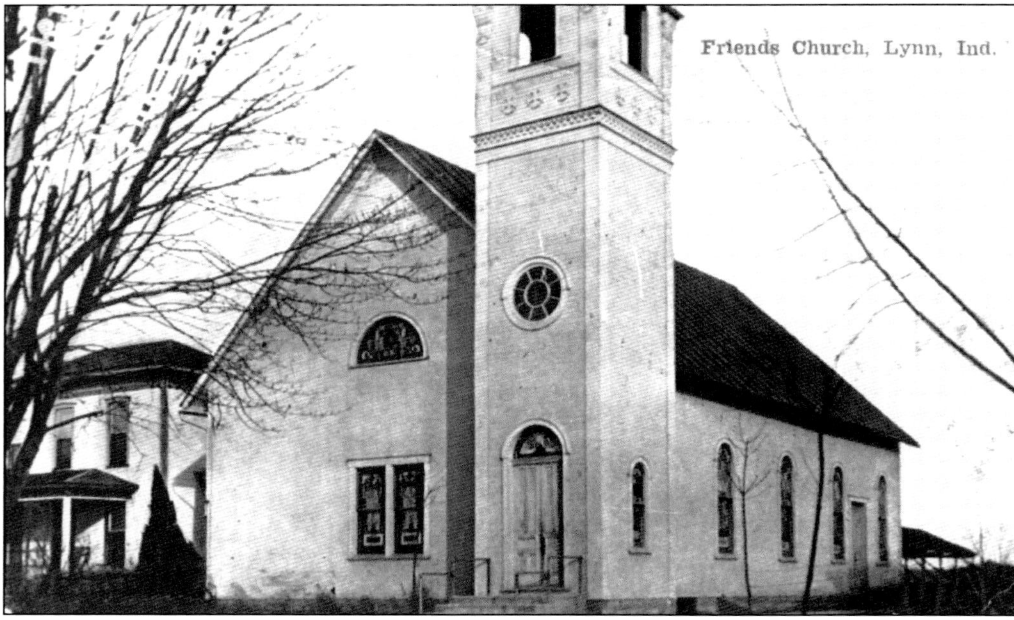

FRIENDS CHURCH. The Friends Church is the oldest congregation in Lynn, having been organized in 1823 at Quaker Lynn, south of the present town. Two meetinghouses were used there. In 1881, a new meetinghouse was erected on the pike south of Lynn. In 1906–1907, the structure depicted here was erected on South Main Street and dedicated on December 8. Additions were made in 1913 and again in 1954. (Gregory P. Hinshaw.)

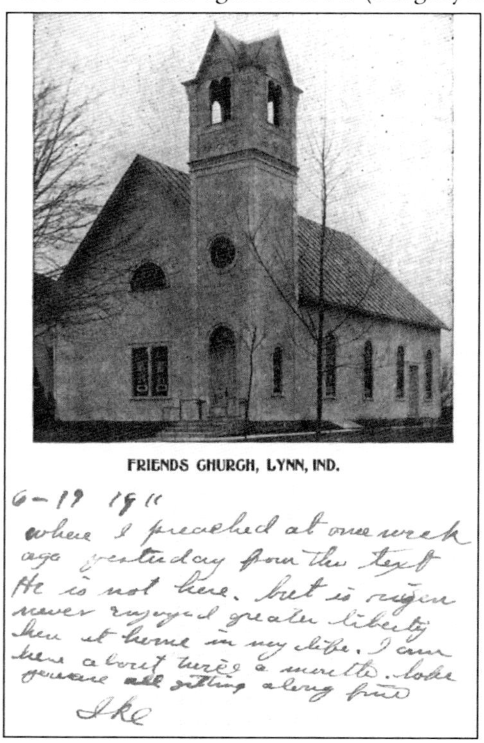

FRIENDS CHURCH. The building depicted here was replaced by a new brick structure between 1971 and 1973. This card was mailed in 1911 by Isaac Hollingsworth, a minister who was a member of this congregation. (Gregory P. Hinshaw.)

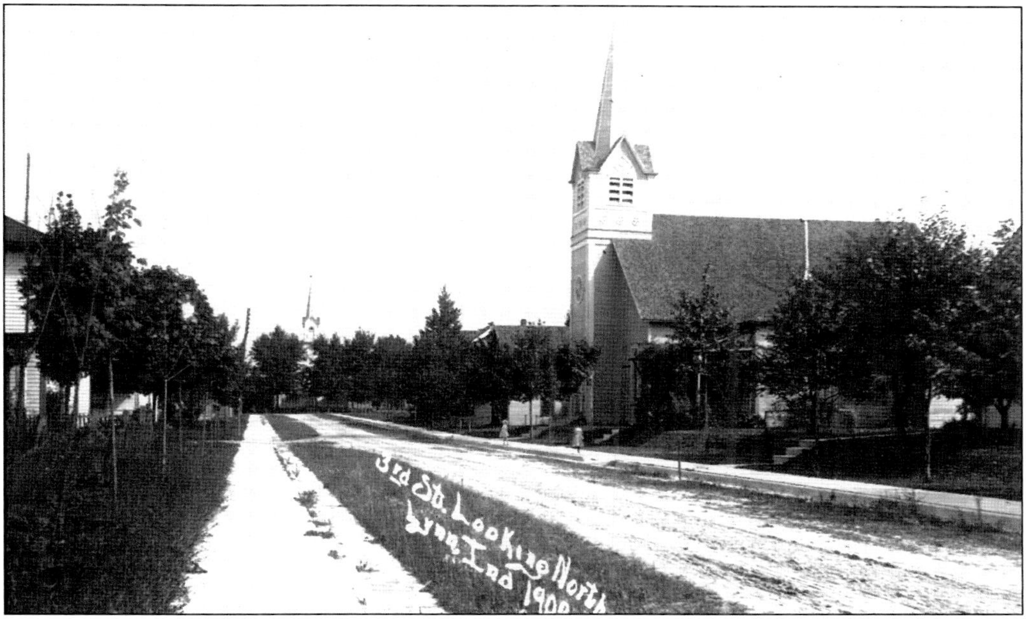

THIRD STREET LOOKING NORTH. Third Street is today known as Franklin Street. At right is the United Brethren Church, built in 1898 and dedicated on October 12. The church was sold in 1919 and was razed long ago. The tower of the First Church of Christ can be seen at the end of the street in the background. (Judy Wilson Wright.)

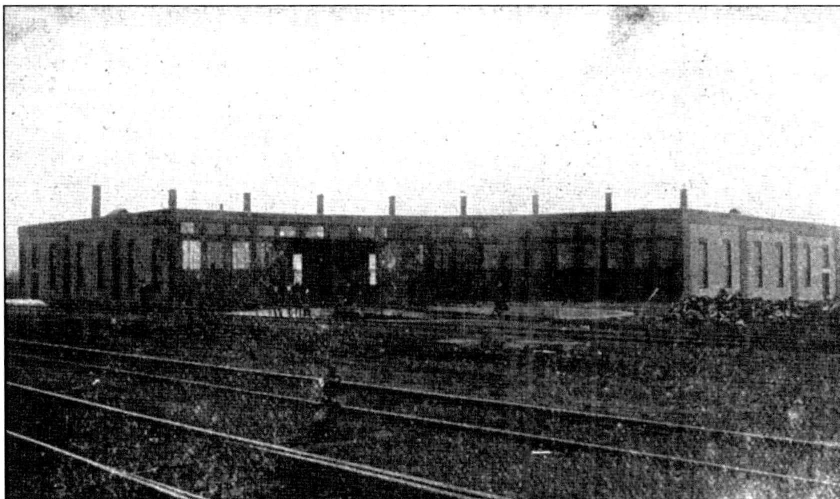

ROUNDHOUSE. The roundhouse was built in 1903 on the Cleveland, Cincinnati, Chicago, and St. Louis Railroad (formerly the Indiana, Bloomington, and Western) on the south side of town. It was razed sometime before 1941. (Tom Harshman.)

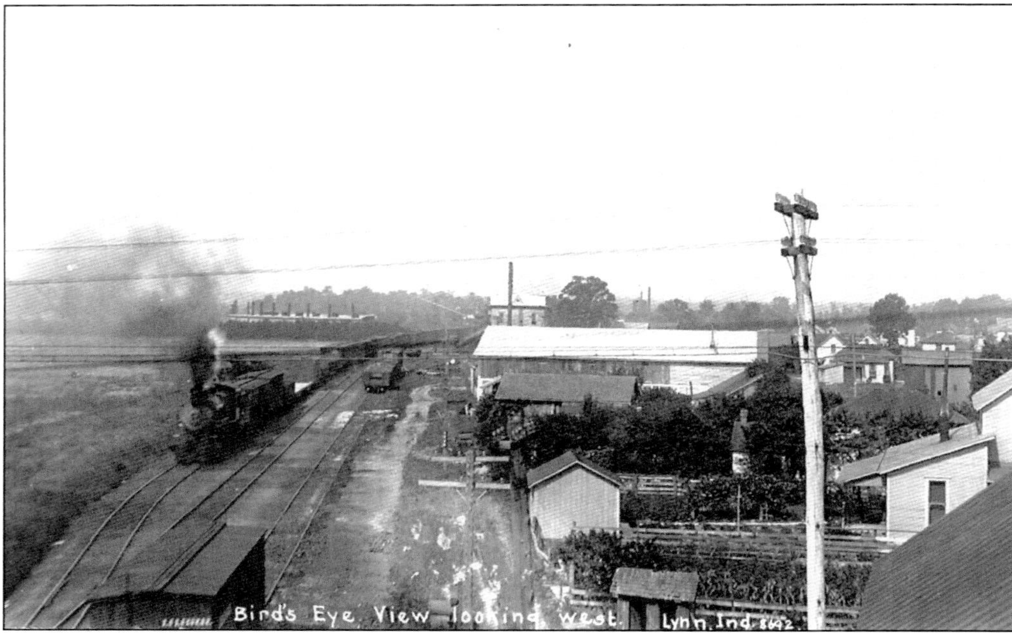

BIRD'S-EYE VIEW LOOKING WEST. This view looks west along the lines of the Cleveland, Cincinnati, Chicago, and St. Louis Railroad from the tower of the elevator on Main Street. The roundhouse is in the distance on the left. (Janice Harvey.)

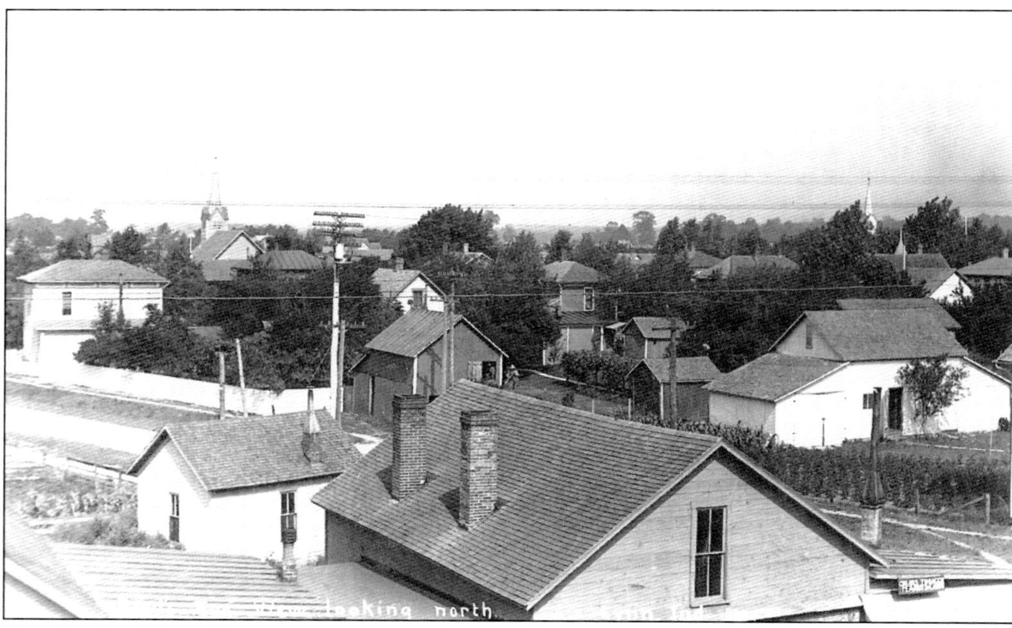

BIRD'S-EYE VIEW LOOKING NORTH. This view looks northwest from the tower of the elevator on South Main Street. The United Brethren Church can be seen at left, and the tower of the First Church of Christ is visible at the right. (Randolph County Historical Society.)

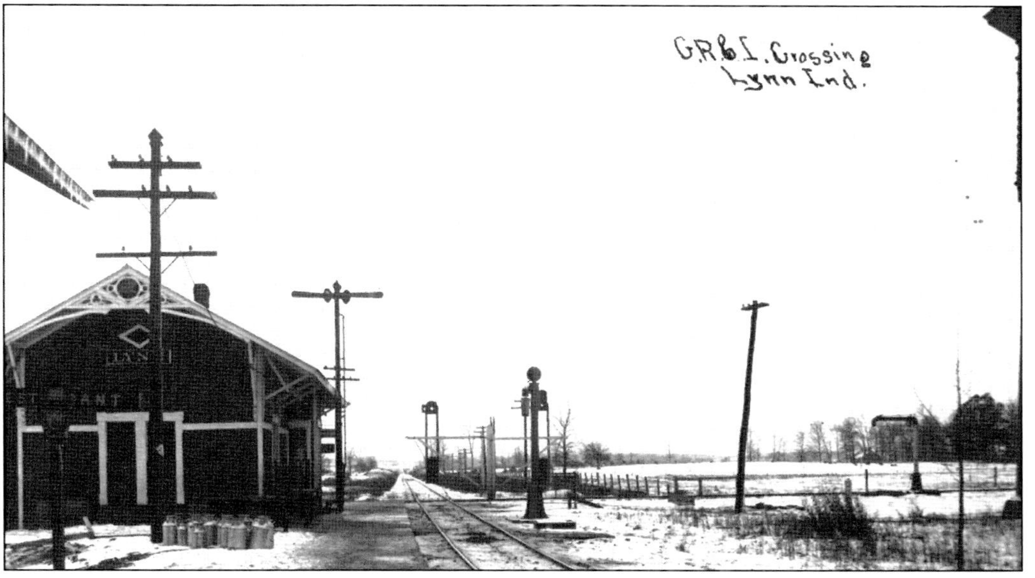

Grand Rapids and Indiana Railroad Crossing. This view depicts the depot at the crossing of the Grand Rapids and Indiana and the Cleveland, Cincinnati, Chicago, and St. Louis Railroads in Lynn. The view looks west. The depot was moved to the north side of the tracks in about 1912. It was closed in 1964 and razed in 1965. The north–south line was abandoned in 1975 and the east–west line was abandoned in 1977. (Gregory P. Hinshaw.)

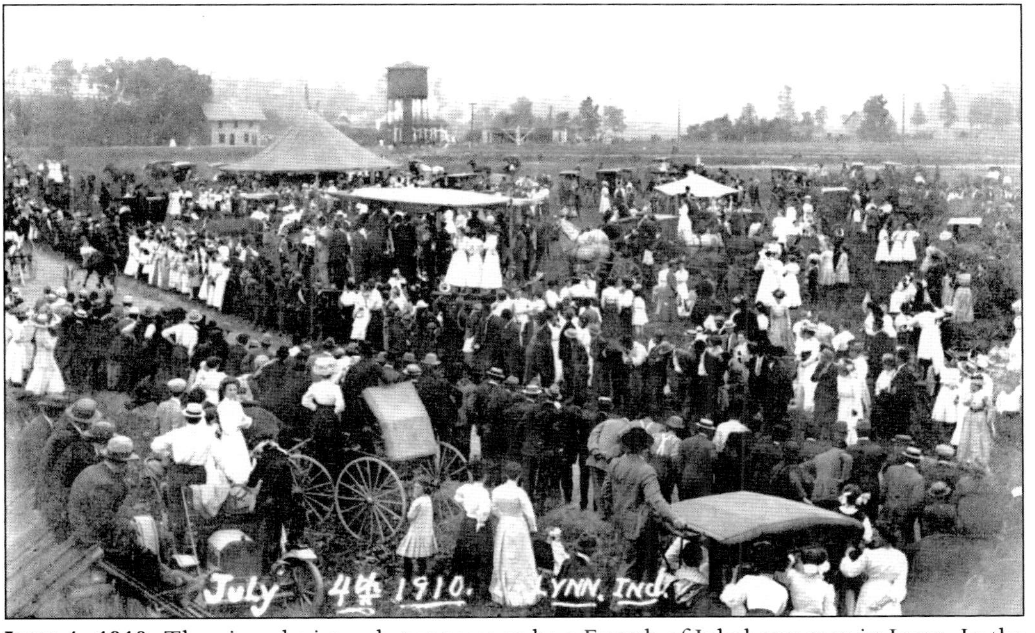

July 4, 1910. The view depicts what appears to be a Fourth of July horse race in Lynn. In the distance is the railroad water tank. Behind it are the depot and a steaming train engine. The water tank was removed in 1955. (Thomas Keesling.)

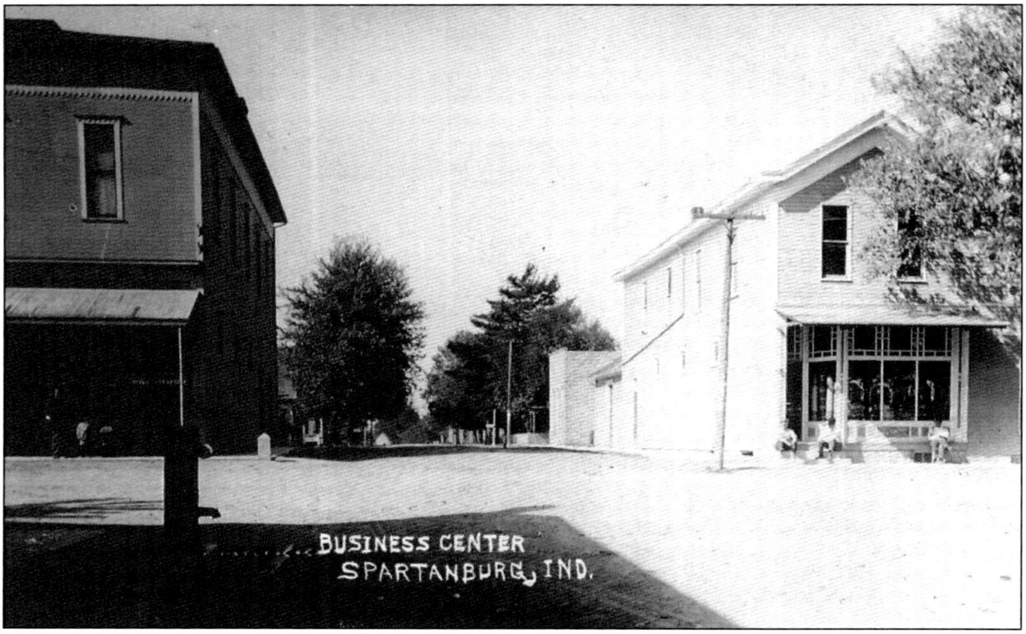

SPARTANBURG, BUSINESS CENTER. This view looks west on Second Street from Main Street. The Spartanburg Hotel, at right, was used for various purposes. It was destroyed by fire in 1974. The block building behind the hotel was the Greensfork Township State Bank. The building at the left was the IOOF hall, erected in 1867. The building was razed to make room for the new Greensfork Township State Bank, completed in 1965. (Tom Harshman.)

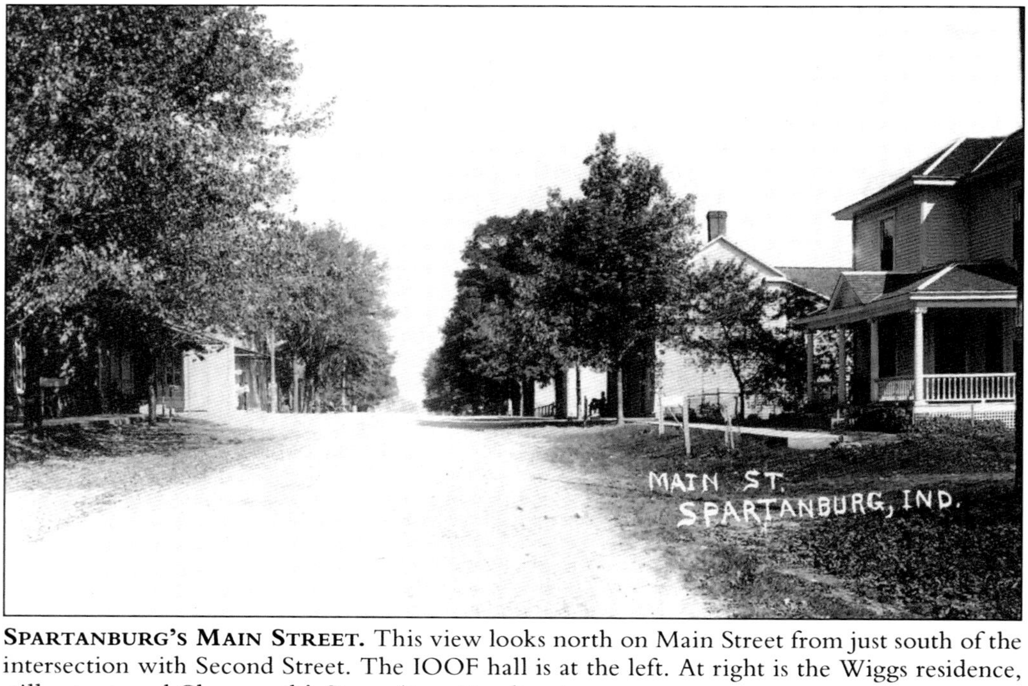

SPARTANBURG'S MAIN STREET. This view looks north on Main Street from just south of the intersection with Second Street. The IOOF hall is at the left. At right is the Wiggs residence, still extant, and Chenoweth's Store. (Jean Keesling.)

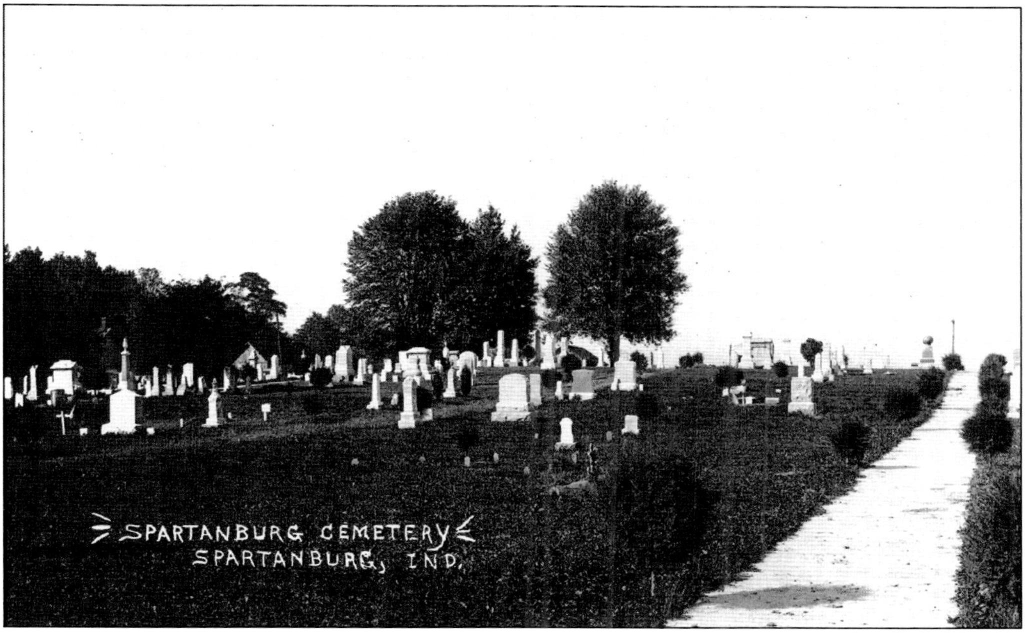

SPARTANBURG CEMETERY. Located on the northeast side of the village, the Spartanburg Cemetery was originally connected with the Methodist Episcopal church. (Thomas Keesling.)

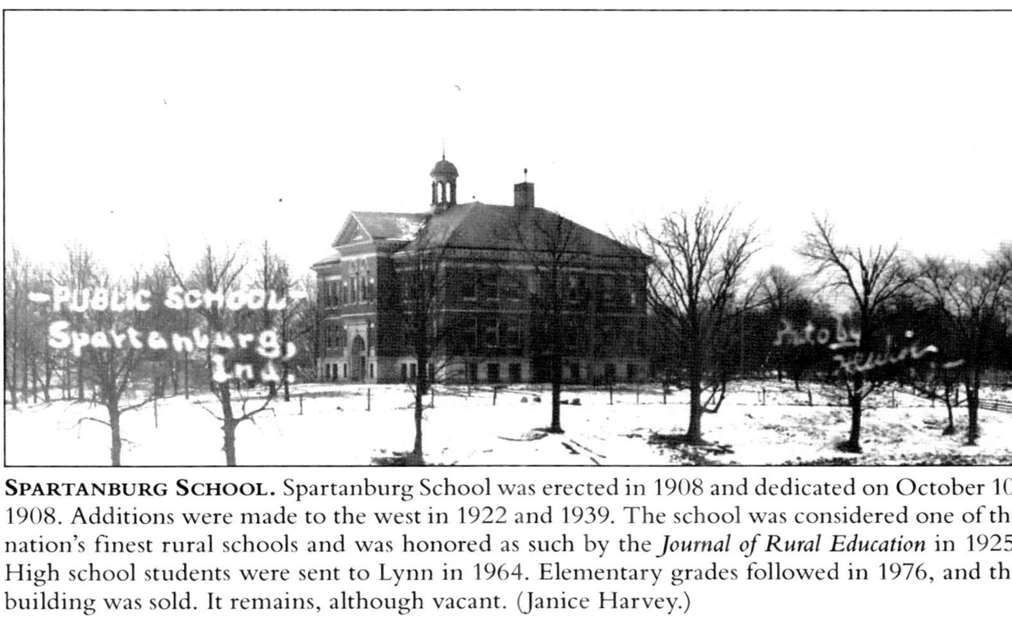

SPARTANBURG SCHOOL. Spartanburg School was erected in 1908 and dedicated on October 10, 1908. Additions were made to the west in 1922 and 1939. The school was considered one of the nation's finest rural schools and was honored as such by the *Journal of Rural Education* in 1925. High school students were sent to Lynn in 1964. Elementary grades followed in 1976, and the building was sold. It remains, although vacant. (Janice Harvey.)

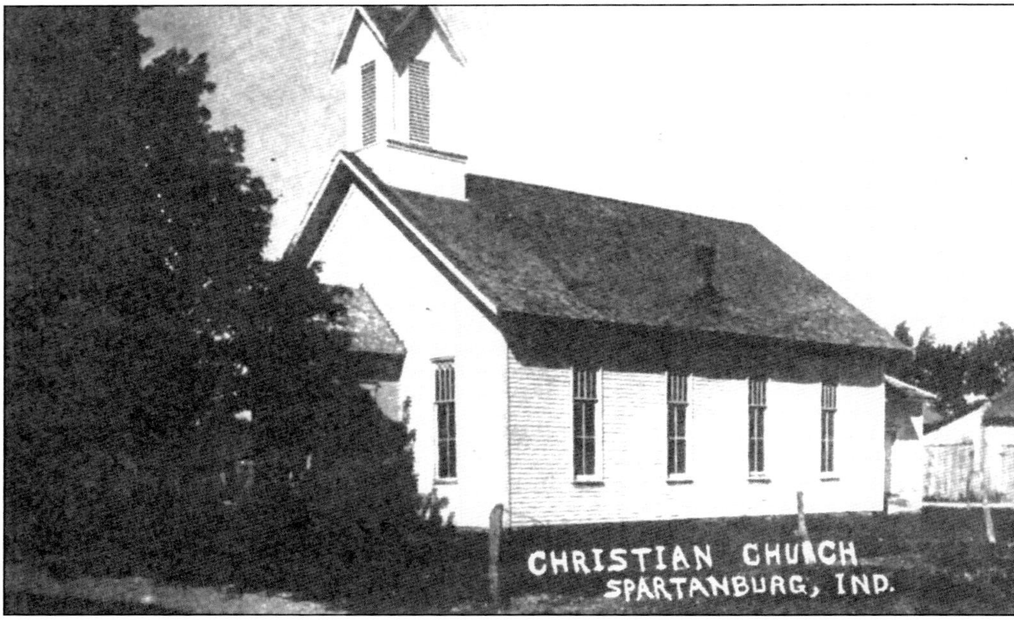

SPARTANBURG CHRISTIAN CHURCH. Spartanburg Christian Church was organized in 1868, although members of the Disciples of Christ had churches in the area long before that date. The structure depicted here was erected in 1868 at the northwest corner of Second and Mill Streets. The building was remodeled in 1903. It was removed in 1920 in preparation for construction of the present brick church. (Linda L. Black.)

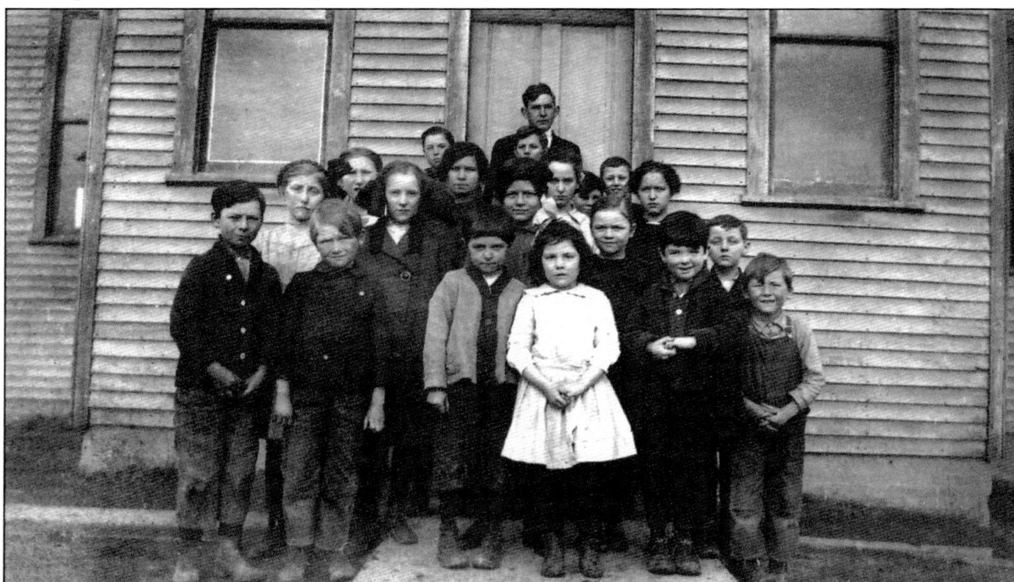

PINHOOK SCHOOL. Pinhook School was located at the southwest corner of 1000 S and Highway 227. The structure shown here was built in 1907 as the sixth schoolhouse on the site. The school closed in 1919. The building was later moved north, where it was attached to the rear of a barn and still stands. The teacher was Glen O. Chenoweth, who served as county superintendent of schools (1929–1949). (Jean Keesling.)

CRETE ELEVATOR. Crete Elevator stood on the west side of the Arba Pike and the south side of the Cleveland, Cincinnati, Chicago, and St. Louis Railroad in the village of Crete. It was damaged by a storm in 1912. The elevator closed in 2003. It was destroyed by fire on March 6, 2004. (Janice Harvey.)

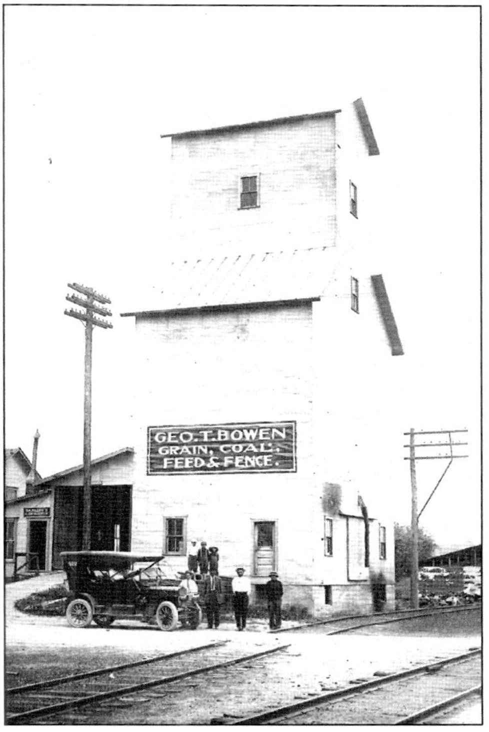

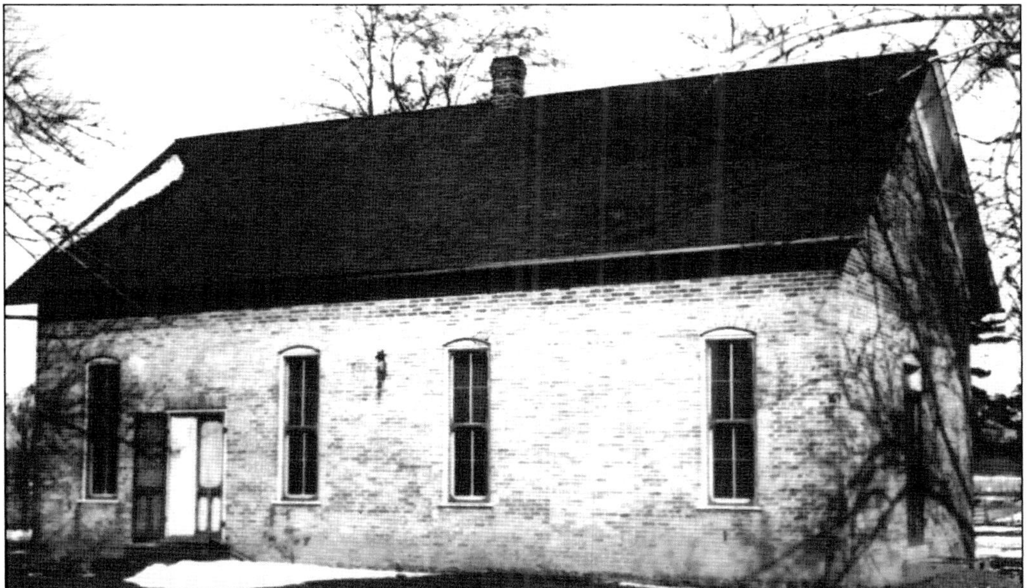

ARBA FRIENDS CHURCH. Arba Friends Church, established in 1815, is the oldest congregation in Randolph County. A pole cabin, erected in 1815, served until 1824, when a log structure was completed. This building was erected in 1854. The structure was remodeled in 1888 and 1904. At some point, the men's door was enclosed. A belfry was added in 1913–1914, a basement was dug in 1937, and an annex was completed in 1975. (Friends Collection, Earlham College.)

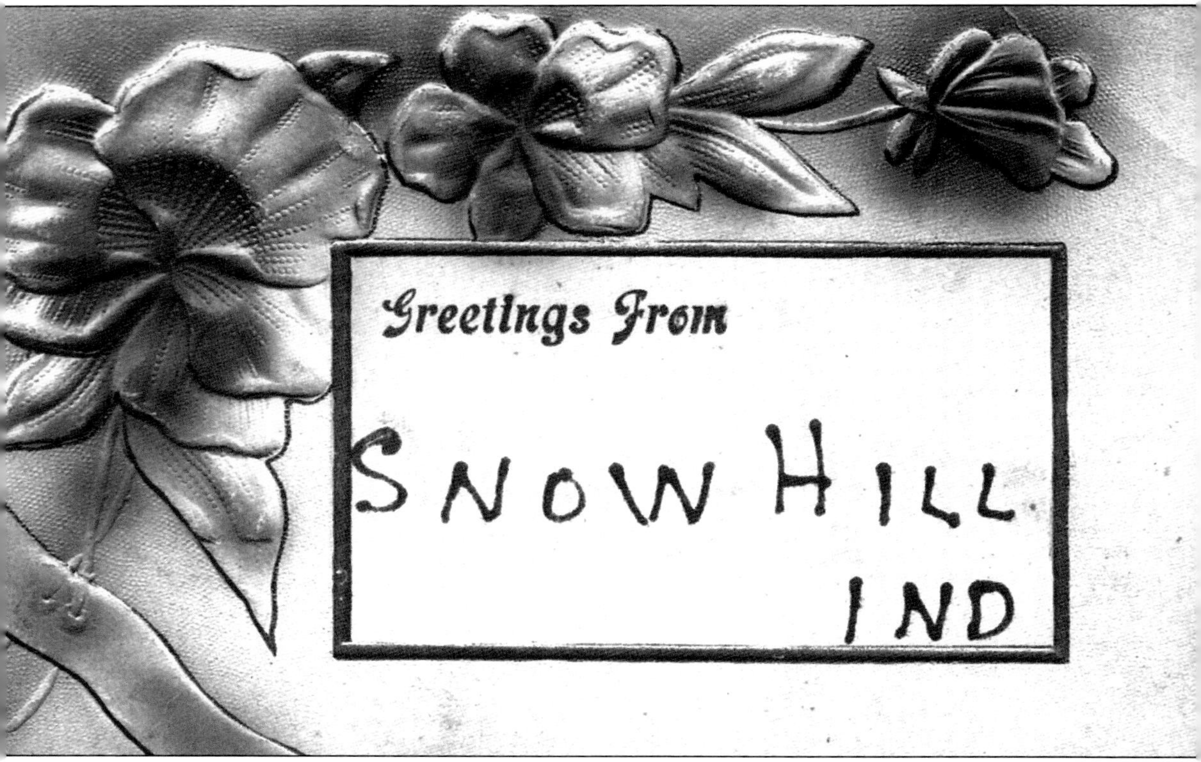

GREETINGS FROM SNOW HILL. The authors have been unable to locate any real-photo postcards from Snow Hill, a village north of Lynn; however, this card has survived. Snow Hill Post Office was established at "old Snow Hill" in 1859. It moved to Hinshaw's Station, one mile to the west, in the 1870s and closed in 1907. (Janice Harvey)

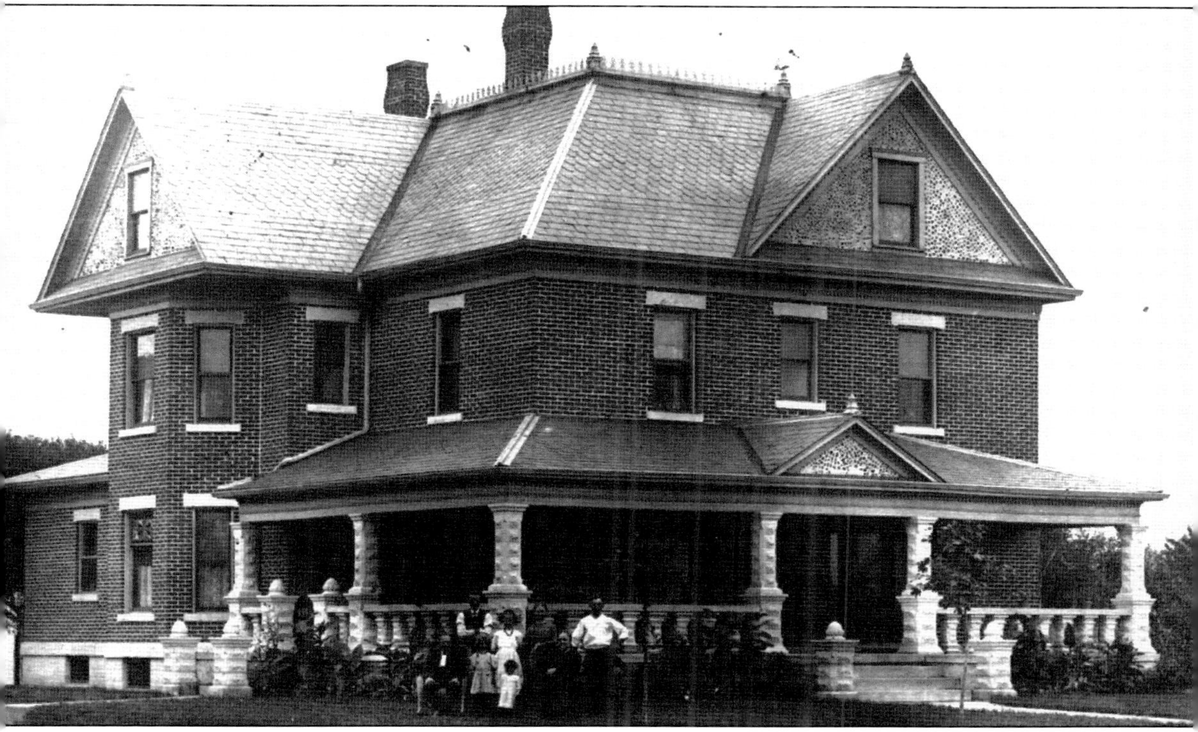

MARTIN COATS RESIDENCE. This card shows the family and brick residence of Martin E. Coats (1865–1948), a Quaker farmer who resided five miles south of Winchester and one mile west of Snow Hill Station. The residence was completed in 1909 and was one of the finest farm residences of the area. The house has been owned for more than a half century by the Bake family. (Gregory P. Hinshaw.)

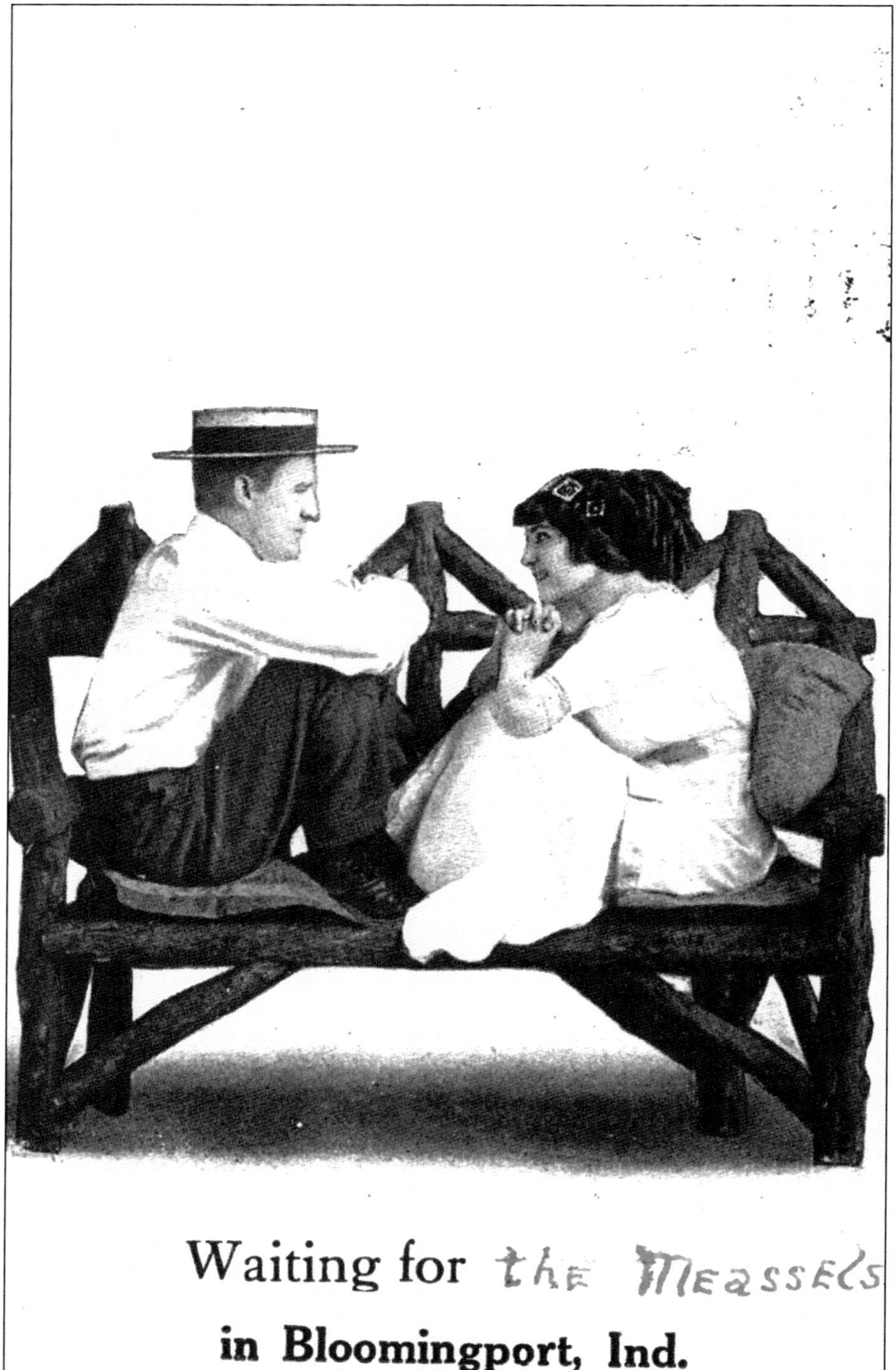

WAITING FOR THE "MEASSELS" IN BLOOMINGPORT. There are no surviving real-photo postcards from the village of Bloomingport, located west of Lynn; however, this humorous card has survived. A post office operated in the village from 1851 until 1905. (Janice Harvey.)

Seven

Modoc, Losantville, Carlos, and Huntsville

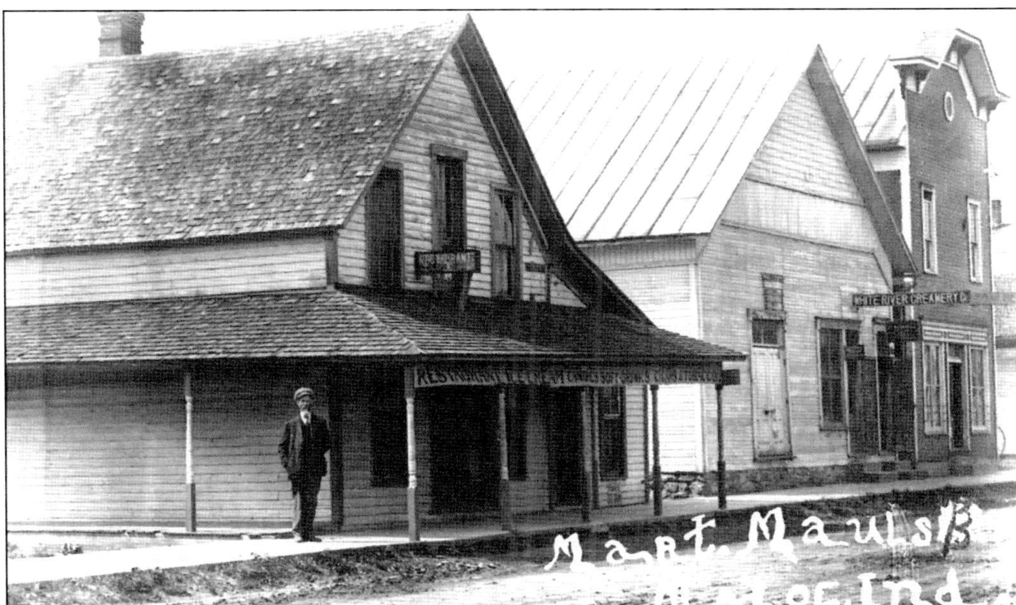

Mart Maulsby. This view looks at the west side of Main Street in Modoc. The first building is the restaurant of Martin Maulsby. The next building was once located north of town and served as the town's school from 1890 until 1911. The building at the right was George W. Dutro's store, which stood at the southwest corner of Main and Wine Streets. The store building burned in the early 20th century. (Randolph County Historical Society.)

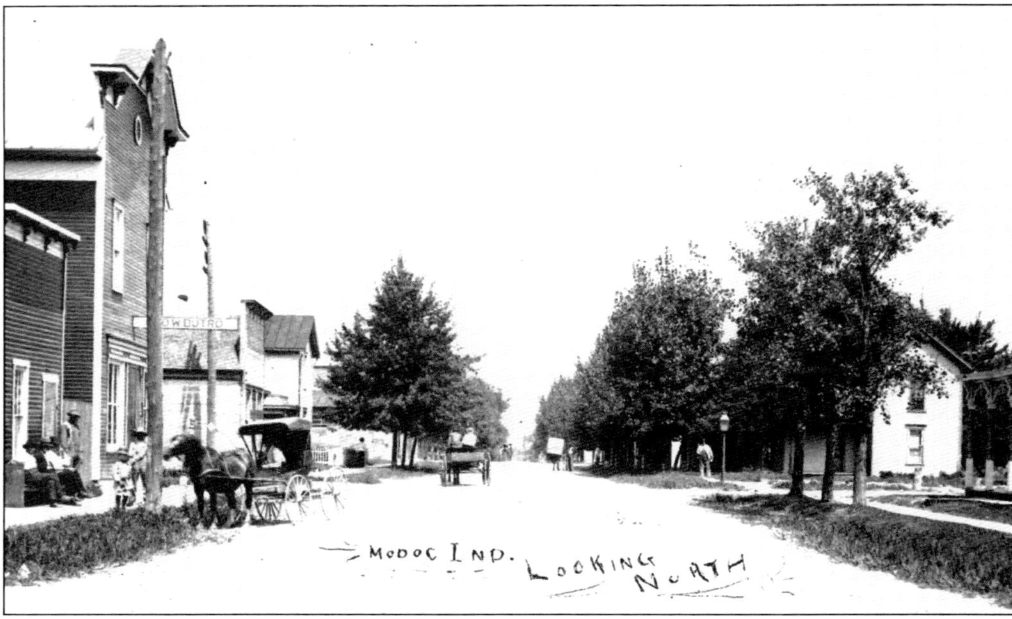

Modoc Looking North. This view looks north on Main Street from just south of Wine Street. Dutro's department store, established in 1902, is located at left. Almost none of the buildings here are extant. (Gregory P. Hinshaw.)

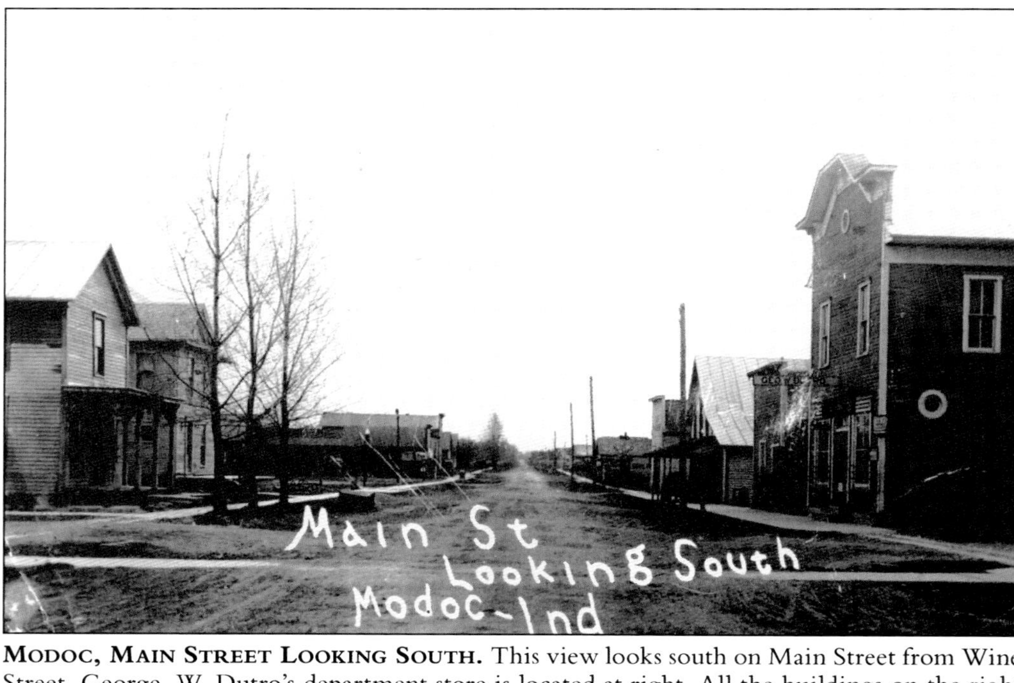

Modoc, Main Street Looking South. This view looks south on Main Street from Wine Street. George. W. Dutro's department store is located at right. All the buildings on the right were razed before 1955. (Gregory P. Hinshaw.)

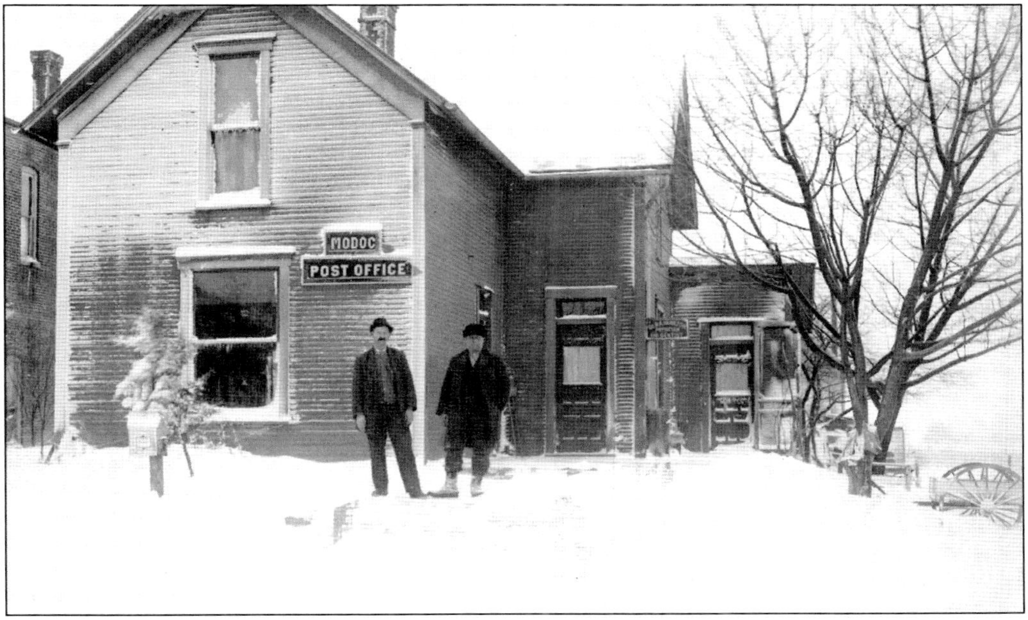

MODOC POST OFFICE. The Modoc Post Office was located on the west side of Main Street south of Conley Street. At the rear of the building was the office of Dr. R. A. Hamilton, physician and dentist. (Jane Lyle.)

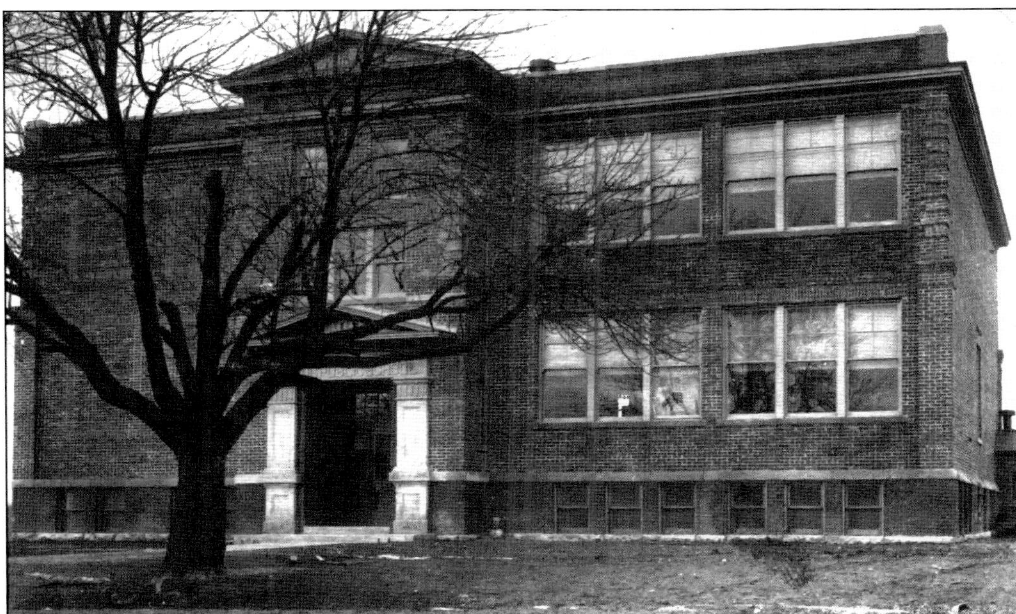

MODOC SCHOOL. A three-room schoolhouse was erected at the northeast corner of what is today U.S. Highway 36 and Indiana Highway 1 in 1890. The building was replaced by the structure depicted here in 1911. The structure was used as a high school until the fall of 1957, when students were sent to the new Union High School. The building was sold in May 1963 and razed soon after. (Gregory P. Hinshaw.)

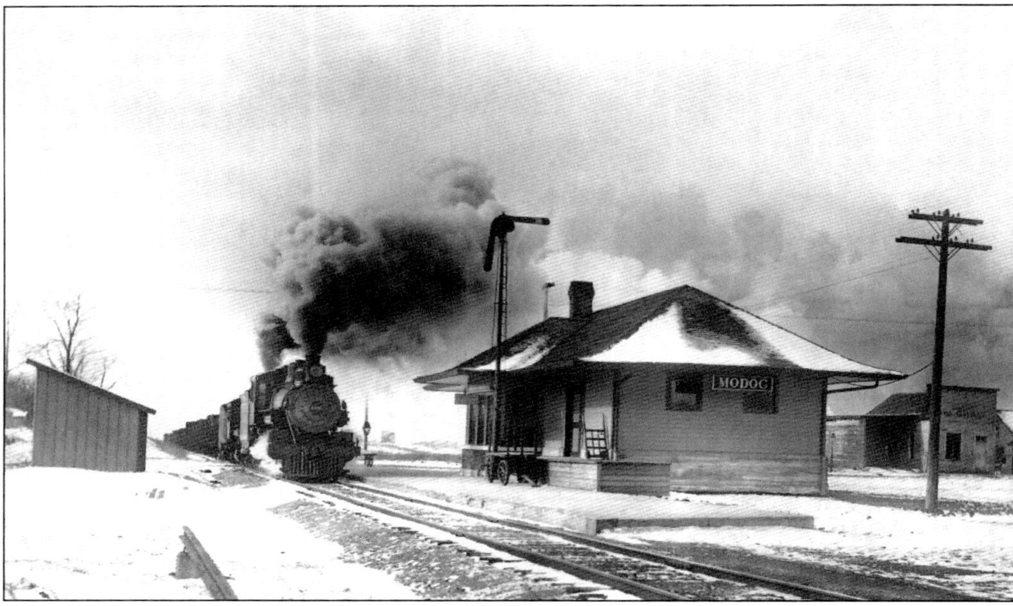

MODOC DEPOT. This depot was located on the north side of the Cleveland, Cincinnati, Chicago, and St. Louis Railroad, on the east side of Main Street. It was built in 1912 to replace a depot that burned in 1911. The building stood into the 1950s. (Jane Lyle.)

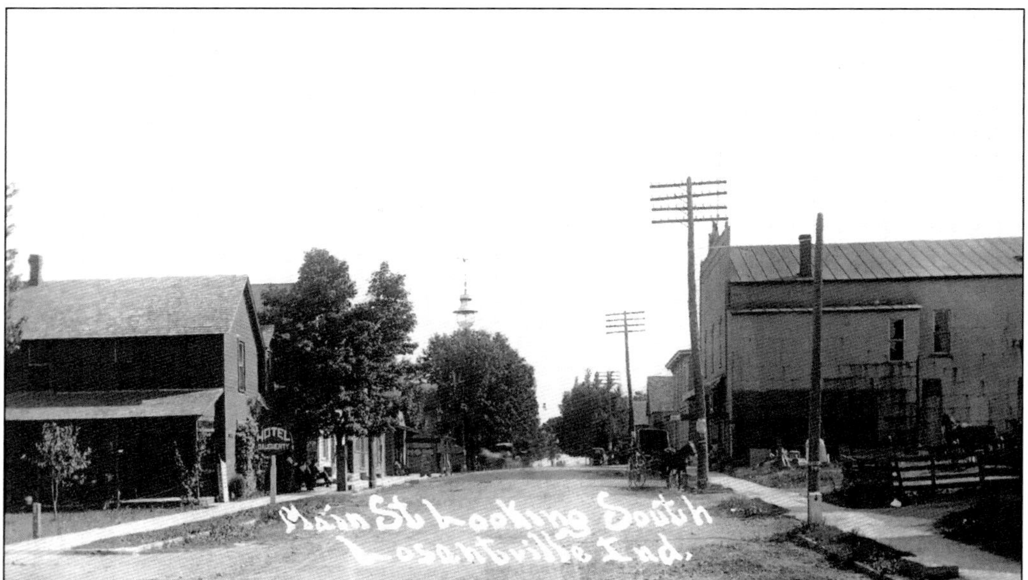

LOSANTVILLE, MAIN STREET LOOKING SOUTH. This view looks south on Main Street from the crossing of the Cleveland, Cincinnati, Chicago, and St. Louis Railroad. At left is the Hotel Daugherty. Beyond the hotel are the post office and the bank. At right are other commercial buildings. None of these are extant today. (Jeffrey Koenker.)

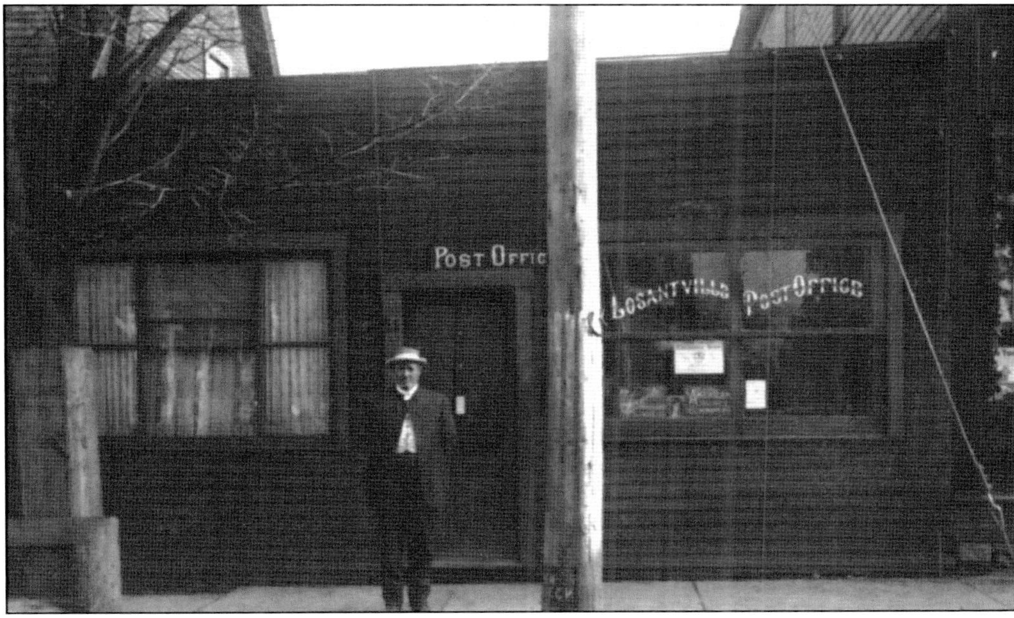

LOSANTVILLE POST OFFICE. Here a man stands near the door of the Losantville Post Office, located on the east side of Main Street. A new post office was constructed in the town in 1961. (Dott Shook.)

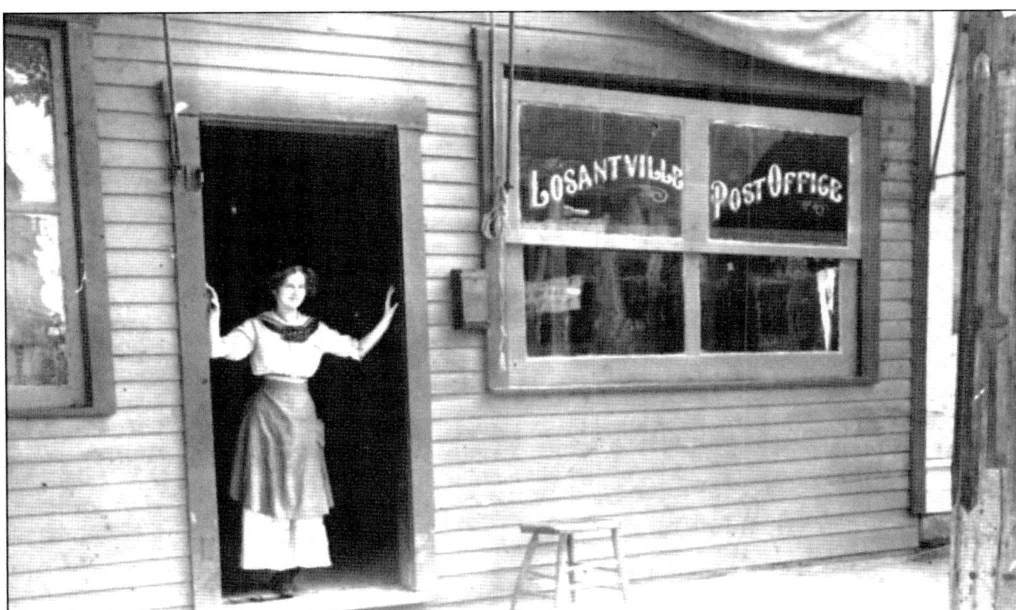

LOSANTVILLE POST OFFICE WITH ARDITH JOHNSON. Here Ardith Johnson stands in the door of the Losantville Post Office. Ardith was the daughter of James N. Johnson, the trustee of Nettle Creek Township. (Dott Shook.)

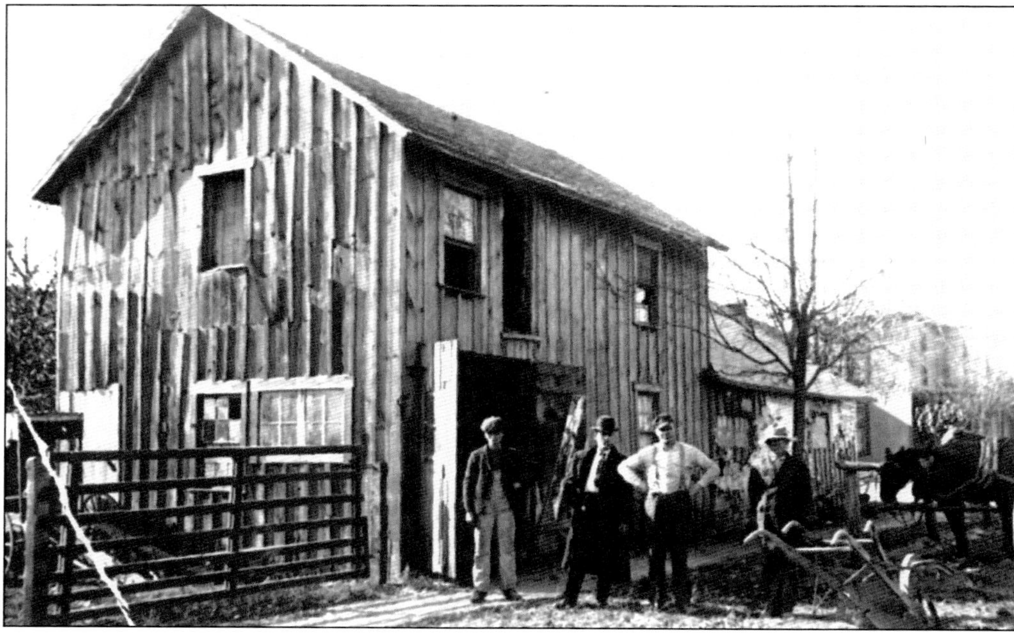

LOSANTVILLE BLACKSMITH SHOP. This scene shows the blacksmith shop of Sylvester Sulteen on Main Street. (Dott Shook.)

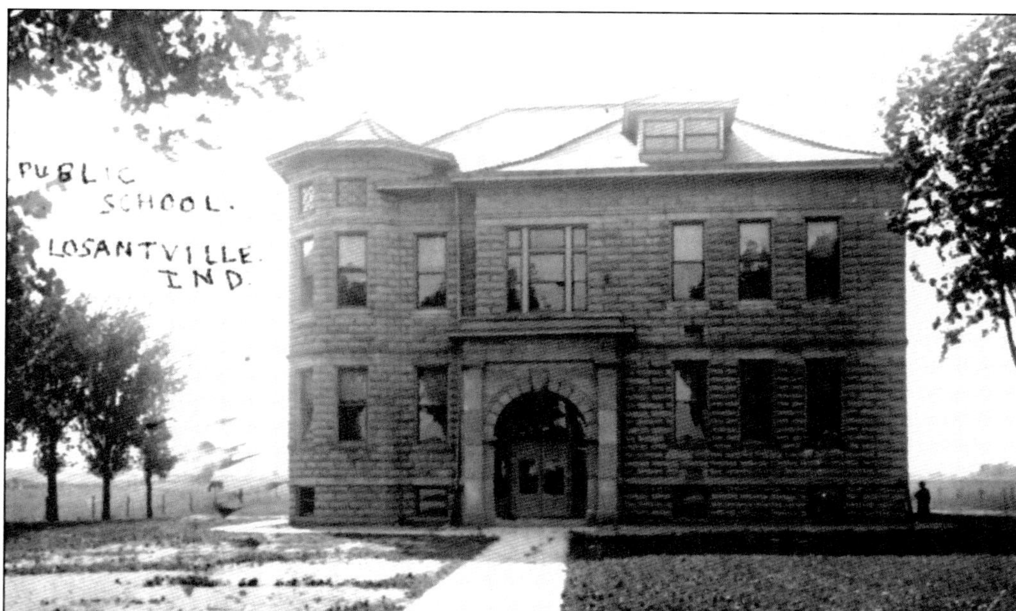

PUBLIC SCHOOL, LOSANTVILLE. This school building, constructed of concrete blocks, was built north of Losantville in 1905 and opened on November 6. An addition was built in 1920. High school students were transferred to Modoc in the fall of 1952. The building continued to house elementary grades until 1957. It was razed in 1958. (Dott Shook.)

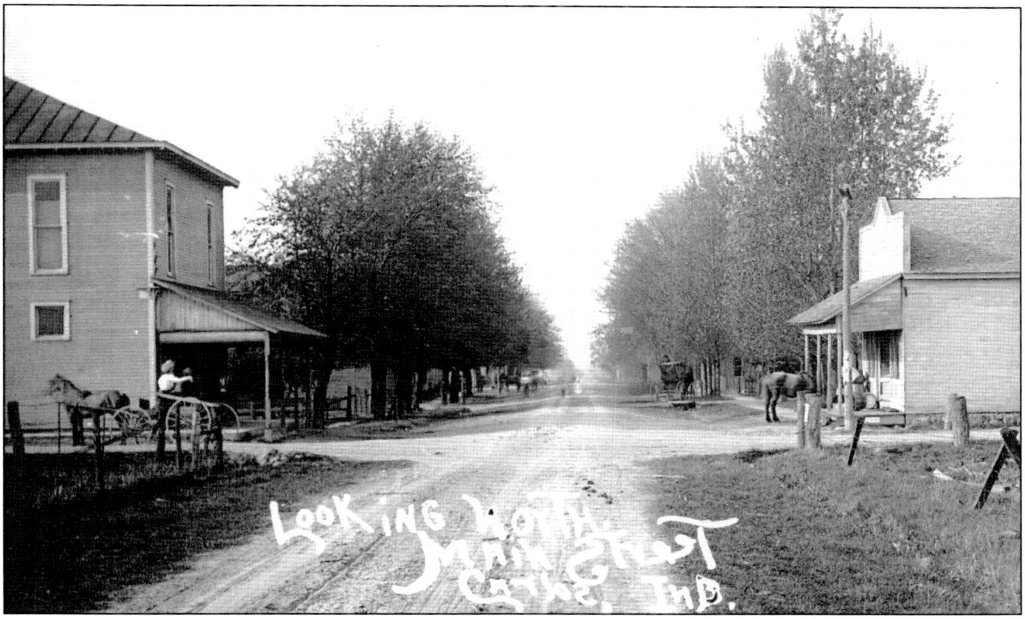

CARLOS, MAIN STREET. This view looks north on Main Street (300 W) from just south of Third Street (950 S). At left is the IOOF hall and general store, built in 1904. At right is the Carlos Grocery. Both of these buildings, although vacant, remain today. (Gregory P. Hinshaw.)

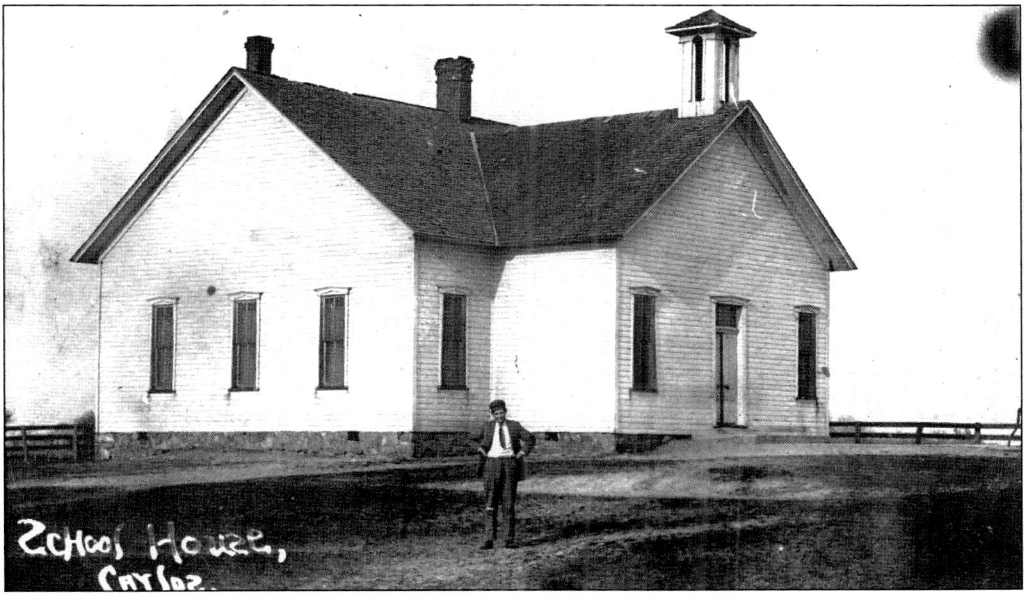

CARLOS SCHOOLHOUSE. This building, a two-room frame schoolhouse, stood just east of Carlos on County Road 950 S. It was used until 1921, when a new brick structure was built. The brick school was used until 1933, when the students were transferred to Lynn and Huntsville. The brick building stood in a state of extreme decay until the 1980s. (Gregory P. Hinshaw.)

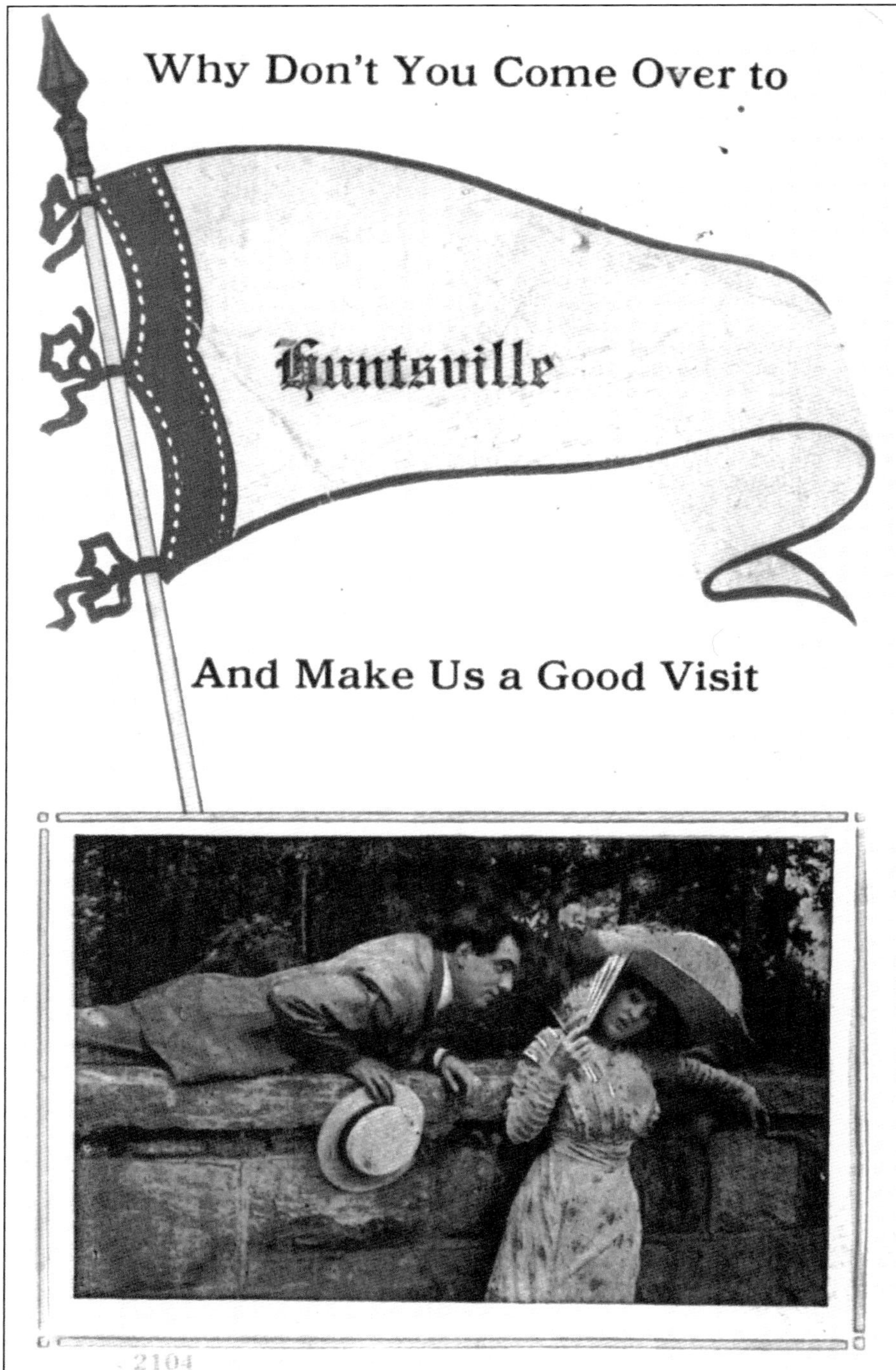

"WHY DON'T YOU COME OVER TO HUNTSVILLE?" The authors have been unable to locate a real-photo postcard from Huntsville; however, this greeting card has survived. Huntsville had a post office, first called Hunt's Cross Roads, then Trenton, from 1832 until 1902. (Judy Wilson Wright.)

Index